1008

D6L
Øidsen

Naming, Necessity,
and Natural Kinds

Naming, Necessity, and Natural Kinds

edited by
STEPHEN P. SCHWARTZ

Cornell University Press
ITHACA AND LONDON

First published 1977 by Cornell University Press.
Published in the United Kingdom by Cornell University Press Ltd.,
2–4 Brook Street, London W1Y 1AA

International Standard Book Number (cloth.) 0-8014-1049-5
International Standard Book Number (paper) 0-8014-9861-9
Library of Congress Catalog Card Number 76-28021
Printed in the United States of America by Vail-Ballou Press, Inc.
Librarians: Library of Congress cataloging information appears on the last page of the book.

To the memory of my great-aunt,
MARJORIE WORTHINGTON

Contents

Preface

The new theory of reference that has recently aroused so much interest, while perhaps not bringing about a revolution, has had the effect of altering the manner and substance of a great deal of philosophy. The theory is plausible and simple and challenges many widely held beliefs. Its proponents have argued, for example, that names and many general terms refer without the mediation of descriptions, that identity statements such as "Tully is Cicero" are not contingent, that there can be synthetic necessary truths discovered a posteriori, and that terms like "gold" and "tiger" do not have definitions in the ordinary sense. In the Introduction to this volume I discuss the challenge the new theory poses to traditional thinking, summarize the arguments for these claims, and try to assess some of its contributions to philosophy.

Two articles by Saul Kripke, "Naming and Necessity" and "Identity and Necessity," are the most complete and influential expressions of the new theory of reference, and have deeply affected current thinking about such topics as reference, naming, natural kinds, necessity, analyticity, and identity. The latter article is included here. Keith Donnellan and Hilary Putnam have also done pioneering work on these topics and in developing the new theory, and they are heavily represented in this book. I have included works by other authors for various reasons. The articles by William Goosens and Gareth Evans develop certain aspects of the new theory in important ways. They depend heavily on Kripke, Donnellan, and Putnam, but also make significant original contributions. The article by Alvin Plantinga deals with a central problem involved in the possible worlds semantics widely used by Kripke, Putnam, and others. Plantinga's approach to possible worlds is helpful in making clear some of the features of this important tool. I have also included two articles that predate the new theory of reference, those by W. V. Quine and Irving Copi. Probably the most important contribution the new theory makes is to increase our understanding of natural kinds and the terms that purport to refer to them. Both Quine and Copi express views about natural kinds that receive tremendous support from the new theory. These two articles and much of Putnam's writings on natural kinds have been cast in a new and more favorable light by Kripke's work.

In making selections I have tried to include statements covering all the major aspects and applications of the new theory, especially its application to natural kind terms. Several of the authors have published much longer works than those that appear here. Both "Naming and Necessity" by Saul Kripke and "The Meaning of 'Meaning' " by Hilary Putnam are more elaborate in their criticisms of traditional thinking, offer more examples, and perhaps attempt to extend the theory somewhat further. I believe, nevertheless, that the articles in this anthology present all the essential aspects, arguments, and notions of the new theory of reference. Those interested in further reading will find other works, including criticisms of the new theory, listed in the Bibliography.

I am grateful to the authors and editors who gave permission for the reprinting of these papers. I would also like to thank Eric Lerner, Richard Creel, Robin Fleming, Walter Horn, James Twiggs, and Keith Donnellan for reading and helping to improve the Introduction, and for their advice and encouragement. Thanks are due also to Diane Creel for helping with the proofreading and indexing.

STEPHEN P. SCHWARTZ

Ithaca, New York

Naming, Necessity,
and Natural Kinds

Introduction

STEPHEN P. SCHWARTZ

Ithaca College

I

According to traditional theories of meaning there is an intension/extension distinction: that is, concepts or meanings associated with general terms and names determine the set of things to which they apply or refer. A general term or name refers to whatever fits the characteristics the term or name means. Recently this tenet has been challenged by several philosophers, foremost among them Saul Kripke, Hilary Putnam, and Keith Donnellan.[1] Among the views of these philosophers is the idea that names have no intension in the traditional sense, that at least nouns meant to designate natural kinds (naturally occurring species) are like names and thus do not have their extensions determined by concepts, and that reference is established by something like a causal chain rather than by associated descriptions. This new theory of reference is the most serious challenge ever to traditional theories of meaning and has important implications for other areas of philosophy.

In this Introduction I will discuss the major features of the new theory and also its effects on areas of philosophy other than semantics. First, however, I will set out the key tenets of the traditional theory in more detail. Following the traditional approach, philosophers have generally started with the meaning of common nouns and extended their views about common nouns to proper names. The new theory of reference on the other hand has gained its greatest impetus from the work of

---

1. See the bibliography for titles of works by these authors other than those reprinted here.

Kripke and Donnellan on proper names, the results of which have led to an extension of the new theory by them and others to many common nouns. My exposition will follow both patterns. In setting out the traditional position I will start with common nouns and then indicate how the theory is extended to proper names, whereas in explicating the new theory I will begin with proper names and then examine its extension to common nouns. In my view the greatest impact of the new theory is on our understanding of the meanings of common nouns, especially those that purport to refer to natural kinds. The differences between the traditional theory and the new theory, however, are more easily understood when their views about proper names are compared; it would in fact be quite difficult to appreciate the force of the new ideas about common nouns without first understanding what the new theorists have to say about proper names.

II

The heart of the traditional theory of meaning is described by Putnam in the following way: "On the traditional view, the meaning of say, 'lemon,' is given by specifying a conjunction of *properties*. For each of these properties, the statement 'lemons have the property P' is an analytic truth; and if $P_1, P_2, \ldots . P_n$ are all of the properties in the conjunction, then 'anything with all of the properties $P_1, \ldots$, is a lemon' is likewise an analytic truth" ("Is Semantics Possible?" p. 103). The conjunction of properties associated with a term such as "lemon" is often called the intension of the term "lemon." This intension determines what it is to be a lemon. Thus according to traditional theories intension determines extension. In the first section of "Meaning and Reference" Putnam also discusses traditional theories of meaning. It was the ancient and medieval tradition, he says, "that the concept corresponding to a term was just a conjunction of predicates, and hence that the concept corresponding to a term must *always* provide a necessary and sufficient condition for falling into the extension of the term" ("Meaning and Reference," pp. 119–120).

According to Putnam, Carnap also espoused a version of the traditional theory because for him "the concept corresponding to a term provided (in the ideal case, where the term had 'complete meaning') a *criterion* for belonging to the extension (not just in the sense of 'necessary and sufficient condition,' but in the strong sense of *way of recognizing* whether a given thing falls into the extension or not)" ("Meaning and Reference," p. 120).

Of course there are differences in terminology and in the way details get worked out among various versions of the traditional theory. According to one contemporary version there is *not* a *conjunction* of properties associated with each term, but there *is* a *cluster* of properties associated with it. For example, it is held that we cannot define "game" by a conjunction of properties such as having a winner and a loser, being entertaining, involving the gaining and losing of points, because some perfectly acceptable games lack some of these features. According to the cluster theory, something is a game because it has enough features from a cluster of properties like these. A cluster theorist would claim that there need not be any property in the cluster that is sufficient for the application of the term, but he nevertheless holds that the cluster taken as a whole determines the extension of the term. Wittgenstein's position that there are only family resemblances among the individuals in the extension of many ordinary terms can be construed as a version of the cluster theory.

The central features, then, of what is here meant by a traditional theory of meaning are the following: (1) Each meaningful term has some meaning, concept, intension, or cluster of features associated with it. It is this meaning that is known or present to the mind when the term is understood. (2) The meaning determines the extension in the sense that something is in the extension of the term if and only if it has the characteristics included in the meaning, concept, intension, or, in the case of the cluster theory, enough of the features. In many contemporary versions, the meaning or concept of the term may include only observable criteria for the application of the term. (3) Analytic truths are based on the meanings of terms. If *P* is a property in the concept of *T,* then the statement "All *T*s are *P*" is true by definition. If the concept of bachelor includes the property of being male, then it is analytic and necessary that all bachelors are male. It should be pointed out here that often the intension of a term is taken to be the essence of the kind of thing named. Since the conjunction of properties associated with "lemon" tells us what it is to be a lemon, and generates necessary truths about lemons, it is thought to be the essence of lemon. A cluster theorist would, of course, deny that there are essences of this sort since there need be no property shared by all and only members of the extension of some term.

Although I do not have space here to provide a historical survey, I will give some examples of the traditional theory as applied to general terms before going on to consider briefly the traditional account of proper names.

Perhaps the best example of the traditional theory of meaning is John Locke's. His view is that with each meaningful term there is associated some abstract idea or definition that determines what things have a right to be called by the name. This abstract idea is what he called the nominal essence of the kind for which the term stands. These nominal essences are of our own making, whereas real essences exist in the things themselves and are made by nature. It is by the nominal essences that we distinguish things into sorts since, according to Locke, we can never come to know the real essences of natural things.

The next thing therefore to be considered is, what kind of signification it is that general words have. For, as it is evident that they do not signify barely one particular thing; for then they would not be general terms, but proper names, so, on the other side, it is as evident they do not signify a plurality; for *man* and *men* would then signify the same. . . . That then which general words signify is a *sort* of things; and each of them does that, by being a sign of an abstract idea in the mind; to which idea, as things existing are found to agree, so they come to be ranked under that name, or, which is all one, be of that sort. Whereby it is evident that the *essences* of the sorts, or, if the Latin word pleases better, *species* of things, are nothing else but these abstract ideas. For the having the essence of any species, being that which makes anything to be of that species; and the conformity to the idea to which the name is annexed being that which gives a right to that name; the having the essence, and the having that conformity, must needs be the same thing.[2]

Locke suggests that analytic propositions are derived from definitions.

Alike trifling it is to predicate any other part of the definition of the term defined, or to affirm any one of the simple ideas of a complex one of the name of the whole complex idea; as, 'All gold is fusible.' For fusibility being one of the simple ideas that goes to the making up the complex one the sound gold stands for, what can it be but playing with sounds, to affirm that of the name gold, which is comprehended in its received signification? . . . And if I know that the name gold stands for this complex idea of body, yellow, heavy, fusible, malleable, it will not much instruct me to put it solemnly afterwards in a proposition, and gravely say, all gold is fusible. Such propositions can only serve to show the disingenuity of one who will go from the definition of his own terms, by reminding him sometimes of it; but carry no knowledge with them, but of the signification of words, however certain they be.[3]

A more recent version of the traditional theory is to be found in C. I. Lewis' book, *An Analysis of Knowledge and Valuation.* Lewis' view is more complicated than Locke's, but is in the same spirit. Lewis distinguishes among several different kinds of meaning. Two of these are intension and extension. "The *denotation* or *extension* of a term is . . . the class of all actual or existent things which the term correctly applies to or names,"[4] he says. "The *connotation* or *intension* of a term is delimited by any correct definition of it. In traditional language, one says that if nothing would be correctly nameable by a term '*T*' unless it possess the attribute *A,* then term '*T*' connotes *A;* and the totality or conjunction of attributes so connoted constitutes the connotation of '*T*'."[5] According to Lewis it is the intension that determines for us whether or not a term applies in a particular

2. John Locke, *An Essay Concerning Human Understanding,* ed., A. C. Fraser (New York: Dover, 1959), Vol. II, p. 22.

3. *Ibid.,* pp. 296–297.

4. *An Analysis of Knowledge and Valuation* (La Salle, Ill.: Open Court, 1946), p. 39.

5. *Ibid.,* p. 40. (Emphasis is mine.)

case; the intension determines the extension, given what happens to exist. "We shall wish to preserve this original sense of 'intension' and, specifically, to identify it with the *criterion in mind* by which it is determined whether the term in question applies or fails to apply in any particular instance." [6]

My last example of traditional thinking is taken from a contemporary logic textbook, written by one of the authors represented in this anthology. Irving Copi, in *Introduction to Logic,* says the following about intension and extension:

> To understand a term is to know how to apply it correctly, but for this it is not necessary to know all of the objects to which it may be correctly applied. It is required only that we have a criterion for deciding of any given object whether it falls within the extension of that term or not. All objects in the extension of a given term have some common properties or characteristics which lead us to use the same term to denote them. . . . The collection of properties shared by all and only those objects in a term's extension is called the *intension* or *connotation* of that term.[7]

Of course, Copi adds that "extension is determined by intension, but not the other way around." [8] It is somewhat ironic that Copi should express this view in his textbook, given what he says in "Essence and Accident," but it is not inappropriate. The view that intension determines extension is the traditional, accepted view.

It was natural for many traditional theorists to extend their treatment to cover ordinary proper names. It is on this aspect of traditional theories that Kripke focuses. According to the conjunction theorists and cluster theorists, each meaningful proper name has associated with it a set of descriptions. The unique thing that satisfies the descriptions or, in the case of the cluster theorist, enough of the descriptions is the referent of the name. When one uses a name the intended referent is determined by the descriptions that are associated with the name being used. As examples of the traditional conjunction theory applied to proper names, Kripke cites Russell and Frege,

---

6. *Ibid.*, p. 43.
7. *Introduction to Logic,* 4th ed. (New York: Macmillan, 1972), p. 125.
8. *Ibid.*, p. 127.

whereas he mentions Wittgenstein and Searle as examples of cluster theorists.[9] The cluster theory of proper names has seemed more plausible to most philosophers than the strict conjunction view of Russell, but Kripke says that the cluster view is just a refinement of the older theory. He cites a well-known passage of Wittgenstein's as a statement of the cluster theory of proper names:

If one says "Moses did not exist", this may mean various things. It may mean: the Israelites did not have a *single* leader when they withdrew from Egypt—or: their leader was not called Moses. . . . But when I make a statement about Moses,—am I always ready to substitute some *one* of those descriptions for "Moses"? I shall perhaps say: by "Moses" I understand the man who did what the Bible relates of Moses, or at any rate a good deal of it. But how much? Have I decided how much must be proved false for me to give up this proposition as false? Has the name "Moses" got a fixed and unequivocal use for me in all possible cases? [10]

Wittgenstein assumes that descriptions will be associated with "Moses" but denies that there is a strict conjunction that can be substituted for the name.

Just as in the case of general terms, the conjunction or cluster of identifying descriptions associated with a name generates necessary truths. If part of what we mean by "Aristotle" is "the teacher of Alexander," then "Aristotle is the teacher of Alexander" is a necessary truth. Although the cluster theorists reject the claim that any one description is necessary of Aristotle, Searle still holds that there are necessary truths about Aristotle generated by the cluster associated with the name "Aristotle."

To put the same point differently, suppose we ask, 'why do we have proper names at all?' Obviously to refer to individuals. 'Yes, but descriptions could do that for us.' But only at the cost of specifying iden-

9. Kripke claims that the clearest statement of the cluster theory of proper names is to be found in John Searle's article, "Proper Names," reprinted in *Philosophy and Ordinary Language,* ed. by C. E. Caton (Urbana: University of Illinois Press, 1963).

10. Ludwig Wittgenstein, *Philosophical Investigations,* trans. by G. E. M. Anscombe (New York: Macmillan, 1953), para. 79, as quoted in "Naming and Necessity," in *Semantics of Natural Language,* ed. by Donald Davidson and Gilbert Harman (Dordrecht: D. Reidel, 1972).

tity conditions every time reference is made: Suppose we agree to drop 'Aristotle' and use, say, 'the teacher of Alexander,' then it is a necessary truth that the man referred to is Alexander's teacher—but it is a contingent fact that Aristotle ever went into pedagogy (though I am suggesting that it is a necessary fact that Aristotle has the logical sum, inclusive disjunction, of properties commonly attributed to him).[11]

Locke, Lewis, Copi, Searle, and Wittgenstein are philosophers who have held or expressed the traditional theory of meaning. While they have differed about some of the details, I do not believe these philosophers felt it necessary to defend the foundations of the theory. Most have just taken it for granted that some version of the conjunction or cluster theory is true. Of course there are many other philosophers whom we could have referred to for statements of the traditional theory. Most modern empiricists such as Berkeley, Hume, Mill, and the logical positivists have held the traditional theory, at least about common nouns. Among contemporary philosophers of language the traditional theory is still strong. Although such philosophers as Jerrold Katz and Richard Montague use more sophisticated technical tools than their predecessors, Putnam claims that they are merely trying to refine traditional thinking.

III

The boldness of the new theory of reference is that it undertakes to refute the traditional theory of meaning. It is no mere refinement. Therefore it is no wonder that the new theory has stirred interest and controversy. Our task here will be first to describe the new theory in detail and then to point to some possible difficulties with it.

The description will be divided into three parts, corresponding to what I consider to be the three main features of the new theory. First, criticism of traditional theories of proper names will be taken up. Then the views of the new theorists about the meaning of general terms and criticisms of traditional thinking in this area will be set out. Lastly, the means by

11. Searle, p. 160, as quoted in "Naming and Necessity."

which reference is achieved according to the new theory will be discussed.

In opposition to the traditional theory, Kripke and Donnellan argue that proper names refer independently of identifying descriptions. One of Donnellan's major contributions has been to show that reference can take place not only in the absence of identifying descriptions but even when the identifying descriptions associated with the name do not correctly apply to the individual to whom the name refers. In "Reference and Definite Descriptions" he makes basically the same sort of point about certain uses of definite descriptions. Donnellan distinguishes between two kinds of use for definite descriptions—the attributive and the referential. When using a definite description attributively, the speaker intends to be saying something about whoever or whatever fits a certain description, without necessarily having any idea who or what it is that fits the description. In the case of the referential use, the speaker has independently a definite idea whom or what he means to be speaking about and uses the description to refer to that individual. A referential description is simply a tool for accomplishing the reference and may succeed in doing this even if the thing referred to fails to fit the description. Donnellan gives a good example of the contrast between the two uses. Consider the use of "Smith's Murderer" in the following two cases.

Suppose first that we come upon poor Smith foully murdered. From the brutal manner of the killing and the fact that Smith was the most lovable person in the world, we might exclaim, "Smith's murderer is insane." I will assume, to make it a simpler case, that in a quite ordinary sense we do not know who murdered Smith. . . . This, I shall say, is an attributive use of the definite description.

On the other hand,

Suppose that Jones has been charged with Smith's murder and has been placed on trial. Imagine that there is a discussion of Jones's odd behavior at his trial. We might sum up our impression of his behavior by saying, "Smith's murderer is insane." If someone asks to whom we are referring, by using this description, the answer here is "Jones."

This, I shall say, is a referential use of the definite description ("Reference and Definite Descriptions," pp. 46–47).

With the referential use of "Smith's Murderer" the speaker is referring to Jones even if it later turns out that he is innocent.

Donnellan's point is important because it shows that descriptions do not always just refer to whoever or whatever happens to fit them. When we use a description referentially we do not mean to be referring to whoever happens to fit it. Rather, we have a definite individual in mind. Likewise, it is argued, when we use a name we are not referring to whoever happens to fit some set of descriptions, although we may believe that the person, place, or thing named does fit the descriptions. When we use a name we use it as a referential description. We use it to refer to some definite individual, independently of whether or not he fits some descriptions. Donnellan points out that if names are used attributively, i.e., if they refer to whoever fits the identifying descriptions associated with them, then we get certain paradoxical results. For example, if a name such as "Thales" refers to whoever fits the identifying description "the philosopher who held that all is water," then if no one in fact held this view, we must say that Thales did not exist. But then, Donnellan asks, "to whom were Aristotle and Herodotus referring? Surely we cannot conclude 'to no one.' It seems to me to make sense that we should discover that Thales was after all a well-digger and that Aristotle and Herodotus were deceived about what he did." [12] Thus we can refer to Thales by using the name "Thales" even though perhaps the only description we can supply is false of him.

Kripke makes the same point about names and in addition claims that they are rigid designators. "Rigid designator" is a term coined by Kripke to mean a designator, such as a name or description, that refers to the same individual with respect to all possible worlds in which that individual exists. If a name is a rigid designator, then it refers to the same individual when being used to describe counterfactual situations as it does when

12. "Proper Names and Identifying Descriptions," in *Semantics of Natural Language*, p. 374.

used to describe the actual world. This means that a name will refer to the same individual whether or not he satisfies some list of commonly associated descriptions.

In other possible worlds or possible counterfactual situations, an individual need have only those properties, if any, that are essential to him. Any of his other properties are contingent, and he will have them in some worlds but not in others. As we have already seen, the traditional theory of proper names entails that at least some combination of the things ordinarily believed of Aristotle are necessarily true of him. When considered carefully, however, this idea is highly doubtful. It is certainly odd to suppose that, for example, Aristotle was necessarily a philosopher, necessarily a teacher of Alexander, necessarily a pupil of Plato, and so on. Aristotle, that very man, might have died in a plague that swept his land when he was a child. His dying thus would have been a great loss to the world, but it is one of those things that given the proper conditions could have happened and can be described. Kripke further criticizes the view that Aristotle necessarily has the properties usually attributed to him.

There is a certain theory, perhaps popular in some views of the philosophy of history, which might both be deterministic and yet at the same time assign a great role to the individual in history. Perhaps Carlyle would associate with the meaning of the name of a great man his achievements. According to such a view it will be necessary, once a certain individual is born, that he is destined to perform various great tasks and so it will be part of the very nature of Aristotle that he should have produced ideas which had a great influence on the western world. Whatever the merits of such a view may be as a view of history or the nature of great men, it does not seem that it should be trivially true on the basis of a theory of proper names.[13]

Since it is not necessarily true of Aristotle, that is, it is not true of Aristotle in every world in which he exists, that he was a philosopher, taught Alexander, or did any, all, or any combination of things usually asserted of him, it is not the case that it is essential to Aristotle that he was a philosopher, taught Alexan-

13. "Naming and Necessity," p. 287.

der, etc. Aristotle is Aristotle whether or not he satisfies some set of descriptions such as "is a philosopher," "taught Alexander," and so on. Thus, the name "Aristotle" if it is rigid refers to that man independently of his satisfying any of the descriptions commonly associated with "Aristotle."

Other evidence brought against the traditional theory of proper names is that we could discover about some individual that few or none of the things commonly believed about him are true in the actual world. For example we could discover that Shakespeare was not the author of those plays attributed to him, was not even literate, and so on, or we could discover of Gödel that he was not the one who discovered what is now called Gödel's proof, that he was not a mathematician, and that some huge fraud had been perpetrated. If the traditional theory were correct and names were not rigid designators, that is, if they referred to whoever or whatever fit certain descriptions commonly associated with them, then "Gödel" would refer to whoever discovered Gödel's proof, and "Shakespeare" to whoever was the author of *Hamlet, Othello,* etc., and thus it would be contradictory to suppose that we could discover that Shakespeare did not write those plays or that Gödel did not discover Gödel's proof. Of course, such a discovery is not likely given the evidence to the contrary, but it is not ruled out simply by the logic of proper names.

The claim that ordinary proper names are rigid designators and are not abbreviations of conjunctions or clusters of descriptions is the first important feature of the new theory of reference. One factor supporting the rigidity of proper names is that, given this view, certain outstanding problems about identity statements are solved. One is that of contingent identity statements. This problem is set out at the beginning of Kripke's paper, "Identity and Necessity," and I will not attempt to summarize his discussion here. Suffice it to say that most philosophers have held that such identities as "The Morning Star is the Evening Star" or "Hesperus is Phosphorus" and "Tully is Cicero" are contingent. According to Kripke, if "Tully" and "Cicero" are rigid, and if the identity "Tully is Cicero" is true, then it is necessarily true and not contingent.[14] If "Tully" and "Cicero" are rigid and both refer to the same individual in the actual world, then since rigid designators refer to the same individual in all possible worlds, there will be no world in which "Tully" refers to an individual other then Cicero. This means that the identity "Tully is Cicero" is true in all worlds in which Tully exists, and thus it is necessarily true. According to Kripke, an identity statement that involves only rigid designators will be necessarily true, if it is true at all. Identity statements with nonrigid designators will generally be contingent. For example, if is a contingent fact that the inventor of bifocals was the first postmaster general.

The major reason that most philosophers have been led to believe that such identities as "Hesperus is Phosphorus" and "Tully is Cicero" are contingent is that they are not analytic. It was an empirical discovery that Hesperus (the Morning Star) is Phosphorus (the Evening Star). It is not a priori that these are the same celestial object. Likewise, it is not a priori that Tully is Cicero, and it is even imaginable that he was not. Kripke is willing to admit, and in fact insists, that the identities mentioned are not analytic or a priori. In spite of this he holds that they *are* necessarily true. Kripke claims that most recent and contemporary philosophers have failed to distinguish the metaphysical notion of necessity from the epistemological notion of *a priority* and the linguistic notion of *analyticity*. If "necessarily true" means true in all possible worlds and a priori means knowable independently of experience, then we are talking about two very different notions, and there is no reason to suppose that their extensions have to be the same. In fact, Kripke claims that "Hesperus is Phosphorus" is necessarily true but is not a priori or analytic. Of course, the claim that there can be synthetic necessary propositions is startling to most contemporary analytic philosophers, but given the persuasiveness of

14. This is slightly inaccurate. "Tully is Cicero" is true in every world in which Tully exists. It is unclear what truth value to assign it in Tullyless worlds. In any case what we must say is that "If Tully exists, then Tully is Cicero" is necessarily true. (See Kripke, "Naming and Necessity", p. 311.)

Kripke's arguments and examples the claim must be taken seriously.

Since Kripke uses the device of possible worlds, he must deal with the problem of transworld identity. Once we start to use the whole apparatus of possible worlds and individuals in possible worlds, it seems we must have some way of re-identifying individuals in various possible worlds in which they exist. This problem has received a great deal of attention lately since the apparatus of possible worlds is fundamental to the kind of metaphysical systems employed in contemporary logic, philosophy of language, and metaphysics. Kripke, in "Identity and Necessity," treats the question of transworld identity as something of a pseudo-problem. He claims that confusion comes from taking "the metaphor of possible worlds much too seriously in some way. It is as if a 'possible world' were like a foreign country, or distant planet way out there. It is as if we see dimly through a telescope various actors on this distant planet" ("Identity and Necessity," p. 80). How can someone out there, on that "distant planet," be identical with someone here? Plantinga, like Kripke, rejects the distant planet metaphor. In "Transworld Identity or Worldbound Individuals?" Plantinga undertakes to defend the view that individuals can exist in various possible worlds. I believe that his arguments give a great deal of support to Kripke's use of the metaphysical apparatus of possible worlds.

In the controversy with the traditional theory of meaning the second major feature of the new theory of reference is perhaps more important than the first. The second feature is the extension of the insights about proper names to common nouns, and in particular to nouns standing for putative natural kinds like "gold," "water," "tiger." According to Kripke such nouns are like proper names in that they are rigid designators. If "gold" is a rigid designator, then it always refers to the same stuff independently of the stuff's superficial phenomenal properties. Furthermore, what it is to be gold cannot be analytically specified by some list of properties, for no matter how much the properties of something resemble what we take to be the superficial properties of gold, the stuff would not be gold unless it were the same kind of substance that is rigidly designated by "gold." It is an empirical hypothesis that gold is the element with atomic number 79, but if this hypothesis is correct then "gold" rigidly designates the element with atomic number 79. Anything else is not gold no matter how much it resembles gold.

Being yellow is just the sort of property that a traditional theorist would include in the definition of "gold." Accordingly, "gold is yellow" would be analytic. Kripke argues, however, that such a statement is not analytic. It is possible that we could discover that gold is not yellow in the actual world. In order to imagine such a discovery, we can suppose that we have all been victim of massive illusions, or some such thing. Such a supposition is outlandish, but the situation is not impossible. One well-known example, to illustrate the fact that statements about natural kinds are almost always synthetic, is the example of the robot cats.[15] It is conceivable that we could discover that all the cats were robots sent from Mars to spy on us. Since this is conceivable, statements such as "cats are animals" are not analytic. A less outlandish example was the discovery that "whales are fish" is false, and thus not analytic. If such statements about natural kinds are not analytic, then we cannot specify the meaning of natural kind terms by conjunctions of properties. That examples of the kind in question have the properties that they do is a matter of nature, not language.

According to the traditional theory, the concept associated with a term functions like the set of identifying descriptions supposedly associated with an ordinary proper name. The new theory of reference holds that the descriptions, if any, associated with a natural kind term do not have a decisive role in deciding whether the term applies in a given case. At best the descriptions associated with such a term are a handy guide in picking out things of the kind named, but the descriptions do not determine what it is to be of the kind. What determines whether some stuff is gold is its atomic structure. Likewise,

15. See Putnam's "It Ain't Necessarily So," reprinted in *Readings in the Philosophy of Language,* ed. by Jay F. Rosenberg and Charles Travis (Englewood Cliffs, N.J.: Prentice-Hall, 1971).

water is H_2O—some stuff is water only if it has the right chemical structure. Biological kinds are determined by genetic structure, and other natural kinds are similarly determined.

Putnam has been the most important influence in the application of the new ideas on reference to natural kind terms. He holds that water, for example, is H_2O in all possible worlds. Thus, water is necessarily H_2O. This means that anything that is not H_2O is not water, even if it satisfies some list of superficial features that we think characterize water. Thus a liquid could be clear, colorless, tasteless, etc., and still not be water, if it is not H_2O. Putnam argues for this position by using his device of Twin Earth. Twin Earth is just like earth except that the lakes and rivers of Twin Earth are filled with some complicated chemical, XYZ, that exactly mimics the superficial properties of H_2O. Such a planet is certainly possible.

Suppose, now, that I discover the microstructure of water—that water is H_2O. At this point I will be able to say that the stuff on Twin Earth that I earlier *mistook* for water isn't really water. In the same way, if you describe, not another planet in the actual universe, but another possible universe in which there is stuff with the chemical formula XYZ which passes the "operational test" for *water,* we shall have to say that that stuff isn't water but merely XYZ. You will not have described a possible world in which "water is XYZ," but merely a possible world in which there are lakes of XYZ, people drink XYZ (and not water), or whatever ("Meaning and Reference," p. 130).

Thus water is H_2O in all possible worlds because nothing would count as a possible world in which some stuff that was not H_2O was water. An example offered by Kripke that reinforces Putnam's point is that of fool's gold. Iron pyrites looks and behaves in many ways like gold, but it is not gold because it is not the element with atomic number 79.

It is not the satisfying of some descriptions, analytically associated with the terms, but the having of a particular chemical nature that makes some liquid water or some metal gold. We have seen that some imposter substance does not have a right to the name "water" just because it superficially resembles water; likewise, some stuff might still be water although it does not resemble other bodies of water, as long as it is H_2O. "On

the other hand if this substance [H_2O] can take another form—
such as the polywater allegedly discovered in the Soviet Union,
with very different identifying marks from that of what we now
call water—it is a form of water because it is the same substance, even though it doesn't have the appearances by which
we originally identified water." [16] Thus we see that if Kripke's
and Putnam's view is correct, the conjunction or cluster of descriptions associated with some natural kind term is neither
necessary nor sufficient for the application of the term.

In that case what is the role of the descriptions that are commonly associated with natural kind terms? Kripke distinguishes
between fixing the reference of a term and giving its definition.
When we fix the reference of a term, we give a description that
helps the hearer pick out what we have in mind. Thus, for example, when teaching someone the meaning of color words, I
may say: "By green we mean the color of that car over there."
The description "the color of that car over there" is meant to
fix the reference of "green" but not to give its meaning in the
sense of supplying a synonym for "green." It does not follow
from the way I have fixed the reference of "green" that it is analytic or necessary that the car is green. I did not mean that
"green" is defined as whatever color that car over there happens to be. If I had meant this, then if someone painted the car
a different color, say red, then "green" would refer to red,
since that happened, then, to be the color of the car. When I
fix the reference of a term, I give a description that is to be
taken as giving the referent of the term, not the meaning in the
traditional sense. I have a definite kind of thing in mind when I
use the term, and now I want to help the audience pick it out.
It is in this way that the descriptions associated with natural
kind terms function. The traditional theorist assumed that descriptions given in connection with natural kind terms were
defining the term, in the sense that anything satisfying the
description falls in the extension of the term. According to
Kripke, such descriptions are typically meant only to fix the
reference. The error of the traditional theorist results from his

---

16. Kripke, "Naming and Necessity," p. 323.

failing to distinguish fixing the reference from giving the meaning.

We have seen that Kripke and Putnam hold that water is necessarily H_2O. H_2O is the nature of water. H_2O is the essence of water. "Water" rigidly designates H_2O, regardless of what superficial properties the H_2O may or may not have. At this point it is very easy to confuse the new theory with a possible refinement of traditional theories. Such a confusion would come about if we then thought that "water is H_2O" were analytic. It might be thought that Kripke and Putnam are merely trying to replace ordinary definitions with scientific ones so that instead of defining water as a clear, colorless liquid, we define it as H_2O. This is not the view of the new theory of reference. One would come closer to the position of Kripke and Putnam if one simply said that "water" has no definition at all, at least in the traditional sense, and is a proper name of a specific substance.

There are at least two very good reasons for supposing that "water is H_2O" or "gold is an element" are not analytic. The first is that they could each turn out to be false. We could discover that there were certain fundamental errors in our chemical theories, or some such thing, and that water was some other complicated chemical. The same kind of thing could happen with gold. Since there is a logical possibility of such an error, the statements are not analytic. We said before that water is necessarily H_2O, but it could not be the case that "water is H_2O" might be false, and yet that water is necessarily H_2O. Thus if we are being most accurate, what we must say is that water is necessarily H_2O if it is H_2O. If our theories are correct and there is no error and water is in fact H_2O, *then* it is necessarily H_2O. Our certainty that water is H_2O is the certainty of a well-established empirical theory—not the certainty that issues from knowledge of a definition; it is not analytic, but if it is true, it is necessary. This means that if water is H_2O, then we have an example of a necessary a posteriori synthetic proposition. When I say that we could discover that water is not H_2O, I mean "could" in the epistemological sense that it is consistent with our present experiences that such a discovery is possible. In the metaphysical sense of possibility, there is no possible world in which we discover that water is not H_2O, if it is H_2O in the actual world.

The second reason for supposing that "water is H_2O" and other similar statements are not analytic is that they are matters of scientific discovery, not of definition. It is a discovery about the world that water is H_2O. What this means is that scientists are sometimes discovering necessary truths—not just contingencies as had been supposed. Furthermore, a scientific investigation into the atomic, chemical, or biological structure of some kind of thing is an investigation into the essence of that kind. The view that discovering essences of natural kinds is one of the tasks of science is well expressed by Irving Copi:

Now modern atomic theory is directly concerned with the insensible parts of things. Through the use of his Periodic Table, interpreted as dealing with atomic number and valency, ". . . Mendeléev was enabled to predict the existence *and properties* . . ." of half a dozen elements whose existence had not been previously known or even suspected. And other scientists have subsequently been able to make similar predictions. Modern science seeks to know the *real* essences of things, and its increasing successes seem to be bringing it progressively nearer to that goal ("Essence and Accident," p. 187).

In a similar vein, Quine's view as expressed in "Natural Kinds" is that a branch of knowledge becomes more scientific the more it depends on underlying structure rather than superficial observable properties for classifying things into kinds.

If the reference of names and natural kind terms is not determined by descriptions, then how is it determined according to the new theory? What determines that "water" designates H_2O and that "Aristotle" designates Aristotle? Without a cogent answer to this question, the new theory would be merely destructive and could not be a genuine alternative to traditional thinking. Unless we see an alternative to determining reference and meaning by descriptions, we will still be tempted to refine the traditional theory further to account for all the difficulties mentioned. It is not, however, necessary that a full-blown alternative theory be worked out. It is sufficient to suggest how an alternative might be worked out, the lines it should take, the general outline, even if the details are left for future thinkers.

Kripke, Donnellan, Putnam, and others do have a general answer to the question of how reference is determined but do not have a fully worked-out theory. This brings us to the third major feature of the new theory of reference. Reference is determined in many cases by causal chains. For example, one way in which a name might be connected to a referent is the following: a name is given to a person in a "baptism" or an initial use with the referent present. It is then handed on from speaker to speaker. As long as we have the right sort of causal chain, that is, as long as the later speakers in the chain intend to use the name with the same reference as the earlier, reference to the person "baptized" is accomplished by use of the name. In this way reference to the initial referent of the name can be achieved even though the later user of the name knows no descriptions uniquely specifying the referent. This pattern seems to fit our ability to use names to refer to well-known contemporary and historical figures. I may not know anything more about Abdul Jabbar than that he is a great basketball player from California, but I can still refer to him because there is a causal chain leading back from my use to Jabbar himself.

As I indicated, work on the causal theory of reference is still in its infancy. Donnellan in "Speaking of Nothing" avoids use of the expression "causal theory" and speaks of his view as "the historical explanation theory" of reference because he does not want to be committed to holding that there are only causal links in the chain of events leading back to the original referent. Gareth Evans, in his paper "The Causal Theory of Names," attempts to work out some of the details of the theory. His view is that the relevant causal chain is not between my current use of the name and the referent, but between the body of knowledge I associate with the name and the referent. In any case, Evans and Donnellan give several indications of why some version of the causal theory must be correct. One criterion for a theory's truth is its ability to solve outstanding philosophical problems. One of the outstanding problems in the theory of reference is that of how to understand statements claiming that someone does not exist. The problem is that the speaker seems to be referring to someone only to deny that they exist. Donnellan argues that truth conditions for such negative existential statements can be given in terms of the historical explanation theory. If instead of a "baptism" the origin of the use of some name N is in a fantasy or story, then even though later users who are unaware of the origin may use N intending to refer to someone, "N does not exist" is true because the name never had a referent. The attraction of the causal theory of reference is that it is simple in outline and seems to promise solution to many problems.

So far we have spoken of the causal theory only with respect to the reference of proper names. Putnam extends the theory to natural kind terms. His view is that we "baptise" what we take to be good examples or paradigms of some substance such as water and then use "water" to refer to whatever has the same nature as the paradigms. When we introduce the term it is not necessary that we know the nature of the stuff we are naming. We hope that such knowledge will come with empirical scientific investigations. The term, once introduced, can be handed on from person to person in the referential chain, maintaining its original reference at each link. Putnam calls a term that is introduced by means of a paradigm and is meant to refer to whatever has the same underlying nature as the paradigm "an indexical term." It follows from the fact that a term is indexical that it is rigid in Kripke's sense.

When Putnam says that a natural kind term is indexical and is thus introduced by means of a paradigm, he does not mean a paradigm in the sense of something that we would all concur in calling by the term in question and that is used as an example in teaching the use of the term. If I point to a glass of clear, colorless liquid and say, "By 'water' I mean that stuff," then the liquid in the glass is serving as my paradigm in Putnam's sense. If, however, the stuff in the glass turns out to be hydrochloric acid, I withdraw my "baptism." I meant to point to some of the same stuff that fills the rivers, lakes, and oceans of earth. According to some versions of the traditional theory, if something is a paradigm in the sense of example used in teaching a term, then it must necessarily be in the extension of the term. I think Putnam would deny that there are any paradigms in this sense. Even if there were some piece of metal that we would all concur in calling gold and be willing to use in teaching the term "gold," it might still turn out that the piece was not gold if it was not sufficiently like other examples of gold in its atomic structure.

The extension of the causal theory to natural kind terms is admitted to be quite rough. Kripke says the following after an account bearing many similarities to Putnam's: "Obviously, there are also artificialities in this whole account. For example, it may be hard to say which items constitute the original sample. Gold may have been discovered independently by various people at various times. I do not feel that any such complications will radically alter the picture." [17] What Kripke is trying to do is present a better picture of how reference takes place than the traditional one, and this can be done without supplying complicated and complete analyses.

These, then, are the three main features of the new theory of reference: proper names are rigid, natural kind terms are like proper names in the way they refer, and reference depends on causal chains. Each feature directly challenges major tenets of traditional thinking about meaning and reference.

IV

What bearing does the new theory of reference have on important philosophical issues outside of the theory of meaning? It has been axiomatic in recent philosophy that one's theory of meaning affects one's views in all the other areas of philosophy, and, indeed, this is so with the new theory of reference. I have already mentioned that it gives a great deal of support to the kind of scientific realism about natural kinds that we find in Quine's "Natural Kinds" and Copi's "Essence and Accident." Also, the use of possible world semantics and all the important results obtained with that method have resulted in the re-

17. "Naming and Necessity," p. 353.

surgence of metaphysics as an important branch of philosophical study. All the talk about what is true in other possible worlds and even the existence of possible worlds is not verifiable in the positivist's sense. In the philosophy of science, adherents of the new theory of reference oppose the widely held view that new discoveries become part of new definitions of terms. According to Kripke, "scientific discoveries of species essence do not constitute a 'change of meaning'; the possibility of such discoveries was part of the original enterprise." [18] But perhaps the most striking and controversial effects of the new theory of reference are in the philosophy of mind. Let us consider these effects in more detail.

The identity theory version of materialism holds that, for example, the proposition "Pain is brain state S" is contingent. This means that the identity theorists hold that if we discover that pain is a brain state, it is not necessarily true that it is. As we have seen, Kripke argues that any identity statement in which both sides are rigid is necessary, and not contingent. Since both "pain" and "brain state S" are rigid, according to Kripke, the identity "Pain is brain state S" must be necessary and not contingent. This means that if pain is brain state S in the actual world, then it is brain state S in every world in which it exists, just as if water is H_2O in the actual world then it is H_2O in every world in which it exists. The identity theorists were led into believing that "Pain is brain state S" is contingent because it is not analytic, but this overlooks the possibility that a proposition could be both synthetic and necessary.

It may seem open to the identity theorist to agree with Kripke by admitting his point that pain is necessarily brain state S if it is brain state S. After all, the identity theorist wants to assert the likelihood of a scientific identity being discovered between pain and brain states of a certain sort analogous to the scientific identity of water and H_2O. Thus the identity theorist, it appears, can admit that the identity in question is necessary if true without substantially altering his position. Kripke argues,

18. *Ibid.*, p. 330.

however, that there are reasons for supposing that the identity between pain and some brain state is not necessary. If his argument is correct, then the identity theory is refuted.

Kripke points out that there is a disanalogy between the statement that water is H_2O and the statement that pain is a brain state. In the case of water there could be a water mimic that is not H_2O. In such a case we could say that this water mimic is not water. It is certainly a contingent fact if it is a fact at all, that everything that looks and tastes like water is H_2O. With pain on the other hand, the situation is different because there can be no such thing as a pain mimic. If something feels like pain then it is a pain. Now it seems possible that someone could have just this feeling, and yet his brain not be in state S. We do not have an explanation for this apparent contingency as we do in the case of water and H_2O. We cannot say of the painful feeling that is occurring without the brain state that it seems superficially to be a pain but actually is not. On the other hand, it also seems possible that a person could be in brain state S and yet feel nothing. The identity theorist is in the uncomfortable position of having to say that although the person feels nothing he is in pain, because being in brain state S is necessarily being in pain. Speaking of the supposed analogy between the identification of sensations with brain states on the one hand and heat and molecular motion on the other, Kripke says the following:

In the case of molecular motion and heat there is something, namely, the sensation of heat, which is an intermediary between the external phenomenon and the observer. In the mental-physical case no such intermediary is possible, since here the physical phenomenon is supposed to be identical with the internal phenomenon itself. . . . To be in the same epistemic situation that would obtain if one had a pain *is* to have a pain; to be in the same epistemic situation that would obtain in the absence of pain *is* not to have a pain. The apparent contingency of the action between the physical state and the corresponding brain state thus can[not] be explained by some sort of qualitative analogue as obtained in the case of heat.[19]

19. *Ibid.*, p. 339.

Besides causing trouble for the identity theorist, the rigidity of mental terms has provided ammunition for those who argue against contemporary versions of philosophical behaviorism. For example, Putnam has used the rigidity of psychological terms to attack Malcolm's criteriological analyses of terms like "pain" and "dreaming." [20] If psychological terms are rigid designators of natural kinds, then they do not involve concepts. Outer criteria of inner states will at best be good indicators of the inner states, not part of the concept of the inner state as Malcolm would hold. Scientists can and do discover better indicators of inner states than gross outward behavior. According to a scientific realist like Putnam, the study of the ordinary use of such terms as "dreaming," "pain," or "thinking" will tell us nothing about dreaming, pain, or thinking. We must study the referents of these terms, and this is an empirical investigation. [21]

V

The application of the new theory of reference to problems in the philosophy of mind, however, brings out two severe difficulties that the new theory must face. They are (1) explaining exactly what the reference of a rigid natural kind term is, and (2) explaining which terms other than proper names are rigid and which are nonrigid, that is, which are natural kind terms and which are not.

The problem of explaining what the reference of a natural kind term is arises because of the nature of rigid designators. A rigid designator refers to the same individual or thing with respect to every possible world in which that thing exists. What is it that is referred to by terms such as "gold" or "pain" if they are rigid? It cannot be the extension of the term because that

20. See for example Putnam's "Dreaming and 'Depth Grammar'," in *Analytical Philosophy*, ed. by R. J. Butler (Oxford: Blackwell, 1962), and Norman Malcolm, *Dreaming* (New York: Humanities Press, 1959).

21. Once one rejects identity materialism and behaviorism, dualism seems to be the only view left. Putnam, however, also rejects dualism. He has tried to work out his own alternative in recent articles. See for example "Minds and Machines" in *Dimensions of Mind*, ed. by Sidney Hook (London: Collier-Macmillan, 1960), pp. 138–164.

varies from world to world. For example, the extension of "gold" in the actual world includes various objects or bits of gold that do not exist in some other worlds where there is gold. In fact, there could be two possible worlds in which the extension of "gold" is entirely disjoint. None of the gold in one world exists in the other and vice versa.[22]

If "gold" does not rigidly refer to its extension, then to what does it rigidly refer? The only candidate, it seems, for "gold" or "pain" to designate is the kind or species itself, so that "gold" would designate the same kind of metal or the same element in every possible world, and "pain" would designate the same kind of sensation in every possible world. The difficulty with this solution is that it leads to treating every common noun as a rigid designator. Thus "bachelor" would designate the same marital status from world to world, "sloop" would designate the same kind of sailboat from world to world, "lawyer" would designate the same kind of occupation from world to world, and so on. It seems to me, however, that there is an important difference between terms like "gold," "water," "tiger," and possibly "pain" on the one hand and terms like "bachelor," "sloop," and "lawyer" on the other. In using the latter we do not have some kind of thing in mind, name it, and then seek to discover what it is we have named as we do in the case of "gold" or "tiger." Rather we have a certain specification or description in mind and define anything that satisfies the description as having a right to the name. In other words terms like "gold" or "tiger" are referential, whereas terms like "lawyer" or "bachelor" are attributive. A term used attributively refers to whatever satisfies a certain concept; thus it obeys the traditional theory of meaning. By "bachelor" I mean any unmarried male of marriageable age. This definition does not represent an empirical discovery about bachelors. It is an analytic specification of what it is to be a bachelor. If we come to call unmarried women bachelors, as some have suggested we do, then our doing so is based not on a discovery about the nature of women and bach-

22. This was originally pointed out by Donnellan in his APA reply to Putnam's "Meaning and Reference." Donnellan, "Substances and Individuals" (Abstract), *Journal of Philosophy*, LXX (Nov. 8, 1973), 711–712.

elors but on a decision to change the definition of "bachelor."

If what I have said is right, then it seems that some version of the traditional theory is more or less correct about such terms as "bachelor," "lawyer," or "sloop." These are names of synthetic, or nonnatural kinds. Borrowing a term from Locke, I will call such kinds "nominal kinds," indicating that they have what Locke would call a nominal essence but lack a biological, chemical, or atomic essence. The error of the traditional theory was in extending its analysis, based on nominal kind terms, to natural kind terms. The analogous error on the part of the new theory of reference is to extend its analysis, based on natural kind terms, to nominal kind terms.[23] The new theory is led into this error because of the failure to clarify what the referent of a natural kind term is.

It seems to me that both the new theory and the traditional approach are necessary if we are to achieve understanding of language. This means that we must be able to answer the deep and difficult question of which terms name natural kinds and which name nominal kinds. In certain instances the answer is obvious, as in the cases of the terms "gold" and "bachelor," but in other more philosophically important cases it is not so clear. For example, are the terms that name kinds of sensations and mental events natural or nominal? The answer is far from clear. Pains are, of course, naturally occurring things, just as bachelors are human beings and not artifacts, but the question is whether the distinctions that we make between various kinds of sensations and mental events are meant to reflect something hidden in the nature of the things, or whether they are from nature's point of view arbitrary and made only by us because of their social or functional significance?

23. Putnam does seem to commit this error. For example, in "The Meaning of 'Meaning'," reprinted in *Language, Mind, and Knowledge,* ed. by Keith Gunderson (Minneapolis: University of Minnesota Press, 1975) he argues that terms for kinds of artifacts are like natural kind terms and are rigid. If I am correct then terms like "pencil," "bottle," "chair," "hammer" are nominal kind terms and we should be able to give an analytical specification of what it is to be a pencil, bottle, chair, etc. The analytical specification would involve superficial characteristics, such as an object's form and function. Putnam holds that virtually every term in the common language is rigid. See also "Is Semantics Possible?", pp. 104–105.

The answer to this question will have a great deal of philosophical significance, both for answering specific questions and for method. If, for example, the terms for kinds of sensations and mental events are nominal kind terms, then philosophical analysis of the meanings of these terms will be relevant to telling us what pain, thought, emotion, etc. are. In the case of nominal kind terms, *"Essence* is expressed by grammar." [24] Goosens correctly delimits the relevance of philosophical analysis.

Philosophers have long viewed what is called "conceptual analysis" as central to their enterprise. . . . For a large number of terms, the association of properties with them is a significant additional feature of understanding them. Here the assumption is widespread that these associations have a core of conventionality—that, in explaining why properties are associated with a term, we must eventually end with "Well, those properties are just what we mean by the term." For underlying trait terms [natural kind terms], which are a part of ordinary language but which are especially prominent in science, it is exactly this additional element of conventionality that is missing, and because of this the analysis of underlying trait terms is different. ("Underlying Trait Terms," pp. 153–154).

A few years ago it was fashionable to engage in philosophical psychology by analyzing the ordinary use of terms like "thinking," "pretending," "imagining," "intending," and so on. As I have indicated, this approach is scorned by scientific realists such as Putnam. In the disagreement about dreaming between Malcolm and Putnam, it is clear that Malcolm is treating "dreaming" as a nominal term and that he takes dreams to be a kind whose essence is to be found in linguistic conventions, whereas Putnam is treating dreams as a natural kind whose essence is discovered by empirical science. The particular question about whether "dream" is a nominal kind or a natural kind term is never addressed by either philosopher. Each just assumes that all of language operates in just one way. I do not pretend to have an answer to the question of whether dreams are a natural or a synthetic class, but this is not just a scientific question either. It depends partly on what we intend by

24. Wittgenstein, *Philosophical Investigations,* para. 371.

"dream." Do we simply refer to some process whose nature is hidden, or do we intend to mean by "dream" anything that fits a certain description, that has certain superficial properties, regardless of its underlying nature? The answer to these questions is going to have a great bearing on what sort of philosophical approach we should take to the question of dreaming.

It is my opinion that traditional thinking about meaning and the new theory of reference need not exclude each other. The new theory is correct about natural kind terms and the traditional theory is correct about nominal kind terms. It is only the belief in the universal application of one view that excludes the other. This means that there is a great deal of cooperation needed in the philosophy of language before we can fully assess the value of Kripke's and Putnam's contribution to the philosophy of mind. In particular, what the philosophers of language must do is tell us how to distinguish nominal kind from natural kind terms, describe the operation of both sorts of terms, and suggest cogent ways of presenting the semantics of both kinds of terms. I hope that this anthology and this Introduction are helpful in stimulating and forwarding such projects.

1 Reference and Definite Descriptions

KEITH S. DONNELLAN

University of California, Los Angeles

I

Definite descriptions, I shall argue, have two possible functions. They are used to refer to what a speaker wishes to talk about, but they are also used quite differently. Moreover, a definite description occurring in one and the same sentence may, on different occasions of its use, function in either way. The failure to deal with this duality of function obscures the genuine referring use of definite descriptions. The best-known theories of definite descriptions, those of Russell and Strawson, I shall suggest, are both guilty of this. Before discussing this distinction in use, I will mention some features of these theories to which it is especially relevant.

On Russell's view a definite description may denote an entity: "if 'C' is a denoting phrase [as definite descriptions are by definition], it may happen that there is one entity x (there cannot be more than one) for which the proposition 'x is identical with C' is true. . . . We may then say that the entity x is the denotation of the phrase 'C'." [1] In using a definite description, then, a speaker may use an expression which denotes some entity, but this is the only relationship between that entity and the use of the definite description recognized by Russell. I shall argue, however, that there are two uses of definite descriptions. The

Reprinted from *The Philosophical Review*, LXXV (July, 1966), 281–304, by permission of the author and editors.
1. "On Denoting," reprinted in *Logic and Knowledge*, ed. by Robert C. Marsh (London: George Allen and Unwin, 1956), p. 51.

definition of denotation given by Russell is applicable to both, but in one of these the definite description serves to do something more. I shall say that in this use the speaker uses the definite description to *refer* to something, and call this use the "referential use" of a definite description. Thus, if I am right, referring is not the same as denoting and the referential use of definite descriptions is not recognized on Russell's view.

Furthermore, on Russell's view the type of expression that comes closest to performing the function of the referential use of definite descriptions turns out, as one might suspect, to be a proper name (in "the narrow logical sense"). Many of the things said about proper names by Russell can, I think, be said about the referential use of definite descriptions without straining senses unduly. Thus the gulf Russell thought he saw between names and definite descriptions is narrower than he thought.

Strawson, on the other hand, certainly does recognize a referential use of definite descriptions. But what I think he did not see is that a definite description may have a quite different role—may be used nonreferentially, even as it occurs in one and the same sentence. Strawson, it is true, points out nonreferential uses of definite descriptions,[2] but which use a definite description has seems to be for him a function of the kind of sentence in which it occurs; whereas, if I am right, there can be two possible uses of a definite description in the same sentence. Thus, in "On Referring," he says, speaking of expressions used to refer, "Any expression of any of these classes [one being that of definite descriptions] can occur as the subject of what would traditionally be regarded as a singular subject-predicate sentence; and would, so occurring, exemplify the use I wish to discuss."[3] So the definite description in, say, the sentence "The Republican candidate for president in 1968 will be a conservative" presumably exemplifies the referential use. But if I am right, we could not say this of the sentence in isolation from some particular occasion on which it is used to state something;

2. "On Referring," reprinted in *Philosophy and Ordinary Language*, ed. by Charles E. Caton (Urbana: University of Illinois Press, 1963), pp. 162–163.
3. *Ibid.*, p. 162.

and then it might or might not turn out that the definite description has a referential use.

Strawson and Russell seem to me to make a common assumption here about the question of how definite descriptions function: that we can ask how a definite description functions in some sentence independently of a particular occasion upon which it is used. This assumption is not really rejected in Strawson's arguments against Russell. Although he can sum up his position by saying, " 'Mentioning' or 'referring' is not something an expression does; it is something that someone can use an expression to do," [4] he means by this to deny the radical view that a "genuine" referring expression *has* a referent, functions to refer, independent of the context of some use of the expression. The denial of this view, however, does not entail that definite descriptions cannot be identified as referring expressions in a sentence unless the sentence is being used. Just as we can speak of a function of a tool that is not at the moment performing its function, Strawson's view, I believe, allows us to speak of the referential function of a definite description in a sentence even when it is not being used. This, I hope to show, is a mistake.

A second assumption shared by Russell's and Strawson's account of definite descriptions is this. In many cases a person who uses a definite description can be said (in some sense) to presuppose or imply that something fits the description.[5] If I state that the king is on his throne, I presuppose or imply that there is a king. (At any rate, it would be an unnatural thing to say for anyone who doubted that there is a king.) Both Russell and Strawson assume that where the presupposition or implication is false, the truth value of what the speaker says is affected. For Russell the statement made is false; for Strawson it has no truth

4. *Ibid.*, p. 170.
5. Here and elsewhere I use the disjunction "presuppose or imply" to avoid taking a stand that would side me with Russell or Strawson on the issue of what the relationship involved is. To take a stand here would be beside my main point as well as being misleading, since later on I shall argue that the presupposition or implication arises in a different way depending upon the use to which the definite description is put. This last also accounts for my use of the vagueness indicator, "in some sense."

value. Now if there are two uses of definite descriptions, it may be that the truth value is affected differently in each case by the falsity of the presupposition or implication. This is what I shall in fact argue. It will turn out, I believe, that one or the other of the two views, Russell's or Strawson's, may be correct about the nonreferential use of definite descriptions, but neither fits the referential use. This is not so surprising about Russell's view, since he did not recognize this use in any case, but it is surprising about Strawson's since the referential use is what he tries to explain and defend. Furthermore, on Strawson's account, the result of there being nothing which fits the description is a failure of reference.[6] This too, I believe, turns out not to be true about the referential use of definite descriptions.

II

There are some uses of definite descriptions which carry neither any hint of a referential use nor any presupposition or implication that something fits the description. In general, it seems, these are recognizable from the sentence frame in which the description occurs. These uses will not interest us, but it is necessary to point them out if only to set them aside.

An obvious example would be the sentence "The present king of France does not exist," used, say, to correct someone's mistaken impression that de Gaulle is the king of France.

A more interesting example is this. Suppose someone were to ask, "Is de Gaulle the king of France?" This is the natural form of words for a person to use who is in doubt as to whether de Gaulle is king or president of France. Given this background to the question, there seems to be no presupposition or implication that someone is the king of France. Nor is the person attempting to refer to someone by using the definite description. On the other hand, reverse the name and description

6. In a footnote added to the original version of "On Referring" (*op. cit.* p. 181) Strawson seems to imply that where the presupposition is false, we still succeed in referring in a "secondary" way, which seems to mean "as we could be said to refer to fictional or make-believe things." But his view is still that we cannot refer in such a case in the "primary" way. This is, I believe, wrong. For a discussion of this modification of Strawson's view see Charles E. Caton, "Strawson on Referring," *Mind*, LXVIII (1959), 539–544.

in the question and the speaker probably would be thought to presuppose or imply this. "Is the king of France de Gaulle?" is the natural question for one to ask who wonders whether it is de Gaulle rather than someone else who occupies the throne of France.[7]

Many times, however, the use of a definite description does carry a presupposition or implication that something fits the description. If definite descriptions do have a referring role, it will be here. But it is a mistake, I think, to try, as I believe both Russell and Strawson do, to settle this matter without further ado. What is needed, I believe, is the distinction I will now discuss.

III

I will call the two uses of definite descriptions I have in mind the attributive use and the referential use. A speaker who uses a definite description attributively in an assertion states something about whoever or whatever is the so-and-so. A speaker who uses a definite description referentially in an assertion, on the other hand, uses the description to enable his audience to pick out whom or what he is talking about and states something about that person or thing. In the first case the definite description might be said to occur essentially, for the speaker wishes to assert something about whatever or whoever fits that description; but in the referential use the definite description is merely one tool for doing a certain job—calling attention to a person or thing—and in general any other device for doing the same job, another description or a name, would do as well. In the attributive use, the attribute of being the so-and-so is all important, while it is not in the referential use.

To illustrate this distinction, in the case of a single sentence, consider the sentence, "Smith's murderer is insane." Suppose first that we come upon poor Smith foully murdered. From the brutal manner of the killing and the fact that Smith was the most lovable person in the world, we might exclaim, "Smith's

---

7. This is an adaptation of an example (used for a somewhat different purpose) given by Leonard Linsky in "Reference and Referents," in *Philosophy and Ordinary Language*, p. 80.

murderer is insane." I will assume, to make it a simpler case, that in a quite ordinary sense we do not know who murdered Smith (though this is not in the end essential to the case). This, I shall say, is an attributive use of the definite description.

The contrast with such a use of the sentence is one of those situations in which we expect and intend our audience to realize whom we have in mind when we speak of Smith's murderer and, most importantly, to know that it is this person about whom we are going to say something.

For example, suppose that Jones has been charged with Smith's murder and has been placed on trial. Imagine that there is a discussion of Jones's odd behavior at his trial. We might sum up our impression of his behavior by saying, "Smith's murderer is insane." If someone asks to whom we are referring, by using this description, the answer here is "Jones." This, I shall say, is a referential use of the definite description.

That these two uses of the definite description in the same sentence are really quite different can perhaps best be brought out by considering the consequences of the assumption that Smith had no murderer (for example, he in fact committed suicide). In both situations, in using the definite description "Smith's murderer," the speaker in some sense presupposes or implies that there is a murderer. But when we hypothesize that the presupposition or implication is false, there are different results for the two uses. In both cases we have used the predicate "is insane," but in the first case, if there is no murderer, there is no person of whom it could be correctly said that we attributed insanity to him. Such a person could be identified (correctly) only in case someone fitted the description used. But in the second case, where the definite description is simply a means of identifying the person we want to talk about, it is quite possible for the correct identification to be made even though no one fits the description we used.[8] We were speaking

8. In "Reference and Referents" (pp. 74–75, 80), Linsky correctly points out that one does not fail to refer simply because the description used does not in fact fit anything (or fits more than one thing). Thus he pinpoints one of the difficulties in Strawson's view. Here, however, I use this fact about referring to make a distinction I believe he does not draw, between two uses of definite descriptions. I later discuss that second passage from Linsky's paper.

about Jones even though he is not in fact Smith's murderer and, in the circumstances imagined, it was his behavior we were commenting upon. Jones might, for example, accuse us of saying false things of him in calling him insane and it would be no defense, I should think, that our description, "the murderer of Smith," failed to fit him.

It is, moreover, perfectly possible for our audience to know to whom we refer, in the second situation, even though they do not share our presupposition. A person hearing our comment in the context imagined might know we are talking about Jones even though he does not think Jones guilty.

Generalizing from this case, we can say, I think, that there are two uses of sentences of the form, "The ϕ is ψ." In the first, if nothing is the ϕ then nothing has been said to be ψ. In the second, the fact that nothing is the ϕ does not have this consequence.

With suitable changes the same difference in use can be formulated for uses of language other than assertions. Suppose one is at a party and, seeing an interesting-looking person holding a martini glass, one asks, "Who is the man drinking a martini?" If it should turn out that there is only water in the glass, one has nevertheless asked a question about a particular person, a question that it is possible for someone to answer. Contrast this with the use of the same question by the chairman of the local Teetotalers Union. He has just been informed that a man is drinking a martini at their annual party. He responds by asking his informant, "Who is the man drinking a martini?" In asking the question the chairman does not have some particular person in mind about whom he asks the question; if no one is drinking a martini, if the information is wrong, no person can be singled out as the person about whom the question was asked. Unlike the first case, the attribute of being the man drinking a martini is all-important, because if it is the attribute of no one, the chairman's question has no straightforward answer.

This illustrates also another difference between the referential and the attributive use of definite descriptions. In the one case we have asked a question about a particular person or thing even though nothing fits the description we used; in the other this is not so. But also in the one case our question can be answered; in the other it cannot be. In the referential use of a definite description we may succeed in picking out a person or thing to ask a question about even though he or it does not really fit the description; but in the attributive use if nothing fits the description, no straightforward answer to the question can be given.

This further difference is also illustrated by commands or orders containing definite descriptions. Consider the order, "Bring me the book on the table." If "the book on the table" is being used referentially, it is possible to fulfill the order even though there is no book on the table. If, for example, there is a book *beside* the table, though there is none *on* it, one might bring that book back and ask the issuer of the order whether this is "the book you meant." And it may be. But imagine we are told that someone has laid a book on our prize antique table, where nothing should be put. The order "Bring me the book on the table" cannot now be obeyed unless there is a book that has been placed on the table. There is no possibility of bringing back a book which was never on the table and having it be the one that was meant, because there is no book that in that sense was "meant." In the one case the definite description was a device for getting the other person to pick the right book; if he is able to pick the right book even though it does not satisfy the description, one still succeeds in his purpose. In the other case, there is, antecedently, no "right book" except one which fits the description; the attribute of being the book on the table is essential. Not only is there no book about which an order was issued, if there is no book on the table, but the order itself cannot be obeyed. When a definite description is used attributively in a command or question and nothing fits the description, the command cannot be obeyed and the question cannot be answered. This suggests some analogous consequence for assertions containing definite descriptions used attributively. Perhaps the analogous result is that the assertion is neither true nor false: this is Strawson's view of what happens when the presupposition of the use of a definite description is false. But if so, Strawson's view works not for definite descriptions used referentially, but for the quite different use, which I have called the attributive use.

I have tried to bring out the two uses of definite descriptions by pointing out the different consequences of supposing that nothing fits the description used. There are still other differences. One is this: when a definite description is used referentially, not only is there in some sense a presupposition or implication that someone or something fits the description, as there is also in the attributive use, but there is a quite different presupposition; the speaker presupposes of some *particular* someone or something that he or it fits the description. In asking, for example, "Who is the man drinking a martini?" where we mean to ask a question about that man over there, we are presupposing that that man over there is drinking a martini— not just that *someone* is a man drinking a martini. When we say, in a context where it is clear we are referring to Jones, "Smith's murderer is insane," we are presupposing that Jones is Smith's murderer. No such presupposition is present in the attributive use of definite descriptions. There is, of course, the presupposition that someone *or other* did the murder, but the speaker does not presupppose of someone in particular—Jones or Robinson, say—that he did it. What I mean by this second kind of presupposition that someone or something in particular fits the description—which is present in a referential use but not in an attributive use—can perhaps be seen more clearly by considering a member of the speaker's audience who believes that Smith was not murdered at all. Now in the case of the referential use of the description, "Smith's murderer," he could accuse the speaker of mistakenly presupposing both that someone or other is the murderer and that also Jones is the murderer, for even though he believes Jones not to have done the deed, he knows that the speaker was referring to Jones. But in the case of the attributive use, he can accuse the speaker of having only the first, less specific presupposition; he cannot pick out some person and claim that the speaker is presupposing that that person is Smith's murderer. Now the more particular presuppositions that we find present in referential uses are clearly not ones we can assign to a definite description in some particular sentence in isolation from a context of use. In order to know that a person presupposes that Jones is Smith's murderer in using the sentence "Smith's murderer is insane," we have to know that he is using the description referentially and also to whom he is referring. The sentence by itself does not tell us any of this.

IV

From the way in which I set up each of the previous examples it might be supposed that the important difference between the referential and the attributive use lies in the beliefs of the speaker. Does he believe of some particular person or thing that he or it fits the description used? In the Smith murder example, for instance, there was in the one case no belief as to who did the deed, whereas in the contrasting case it was believed that Jones did it. But this is, in fact, not an essential difference. It is possible for a definite description to be used attributively even though the speaker (and his audience) believes that a certain person or thing fits the description. And it is possible for a definite description to be used referentially where the speaker believes that nothing fits the description. It is true—and this is why, for simplicity, I set up the examples the way I did—that if a speaker does not believe that anything fits the description or does not believe that he is in a position to pick out what does fit the description, it is likely that he is not using it referentially. It is also true that if he and his audience would pick out some particular thing or person as fitting the description, then a use of the definite description is very likely referential. But these are only presumptions and not entailments.

To use the Smith murder case again, suppose that Jones is on trial for the murder and I and everyone else believe him guilty. Suppose that I comment that the murderer of Smith is insane, but instead of backing this up, as in the example previously used, by citing Jones's behavior in the dock, I go on to outline reasons for thinking that *anyone* who murdered poor Smith in that particularly horrible way must be insane. If now it

turns out that Jones was not the murderer after all, but someone else was, I think I can claim to have been right if the true
murderer is after all insane. Here, I think, I would be using the
definite description attributively, even though I believe that a
particular person fits the description.

It is also possible to think of cases in which the speaker does
not believe that what he means to refer to by using the definite
description fits the description, or to imagine cases in which the
definite description is used referentially even though the
speaker believes *nothing* fits the description. Admittedly, these
cases may be parasitic on a more normal use; nevertheless, they
are sufficient to show that such beliefs of the speaker are not
decisive as to which use is made of a definite description.

Suppose the throne is occupied by a man I firmly believe to
be not the king, but a usurper. Imagine also that his followers
as firmly believe that he is the king. Suppose I wish to see this
man. I might say to his minions, "Is the king in his counting-
house?" I succeed in referring to the man I wish to refer to
without myself believing that he fits the description. It is not
even necessary, moreover, to suppose that his followers believe
him to be the king. If they are cynical about the whole thing,
know he is not the king, I may still succeed in referring to the
man I wish to refer to. Similarly, neither I nor the people I
speak to may suppose that *anyone* is the king and, finally, each
party may know that the other does not so suppose and yet the
reference may go through.

V

Both the attributive and the referential use of definite descriptions seem to carry a presupposition or implication that
there is something which fits the description. But the reasons
for the existence of the presupposition or implication are different in the two cases.

There is a presumption that a person who uses a definite
description referentially believes that what he wishes to refer to
fits the description. Because the purpose of using the description is to get the audience to pick out or think of the right thing
or person, one would normally choose a description that he

believes the thing or person fits. Normally a misdescription of that to which one wants to refer would mislead the audience. Hence, there is a presumption that the speaker believes *something* fits the description—namely, that to which he refers.

When a definite description is used attributively, however, there is not the same possibility of misdescription. In the example of "Smith's murderer" used attributively, there was not the possibility of misdescribing Jones or anyone else; we were not referring to Jones nor to anyone else by using the description. The presumption that the speaker believes *someone* is Smith's murderer does not arise here from a more specific presumption that he believes Jones or Robinson or someone else whom he can name or identify is Smith's murderer.

The presupposition or implication is borne by a definite description used attributively because if nothing fits the description the linguistic purpose of the speech act will be thwarted. That is, the speaker will not succeed in saying something true, if he makes an assertion; he will not succeed in asking a question that can be answered, if he has asked a question; he will not succeed in issuing an order that can be obeyed, if he has issued an order. If one states that Smith's murderer is insane, when Smith has no murderer, and uses the definite description nonreferentially, then one fails to say anything *true*. If one issues the order "Bring me Smith's murderer" under similar circumstances, the order cannot be obeyed; nothing would count as obeying it.

When the definite description is used referentially, on the other hand, the presupposition or implication stems simply from the fact that normally a person tries to describe correctly what he wants to refer to because normally this is the best way to get his audience to recognize what he is referring to. As we have seen, it is possible for the linguistic purpose of the speech act to be accomplished in such a case even though nothing fits the description; it is possible to say something true or to ask a question that gets answered or to issue a command that gets obeyed. For when the definite description is used referentially, one's audience may succeed in seeing to what one refers even though neither it nor anything else fits the description.

VI

The result of the last section shows something to be wrong with the theories of both Russell and Strawson; for though they give differing accounts of the implication or presupposition involved, each gives only one. Yet, as I have argued, the presupposition or implication is present for a quite different reason, depending upon whether the definite description is used attributively or referentially, and exactly what presuppositions or implications are involved is also different. Moreover, neither theory seems a correct characterization of the referential use. On Russell's there is a logical entailment: "The ϕ is ψ" entails "There exists one and only one ϕ." Whether or not this is so for the attributive use, it does not seem true of the referential use of the definite description. The "implication" that something is the ϕ, as I have argued, does not amount to an entailment; it is more like a presumption based on what is *usually* true of the use of a definite description to refer. In any case, of course, Russell's theory does not show—what is true of the referential use—that the implication that *something* is the ϕ comes from the more specific implication that *what is being referred to* is the ϕ. Hence, as a theory of definite descriptions, Russell's view seems to apply, if at all, to the attributive use only.

Russell's definition of denoting (a definite description denotes an entity if that entity fits the description uniquely) is clearly applicable to either use of definite descriptions. Thus whether or not a definite description is used referentially or attributively, it may have a denotation. Hence, denoting and referring, as I have explicated the latter notion, are distinct and Russell's view recognizes only the former. It seems to me, moreover, that this is a welcome result, that denoting and referring should not be confused. If one tried to maintain that they are the same notion, one result would be that a speaker might be referring to something without knowing it. If someone said, for example, in 1960 before he had any idea that Mr. Goldwater would be the Republican nominee in 1964, "The Republican candidate for president in 1964 will be a conservative" (perhaps on the basis of an analysis of the views of party leaders), the definite description here would *denote* Mr. Goldwater. But would we wish to say that the speaker had referred to, mentioned, or talked about Mr. Goldwater? I feel these terms would be out of place. Yet if we identify referring and denoting, it ought to be possible for it to turn out (after the Republican Convention) that the speaker had, unknown to himself, referred in 1960 to Mr. Goldwater. On my view, however, while the definite description used did *denote* Mr. Goldwater (using Russell's definition), the speaker used it *attributively* and did not *refer* to Mr. Goldwater.

Turning to Strawson's theory, it was supposed to demonstrate how definite descriptions are referential. But it goes too far in this direction. For there are nonreferential uses of definite descriptions also, even as they occur in one and the same sentence. I believe that Strawson's theory involves the following propositions:

(1) If someone asserts that the ϕ is ψ he has not made a true or false statement if there is no ϕ.[9]

---

9. In "A Reply to Mr. Sellars," *Philosophical Review*, LXIII (1954), 216–231, Strawson admits that we do not always refuse to ascribe truth to what a person says when the definite description he uses fails to fit anything (or fits more than one thing). To cite one of his examples, a person who said, "The United States Chamber of Deputies contains representatives of two major parties," would be allowed to have said something true even though he had used the wrong title. Strawson thinks this does not constitute a genuine problem for his view. He thinks that what we do in such cases, "where the speaker's intended reference is pretty clear, is simply to amend his statement in accordance with his guessed intentions and assess the amended statement for truth or falsity; we are not awarding a truth value at all to the original statement" (p. 230).

The notion of an "amended statement," however, will not do. We may note, first of all, that the sort of case Strawson has in mind could arise only when a definite description is used referentially. For the "amendment" is made by seeing the speaker's intended reference. But this could happen only if the speaker had an intended reference, a particular person or thing in mind, independent of the description he used. The cases Strawson has in mind are presumably not cases of slips of the tongue or the like; presumably they are cases in which a definite description is used because the speaker believes, though he is mistaken, that he is describing correctly what he wants to refer to. We supposedly amend the statement by knowing to what he intends to refer. But what description is to be used in the amended statement? In the example, perhaps, we could use "the United States Congress." But his description might be one the speaker would not even accept as correctly describing what he wants to

(2) If there is no ϕ then the speaker has failed to refer to anything.[10]

(3) The reason he has said nothing true or false is that he has failed to refer.

Each of these propositions is either false or, at best, applies to only one of the two uses of definite descriptions.

Proposition (1) is possibly true of the attributive use. In the example in which "Smith's murderer is insane" was said when Smith's body was first discovered, an attributive use of the definite description, there was no person to whom the speaker referred. If Smith had no murderer, nothing true was said. It is quite tempting to conclude, following Strawson, that nothing true *or* false was said. But where the definite description is used referentially, something true may well have been said. It is possible that something true was said of the person or thing referred to.[11]

Proposition (2) is, as we have seen, simply false. Where a definite description is used referentially it is perfectly possible to refer to something though nothing fits the description used.

The situation with proposition (3) is a bit more complicated. It ties together, on Strawson's view, the two strands given in (1) and (2). As an account of why, when the presupposition is false, nothing true or false has been stated, it clearly cannot work for the attributive use of definite descriptions, for the reason it

---

refer to, because he is misinformed about the correct title. Hence, this is not a case of deciding what the speaker meant to say as opposed to what he in fact said, for the speaker did not mean to say "the United States Congress." If this is so, then there is no bar to the "amended" statement containing any description that does correctly pick out what the speaker intended to refer to. It could be, e.g., "The lower house of the United States Congress." But this means that there is no one unique "amended" statement to be assessed for truth value. And, in fact, it should now be clear that the notion of the amended statement really plays no role anyway. For if we can arrive at the amended statement only by first knowing to what the speaker intended to refer, we can assess the truth of what he said simply by deciding whether what he intended to refer to has the properties he ascribed to it.

10. As noted earlier (fn. 6), Strawson may allow that one has possibly referred in a "secondary" way, but, if I am right, the fact that there is no ϕ does not preclude one from having referred in the same way one does if there is a ϕ.

11. For a further discussion of the notion of saying something true *of* someone or something, see sec. VIII (p. 60).

supplies is that reference has failed. It does not then give the reason why, if indeed this is so, a speaker using a definite description attributively fails to say anything true or false if nothing fits the description. It does, however, raise a question about the referential use. Can reference fail when a definite description is used referentially?

I do not fail to refer merely because my audience does not correctly pick out what I am referring to. I can be referring to a particular man when I use the description "the man drinking a martini," even though the people to whom I speak fail to pick out the right person or any person at all. Nor, as we have stressed, do I fail to refer when nothing fits the description. But perhaps I fail to refer in some extreme circumstances, when there is nothing that *I* am willing to pick out as that to which I referred.

Suppose that I think I see at some distance a man walking and ask, "Is the man carrying a walking stick the professor of history?" We should perhaps distinguish four cases at this point. (a) There is a man carrying a walking stick; I have then referred to a person and asked a question about him that can be answered if my audience has the information. (b) The man over there is not carrying a walking stick, but an umbrella; I have still referred to someone and asked a question that can be answered, though if my audience sees that it is an umbrella and not a walking stick, they may also correct my apparently mistaken impression. (c) It is not a man at all, but a rock that looks like one; in this case, I think I still have referred to something, to the thing over there that happens to be a rock but that I took to be a man. But in this case it is not clear that my question can be answered correctly. This, I think, is not because I have failed to refer, but rather because, given the true nature of what I referred to, my question is not appropriate. A simple "No, that is not the professor of history" is at least a bit misleading if said by someone who realizes that I mistook a rock for a person. It may, therefore, be plausible to conclude that in such a case I have not asked a question to which there is a straightforwardly correct answer. But if this is true, it is not because nothing fits the description I used, but rather because what I referred to is a rock and my question has no correct answer when asked of a rock. (d) There is finally the case in which there is nothing at all where I thought there was a man with a walking stick; and perhaps here we have a genuine failure to refer at all, even though the description was used for the purpose of referring. There is no rock, nor anything else, to which I meant to refer; it was, perhaps, a trick of light that made me think there was a man there. I cannot say of anything, "That is what I was referring to, though I now see that it's not a man carrying a walking stick." This failure of reference, however, requires circumstances much more radical than the mere non-existence of anything fitting the description used. It requires that there be nothing of which it can be said, "That is what he was referring to." Now perhaps also in such cases, if the speaker has asserted something, he fails to state anything true or false if there is nothing that can be identified as that to which he referred. But if so, the failure of reference and truth value does not come about merely because nothing fits the description he used. So (3) may be true of some cases of the referential use of definite descriptions; it may be true that a failure of reference results in a lack of truth value. But these cases are of a much more extreme sort than Strawson's theory implies.

I conclude, then, that neither Russell's nor Strawson's theory represents a correct account of the use of definite descriptions—Russell's because it ignores altogether the referential use, Strawson's because it fails to make the distinction between the referential and the attributive and mixes together truths about each (together with some things that are false).

VII

It does not seem possible to say categorically of a definite description in a particular sentence that it is a referring expression (of course, one could say this if he meant that it *might* be used to refer). In general, whether or not a definite description is used referentially or attributively is a function of the speaker's intentions in a particular case. "The murderer of Smith" may be used either way in the sentence "The murderer of Smith is insane." It does not appear plausible to account for this, either, as an ambiguity in the sentence. The grammatical structure of the sentence seems to me to be the same whether the description is used referentially or attributively: that is, it is not syntactically ambiguous. Nor does it seem at all attractive to suppose an ambiguity in the meaning of the words; it does not appear to be semantically ambiguous. (Perhaps we could say that the sentence is pragmatically ambiguous: the distinction between roles that the description plays is a function of the speaker's intentions.) These, of course, are intuitions; I do not have an argument for these conclusions. Nevertheless, the burden of proof is surely on the other side.

This, I think, means that the view, for example, that sentences can be divided up into predicates, logical operators, and referring expressions is not generally true. In the case of definite descriptions one cannot always assign the referential function in isolation from a particular occasion on which it is used.

There may be sentences in which a definite description can be used only attributively or only referentially. A sentence in which it seems that the definite description could be used only attributively would be "Point out the man who is drinking my martini." I am not so certain that any can be found in which the definite description can be used only referentially. Even if there are such sentences, it does not spoil the point that there are many sentences, apparently not ambiguous either syntactically or semantically, containing definite descriptions that can be used either way.

If it could be shown that the dual use of definite descriptions can be accounted for by the presence of an ambiguity, there is still a point to be made against the theories of Strawson and Russell. For neither, so far as I can see, has anything to say about the possibility of such an ambiguity and, in fact, neither seems compatible with such a possibility. Russell's does not recognize the possibility of the referring use, and Strawson's, as I have tried to show in the last section, combines elements from each use into one unitary account. Thus the view that there is an ambiguity in such sentences does not seem any more attractive to these positions.

VIII

Using a definite description referentially, a speaker may say something true even though the description correctly applies to nothing. The sense in which he may say something true is the sense in which he may say something true about someone or something. This sense is, I think, an interesting one that needs investigation. Isolating it is one of the by-products of the distinction between the attributive and referential uses of definite descriptions.

For one thing, it raises questions about the notion of a statement. This is brought out by considering a passage in a paper by Leonard Linsky in which he rightly makes the point that one can refer to someone although the definite description used does not correctly describe the person:

. . . said of a spinster that "Her husband is kind to her" is neither true nor false. But a speaker might very well be referring to someone using these words, for he may think that someone is the husband of the lady (who in fact is a spinster). Still, the statement is neither true nor false, for it presupposes that the lady has a husband, which she has not. This last refutes Strawson's thesis that if the presupposition of existence is not satisfied, the speaker has failed to refer.[12]

There is much that is right in this passage. But because Linsky does not make the distinction between the referential and the attributive uses of definite descriptions, it does not represent a wholly adequate account of the situation. A perhaps minor point about this passage is that Linsky apparently thinks it sufficient to establish that the speaker in his example is referring to someone by using the definite description "her husband," that he *believe* that someone is her husband. This will only approximate the truth provided that the "someone" in the de-

12. "Reference and Referents," p. 80. It should be clear that I agree with Linsky in holding that a speaker may refer even though the "presupposition of existence" is not satisfied. And I agree in thinking this an objection to Strawson's view. I think, however, that this point, among others, can be used to define two distinct uses of definite descriptions which, in turn, yields a more general criticism of Strawson. So, while I develop here a point of difference, which grows out of the distinction I want to make, I find myself in agreement with much of Linsky's article.

scription of the belief means "someone in particular" and is not merely the existential quantifier, "there is someone or other." For in both the attributive and the referental use the belief that someone *or other* is the husband of the lady is very likely to be present. If, for example, the speaker has just met the lady and, noticing her cheerfulness and radiant good health, makes his remark from his conviction that these attributes are always the result of having good husbands, he would be using the definite description attributively. Since she has no husband, there is no one to pick out as the person to whom he was referring. Nevertheless, the speaker believed that *someone or other* was her husband. On the other hand, if the use of "her husband" was simply a way of referring to a man the speaker has just met whom he assumed to be the lady's husband, he would have referred to that man even though neither he nor anyone else fits the description. I think it is likely that in this passage Linsky did mean by "someone," in his description of the belief, "someone in particular." But even then, as we have seen, we have neither a sufficient nor a necessary condition for a referential use of the definite description. A definite description can be used attributively even when the speaker believes that some particular thing or person fits the description, and it can be used referentially in the absence of this belief.

My main point, here, however, has to do with Linsky's view that because the presupposition is not satisfied, the *statement* is neither true nor false. This seems to me possibly correct *if* the definite description is thought of as being used attributively (depending upon whether we go with Strawson or Russell). But when we consider it as used referentially, this categorical assertion is no longer clearly correct. For the man the speaker referred to may indeed be kind to the spinster; the speaker may have said something true about that man. Now the difficulty is in the notion of "the statement." Suppose that we know that the lady is a spinster, but nevertheless know that the man referred to by the speaker is kind to her. It seems to me that we shall, on the one hand, want to hold that the speaker said something true, but be reluctant to express this by "It is true that her husband is kind to her."

This shows, I think, a difficulty in speaking simply about "the statement" when definite descriptions are used referentially. For the speaker stated something, in this example, about a particular person, and his statement, we may suppose, was true. Nevertheless, we should not like to agree with his statement by using the sentence he used; we should not like to identify the true statement via the speaker's words. The reason for this is not so hard to find. If we say, in this example, "It is true that her husband is kind to her," *we* are now using the definite description either attributively or referentially. But we should not be subscribing to what the original speaker truly said if we use the description attributively, for it was only in its function as referring to a particular person that the definite description yields the possibility of saying something true (since the lady has no husband). Our reluctance, however, to endorse the original speaker's statement by using the definite description referentially to refer to the same person stems from quite a different consideration. For if we too were laboring under the mistaken belief that this man was the lady's husband, we could agree with the original speaker using his exact words. (Moreover, it is possible, as we have seen, deliberately to use a definite description to refer to someone we believe not to fit the description.) Hence, our reluctance to use the original speaker's words does not arise from the fact that if we did we should not succeed in stating anything true or false. It rather stems from the fact that when a definite description is used referentially there is a presumption that the speaker believes that what he refers to fits the description. Since we, who know the lady to be a spinster, would not normally want to give the impression that we believe otherwise, we would not like to use the original speaker's way of referring to the man in question.

How then would we express agreement with the original speaker without involving ourselves in unwanted impressions about our beliefs? The answer shows another difference between the referential and attributive uses of definite descriptions and brings out an important point about genuine referring.

When a speaker says, "The ϕ is ψ," where "the ϕ" is used attributively, if there is no ϕ, we cannot correctly report the speaker as having said *of* this or that person or thing that it is ψ. But if the definite description is used referentially we can report the speaker as having attributed ψ to something. And *we* may refer to what the speaker referred to, using whatever description or name suits our purpose. Thus, if a speaker says, "Her husband is kind to her," referring to the man he was just talking to, and if that man is Jones, we may report him as having said *of Jones* that he is kind to her. If Jones is also the president of the college, we may report the speaker as having said *of the president of the college* that he is kind to her. And finally, if we are talking to Jones, we may say, referring to the original speaker, "He said of you that *you* are kind to her." It does not matter here whether or not the woman has a husband or whether, if she does, Jones is her husband. If the original speaker referred to Jones, he said of him that he is kind to her. Thus where the definite description is used referentially, but does not fit what was referred to, we can report what a speaker said and agree with him by using a description or name which does fit. In doing so we need not, it is important to note, choose a description or name which the original speaker would agree fits what he was referring to. That is, we can report the speaker in the above case to have said truly of Jones that he is kind to her even if the original speaker did not know that the man he was referring to is named Jones or even if he thinks he is not named Jones.

Returning to what Linsky said in the passage quoted, he claimed that, were someone to say "Her husband is kind to her," when she has no husband, *the statement* would be neither true nor false. As I have said, this is a likely view to hold if the definite description is being used attributively. But if it is being used referentially it is not clear what is meant by "the statement." If we think about what the speaker said about the person he referred to, then there is no reason to suppose he has not said something true or false about him, even though he is not the lady's husband. And Linsky's claim would be wrong. On the other hand, if we do not identify the statement in this way, what is the statement that the speaker made? To say that the statement he made was that her husband is kind to her lands us in difficulties. For we have to decide whether in using the definite description here in the identification of the statement, we are using it attributively or referentially. If the former, then we misrepresent the linguistic performance of the speaker; if the latter, then we are ourselves referring to someone and reporting the speaker to have said something of that person, in which case we are back to the possibility that he did say something true or false of that person.

I am thus drawn to the conclusion that when a speaker uses a definite description referentially he may have stated something true or false even if nothing fits the description, and that there is not a clear sense in which he has made a statement which is neither true nor false.

IX

I want to end by a brief examination of a picture of what a genuine referring expression is that one might derive from Russell's views. I want to suggest that this picture is not so far wrong as one might suppose and that strange as this may seem, some of the things we have said about the referential use of definite descriptions are not foreign to this picture.

Genuine proper names, in Russell's sense, would refer to something without ascribing any properties to it. They would, one might say, refer to the thing itself, not simply the thing in so far as it falls under a certain description.[13] Now this would seem to Russell something a definite description could not do, for he assumed that if definite descriptions were capable of referring at all, they would refer to something only in so far as that thing satisfied the description. Not only have we seen this assumption to be false, however, but in the last section we saw something more. We saw that when a definite description is used referentially, a speaker can be reported as having said something *of* something. And in reporting what it was of which he said something we are not restricted to the description he used, or synonyms of it; we may ourselves refer to it using any

13. Cf. "The Philosophy of Logical Atomism," reprinted in *Logic and Knowledge*, p. 200.

descriptions, names, and so forth, that will do the job. Now this seems to give a sense in which we are concerned with the thing itself and not just the thing under a certain description, when we report the linguistic act of a speaker using a definite description referentially. That is, such a definite description comes closer to performing the function of Russell's proper names than certainly he supposed.

Secondly, Russell thought, I believe, that whenever we use descriptions, as opposed to proper names, we introduce an element of generality which ought to be absent if what we are doing is referring to some particular thing. This is clear from his analysis of sentences containing definite descriptions. One of the conclusions we are supposed to draw from that analysis is that such sentences express what are in reality completely general propositions: there is a ϕ and only one such and any ϕ is ψ. We might put this in a slightly different way. If there is anything which might be identified as reference here, it is reference in a very weak sense—namely, reference to *whatever* is the one and only one ϕ, if there is any such. Now this is something we might well say about the attributive use of definite descriptions, as should be evident from the previous discussion. But this lack of particularity is absent from the referential use of definite descriptions precisely because the description is here merely a device for getting one's audience to pick out or think of the thing to be spoken about, a device which may serve its function even if the description is incorrect. More importantly perhaps, in the referential use as opposed to the attributive, there is a *right* thing to be picked out by the audience and its being the right thing is not simply a function of its fitting the description.

2 Identity and Necessity

SAUL KRIPKE

The Rockefeller University

A problem which has arisen frequently in contemporary philosophy is: "How are *contingent* identity statements possible?" This question is phrased by analogy with the way Kant phrased his question "How are synthetic a priori judgments possible?" In both cases, it has usually been taken for granted in the one case by Kant that synthetic a priori judgments were possible, and in the other case in contemporary philosophical literature that contingent statements of identity are possible. I do not intend to deal with the Kantian question except to mention this analogy: After a rather thick book was written trying to answer the question how synthetic a priori judgments were possible, others came along later who claimed that the solution to the problem was that synthetic a priori judgments were, of course, impossible and that a book trying to show otherwise was written in vain. I will not discuss who was right on the possibility of synthetic a priori judgments. But in the case of contingent statements of identity, most philosophers have felt that the notion of a contingent identity statement ran into something like the following paradox. An argument like the following can be given against the possibility of contingent identity statements:[1]

Reprinted by permission of New York University Press from *Identity and Individuation*, edited by Milton K. Munitz, © 1971 by New York University, pp. 135–164.

1. This paper was presented orally, without a written text, to the New York University lecture series on identity which makes up the volume *Identity and Individuation*. The lecture was taped, and the present paper represents a transcription of these tapes, edited only slightly with no attempt to change the style of the original. If the reader imagines the sentences of this paper as being de-

First, the law of the substitutivity of identity says that, for any objects x and y, if x is identical to y, then if x has a certain property F, so does y:

(1) $(x)(y)[(x=y) \supset (Fx \supset Fy)]$

On the other hand, every object surely is necessarily self-identical:

(2) $(x) \square (x=x)$

But

(3) $(x)(y)[(x=y) \supset [\square (x=x) \supset \square(x=y)]$ $\} \quad F\mathcal{L} = \square(x = \mathcal{L})$

is a substitution instance of (1), the substitutivity law. From (2) and (3), we can conclude that, for every x and y, if x equals y, then, it is necessary that x equals y:

(4) $(x)(y)((x=y) \supset \square(x=y))$

This is because the clause $\square(x=x)$ of the conditional drops out because it is known to be true.

This is an argument which has been stated many times in recent philosophy. Its conclusion, however, has often been regarded as highly paradoxical. For example, David Wiggins, in his paper, "Identity-Statements," says,

Now there undoubtedly exist contingent identity-statements. Let $a=b$ be one of them. From its simple truth and (5) [= (4) above] we can derive '$\square(a=b)$'. But how then can there be any contingent identity-statements? [2]

---

livered, extemporaneously, with proper pauses and emphases, this may facilitate his comprehension. Nevertheless, there may still be passages which are hard to follow, and the time allotted necessitated a condensed presentation of the argument. (A longer version of some of these views, still rather compressed and still representing a transcript of oral remarks, has appeared in *Semantics of Natural Language*, ed. by Donald Davidson and Gilbert Harman, [Dordrecht: D. Reidel, 1972].) Occasionally, reservations, amplifications and gratifications of my remarks had to be repressed, especially in the discussion of theoretical identification and the mind-body problem. The footnotes, which were added to the original, would have become even more unwieldy if this had not been done.

2. R. J. Butler, ed., *Analytical Philosophy, Second Series* (Oxford: Blackwell, 1965), p. 41.

He then says that five various reactions to this argument are possible, and rejects all of these reactions, and reacts himself. I do not want to discuss all the possible reactions to this statement, except to mention the second of those Wiggins rejects. This says,

We might accept the result and plead that provided 'a' and 'b' are proper names nothing is amiss. The consequence of this is that no contingent identity-statements can be made by means of proper names.

And then he says that he is discontented with this solution and many other philosophers have been discontented with this solution, too, while still others have advocated it.

What makes the statement (4) seem surprising? It says, for any objects x and y, if x is y, then it is necessary that x is y. I have already mentioned that someone might object to this argument on the grounds that premise (2) is already false, that it is not the case that everything is necessarily self-identical. Well, for example, am I myself necessarily self-identical? Someone might argue that in some situations which we can imagine I would not even have existed and therefore the statement "Saul Kripke is Saul Kripke" would have been false or it would not be the case that I was self-identical. Perhaps, it would have been neither true nor false, in such a world, to say that Saul Kripke is self-identical. Well, that may be so, but really it depends on one's philosophical view of a topic that I will not discuss, that is, what is to be said about truth values of statements mentioning objects that do not exist in the actual world or any given possible world or counterfactual situation. Let us interpret necessity here weakly. We can count statements as necessary if whenever the objects mentioned therein exist, the statement would be true. If we wished to be very careful about this, we would have to go into the question of existence as a predicate and ask if the statement can be reformulated in the form: For every x it is necessary that, if x exists, then x is self-identical. I will not go into this particular form of subtlety here because it is not going to be relevant to my main theme. Nor am I really going to consider formula (4). Anyone who believes formula (2) is, in my opinion, committed to formula (4). If x and y are the same things and we can talk about modal properties of an object at all, that is, in the usual parlance, we can speak of modality *de re* and an object *necessarily* having certain properties as such, then formula (1), I think, has to hold. Where x is any property at all, including a property involving modal operators, and if x and y are the same object and x had a certain property F, then y has to have the same property F. And this is so even if the property F is itself of the form of necessarily having some other property G, in particular that of necessarily being identical to a certain object. Well, I will not discuss the formula (4) itself because by itself it does not assert, of any particular true statement of identity, that it is necessary. It does not say anything about *statements* at all. It says for every *object* x and *object* y, if x and y are the same object, then it is necessary that x and y are the same object. And this, I think, if we think about it (anyway, if someone does not think so, I will not argue for it here), really amounts to something very little different from the statement (2). Since x, by definition of identity, is the only object identical with x, "$(y)(y=x \supset Fy)$" seems to me to be little more than a garrulous way of saying 'Fx', and thus $(x)(y)(y=x \supset Fx)$ says the same as $(x)Fx$ no matter what 'F' is—in particular, even if 'F' stands for the property of necessary identity with x. So if x has this property (of necessary identity with x), trivially everything identical with x has it, as (4) asserts. But, from statement (4) one may apparently be able to deduce that various particular statements of identity must be necessary and this is then supposed to be a very paradoxical consequence.

Wiggins says, "Now there undoubtedly exist contingent identity-statements." One example of a contingent identity statement is the statement that the first Postmaster General of the United States is identical with the inventor of bifocals, or that both of these are identical with the man claimed by the *Saturday Evening Post* as its founder (*falsely* claimed, I gather, by the way). Now some such statements are plainly contingent. It plainly is a contingent fact that one and the same man both invented bifocals and took on the job of Postmaster General of the United States. How can we reconcile this with the truth of statement (4)? Well, that, too, is an issue I do not want to go into in detail except to be very dogmatic about it. It was I think settled quite well by Bertrand Russell in his notion of the scope of a description. According to Russell, one can, for example, say with propriety that the author of *Hamlet* might not have written *Hamlet,* or even that the author of *Hamlet* might not have been the author of *Hamlet.* Now here, of course, we do not deny the necessity of the identity of an object with itself; but we say it is true concerning a certain man that he in fact was the unique person to have written *Hamlet* and secondly that the man, who in fact was the man who wrote *Hamlet,* might not have written *Hamlet.* In other words, if Shakespeare had decided not to write tragedies, he might not have written *Hamlet.* Under these circumstances, the man who in fact wrote *Hamlet* would not have written *Hamlet.* Russell brings this out by saying that in such a statement, the first occurrence of the description "the author of *Hamlet*" has large scope.[3] That is, we say "The author of *Hamlet* has the following property: that he might not have written *Hamlet.*" We *do not* assert that the following statement might have been the case, namely that the author of *Hamlet* did not write *Hamlet,* for that is not true. That would be to say that it might have been the case that someone wrote *Hamlet* and yet did not write *Hamlet,* which would be a contradiction. Now, aside from the details of Russell's particular formulation of it, which depends on his theory of descriptions, this seems to be the distinction that any theory of descriptions has to make. For example, if someone were to meet the President of Harvard and take him to be a Teaching Fellow, he might say: "I took the President of Harvard for a Teaching Fellow." By this he does not mean that he took the proposition "The President of Harvard is a Teaching Fellow" to be true. He could have meant this, for example, had he believed that some sort of democratic system had gone so far at Harvard that the President of it decided to take on the task of being a Teaching Fellow. But that probably is not what he means. What he means instead, as Russell points out, is "Someone is President of Harvard and I

---

3. The second occurrence of the description has small scope.

took him to be a Teaching Fellow." In one of Russell's examples someone says, "I thought your yacht is much larger than it is." And the other man replies, "No, my yacht is not much larger than it is."

Provided that the notion of modality *de re,* and thus of quantifying into modal contexts, makes any sense at all, we have quite an adequate solution to the problem of avoiding paradoxes if we substitute descriptions for the universal quantifiers in (4) because the only consequence we will draw,[4] for example, in the bifocals case, is that there is a man who both happened to have invented bifocals and happened to have been the first Postmaster General of the United States, and is necessarily self-identical. There is an object x such that x invented bifocals, and as a matter of contingent fact an object y, such that y is the first Postmaster General of the United States, and finally, it is necessary, that x is y. What are x and y here? Here, x and y are both Benjamin Franklin, and it can certainly be necessary that Benjamin Franklin is identical with himself. So, there is no problem in the case of descriptions if we accept Russell's notion of scope.[5] And I just dogmatically want to drop that question here

4. In Russell's theory, $F(\imath xGx)$ follows from $(x)Fx$ and $(\exists!x)Gx$, provided that the description in $F(\imath xGx)$ has the entire context for its scope (in Russell's 1905 terminology, has a 'primary occurrence'). Only then is $F(\imath xGx)$ 'about' the denotation of '$\imath xGx$'. Applying this rule to (4), we get the results indicated in the text. Notice that, in the ambiguous form $\Box(\imath xGx = \imath xHx)$, if one or both of the descriptions have 'primary occurrences' the formula does not assert the necessity of $\imath xGx = \imath xHx$; if both have secondary occurrences, it does. Thus in a language without explicit scope indicators, descriptions must be construed with the smallest possible scope—only then will $\sim A$ be the negation of A, $\Box A$ the necessitation of A, and the like.

5. An earlier distinction with the same purpose was, of course, the medieval one of *de dicto–de re*. That Russell's distinction of scope eliminates modal paradoxes has been pointed out by many logicians, especially Smullyan.

So as to avoid misunderstanding, let me emphasize that I am of course not asserting that Russell's notion of scope solves Quine's problem of 'essentialism'; what it does show, especially in conjunction with modern model-theoretic approaches to modal logic, is that quantified modal logic need not deny the truth of all instances of $(x)(y)(x=y\cdot \supset \cdot Fx \supset Fy)$, nor of all instances of '$(x)(Gx \supset Ga)$' (where 'a' is to be replaced by a nonvacuous definite description whose scope is all of 'Ga'), in order to avoid making it a necessary truth that one and the same man invented bifocals and headed the original Postal Department. Russell's contextual definition of description need not be adopted in order to ensure these results; but other logical theories, Fregean or other, which take descrip-

and go on to the question about names which Wiggins raises. And Wiggins says he might accept the result and plead that, provided *a* and *b* are proper names, nothing is amiss. And then he rejects this.

Now what is the special problem about proper names? At least if one is not familiar with the philosophical literature about this matter, one naively feels something like the following about proper names. First, if someone says "Cicero was an orator," then he uses the name 'Cicero' in that statement simply to pick out a certain object and then to ascribe a certain property to the object, namely, in this case, he ascribes to a certain man the property of having been an orator. If someone else uses another name, such as, say, 'Tully', he is still speaking about the same man. One ascribes the same property, if one says "Tully is an orator," to the same man. So to speak, the fact, or state of affairs, represented by the statement is the same whether one says "Cicero is an orator" or one says "Tully is an orator." It would, therefore, seem that the function of names is *simply* to refer, and not to describe the objects so named by such properties as "being the inventor of bifocals" or "being the first Postmaster General." It would seem that Leibniz' law and the law (1) should not only hold in the universally quantified form, but also in the form "if *a* = *b* and *Fa*, then *Fb*," wherever '*a*' and '*b*' stand in place of names and '*F*' stands in place of a predicate expressing a genuine property of the object:

$$(a = b \cdot Fa) \supset Fb$$

We can run the same argument through again to obtain the conclusion where '*a*' and '*b*' replace any names, "If *a* = *b*, then

---

tions as primitive must somehow express the same logical facts. Frege showed that a simple, non-iterated context containing a definite description with small scope, which cannot be interpreted as being 'about' the denotation of the description, can be interpreted as about its 'sense'. Some logicians have been interested in the question of the conditions under which, in an intensional context, a description with small scope is equivalent to the same one with large scope. One of the virtues of a Russellian treatment of descriptions in modal logic is that the answer (roughly that the description be a 'rigid designator' in the sense of this lecture) then often follows from the other postulates for quantified modal logic: no special postulates are needed, as in Hintikka's treatment. Even if descriptions are taken as primitive, special postulation of when scope is irrelevant can often be deduced from more basic axioms.

necessarily *a* = *b*." And so, we could venture this conclusion: that whenever '*a*' and '*b*' are proper names, if *a* is *b*, that it is necessary that *a* is *b*. Identity statements between proper names have to be necessary if they are going to be true at all. This view in fact has been advocated, for example, by Ruth Barcan Marcus in a paper of hers on the philosophical interpretation of modal logic.[6] According to this view, whenever, for example, someone makes a correct statement of identity between two names, such as, for example, that Cicero is Tully, his statement has to be necessary if it is true. But such a conclusion *seems* plainly to be false. (I, like other philosophers, have a habit of understatement in which "it seems plainly false" means "it is plainly false." Actually, I think the view is true, though not quite in the form defended by Mrs. Marcus.) At any rate, it seems plainly false. One example was given by Professor Quine in his reply to Professor Marcus at the symposium: "I think I see trouble anyway in the contrast between proper names and descriptions as Professor Marcus draws it. The paradigm of the assigning of proper names is tagging. We may tag the planet Venus some fine evening with the proper name 'Hesperus'. We may tag the same planet again someday before sun rise with the proper name 'Phosphorus'." (Quine thinks that something like that actually was done once.) "When, at last, we discover that we have tagged the same planet twice, our discovery is empirical, and not because the proper names were descriptions." According to what we are told, the planet Venus seen in the morning was originally thought to be a star and was called "the Morning Star," or (to get rid of any question of using a description) was called 'Phosphorus'. One and the same planet, when seen in the evening, was thought to be another star, the Evening Star, and was called "Hesperus." Later on, astronomers discovered that Phosphorus and Hesperus were one and the same. Surely no amount of a priori ratiocination on their part could conceivably have made it possible for them to deduce that Phosphorus is Hesperus. In fact, given the information they had, it might have turned out the other way. Therefore, it

6. "Modalities and Intensional Languages," *Boston Studies in the Philosophy of Science,* Vol. 1 (New York: Humanities Press, 1963), pp. 71ff. See also the "Comments" by Quine and the ensuing discussion.

is argued, the statement 'Hesperus is Phosphorus' has to be an ordinary contingent, empirical truth, one which might have come out otherwise, and so the view that true identity statements between names are necessary has to be false. Another example which Quin_ gives in *Word and Object* is taken from Professor Schrödinger, the famous pioneer of quantum mechanics: A certain mountain can be seen from both Tibet and Nepal. When seen from one direction it was called 'Gaurisanker'; when seen from another direction, it was called 'Everest'; and then, later on, the empirical discovery was made that Gaurisanker *is* Everest. (Quine further says that he gathers the example is actually geographically incorrect. I guess one should not rely on physicists for geographical information.)

Of course, one possible reaction to this argument is to deny that names like 'Cicero', 'Tully', 'Gaurisanker', and 'Everest' really are proper names. Look, someone might say (someone has said it: his name was 'Bertrand Russell'), just because statements like "Hesperus is Phosphorus" and "Gaurisanker is Everest" are contingent, we can see that the names in question are not really purely referential. You are not, in Mrs. Marcus' phrase, just 'tagging' an object; you are actually describing it. What does the contingent fact that Hesperus is Phosphorus amount to? Well, it amounts to the fact that *the* star in a certain portion of the sky in the evening is *the* star in a certain portion of the sky in the morning. Similarly, the contingent fact that Guarisanker is Everest amounts to the fact that the mountain viewed from such and such an angle in Nepal is the mountain viewed from such and such another angle in Tibet. Therefore, such names as 'Hesperus' and 'Phosphorus' can only be abbreviations for descriptions. The term 'Phosphorus' *has* to mean "the star seen . . . ," or (let us be cautious because it actually turned out not to be a star), "the *heavenly body* seen from such and such a position at such and such a time in the morning," and the name 'Hesperus' has to mean "the heavenly body seen in such and such a position at such and such a time in the evening." So, Russell concludes, if we want to reserve the term "name" for things which really just name an object without describing it, the only real proper names we can have are names of our own immediate sense data, objects of our own 'immediate acquaintance'. The only such names which occur in language are demonstratives like "this" and "that." And it is easy to see that this requirement of necessity of identity, understood as exempting identities between names from all imaginable doubt, can indeed be guaranteed only for demonstrative names of immediate sense data; for only in such cases can an identity statement between two different names have a general immunity from Cartesian doubt. There are some other things Russell has sometimes allowed as objects of acquaintance, such as one's self; we need not go into details here. Other philosophers (for example, Mrs. Marcus in her reply, at least in the verbal discussion as I remember it—I do not know if this got into print, so perhaps this should not be 'tagged' on her [7]) have said, "If names are really just tags, genuine tags, then a good dictionary should be able to tell us that they are names of the same object." You have an object *a* and an object *b* with names 'John' and 'Joe'. Then, according to Mrs. Marcus, a dictionary should be able to tell you whether or not 'John' and 'Joe' are names of the same object. Of course, I do not know what ideal dictionaries should do, but ordinary proper names do not seem to satisfy this requirement. You certainly *can,* in the case of ordinary proper names, make quite empirical discoveries that, let's say, Hesperus is Phosphorus, though we thought otherwise. We can be in doubt as to whether Gaurisanker is Everest or Cicero is in fact Tully. Even now, we could conceivably discover that we were wrong in supposing that Hesperus was Phosphorus. Maybe the astronomers made an error. So it seems that this view is wrong and that if by a name we do not mean some artificial notion of names such as Russell's, but a proper name in the ordinary sense, then there can be contingent identity statements using proper names, and the view to the contrary seems plainly wrong.

In recent philosophy a large number of other identity statements have been emphasized as examples of contingent identity statements, different, perhaps, from either of the types I

7. It should. See her remark on p. 115, *Boston Studies in the Philosophy of Science,* Vol. 1, in the discussion following the papers.

have mentioned before. One of them is, for example, the statement "Heat is the motion of molecules." First, science is supposed to have discovered this. Empirical scientists in their investigations have been supposed to discover (and, I suppose, they did) that the external phenomenon which we call "heat" is, in fact, molecular agitation. Another example of such a discovery is that water is H_2O, and yet other examples are that gold is the element with such and such an atomic number, that light is a stream of photons, and so on. These are all in some sense of "identity statement" identity statements. Second, it is thought, they are plainly contingent identity statements, just because they were scientific discoveries. After all, heat might have turned out not to have been the motion of molecules. There were other alternative theories of heat proposed, for example, the caloric theory of heat. If these theories of heat had been correct, then heat would not have been the motion of molecules, but instead, some substance suffusing the hot object, called "caloric." And it was a matter of course of science and not of any logical necessity that the one theory turned out to be correct and the other theory turned out to be incorrect.

So, here again, we have, apparently, another plain example of a contingent identity statement. This has been supposed to be a very important example because of its connection with the mind-body problem. There have been many philosophers who have wanted to be materialists, and to be materialists in a particular form, which is known today as "the identity theory." According to this theory, a certain mental state, such as a person's being in pain, is identical with a certain state of his brain (or, perhaps, of his entire body, according to some theorists), at any rate, a certain material or neural state of his brain or body. And so, according to this theory, my being in pain at this instant, if I were, would be identical with my body's being or my brain's being in a certain state. Others have objected that this cannot be because, after all, we can imagine my pain existing even if the state of the body did not. We can perhaps imagine my not being embodied at all and still being in pain, or, conversely, we could imagine my body existing and being in the very same state even if there were no pain. In fact, conceivably, it could be in this state even though there were no mind 'back of it', so to speak, at all. The usual reply has been to concede that all of these things might have been the case, but to argue that these are irrelevant to the question of the identity of the mental state and the physical state. This identity, it is said, is just another contingent scientific identification, similar to the identification of heat with molecular motion, or water with H_2O. Just as we can imagine heat without any molecular motion, so we can imagine a mental state without any corresponding brain state. But, just as the first fact is not damaging to the identification of heat and the motion of molecules, so the second fact is not at all damaging to the identification of a mental state with the corresponding brain state. And so, many recent philosophers have held it to be very important for our theoretical understanding of the mind-body problem that there can be contingent identity statements of this form.

To state finally what *I* think, as opposed to what seems to be the case, or what others think, I think that in both cases, the case of names and the case of the theoretical identifications, the identity statements are necessary and not contingent. That is to say, they are necessary if *true;* of course, false identity statements are not necessary. How can one possibly defend such a view? Perhaps I lack a complete answer to this question, even though I am convinced that the view is true. But to begin an answer, let me make some distinctions that I want to use. The first is between a *rigid* and a *nonrigid designator.* What do these terms mean? As an example of a nonrigid designator, I can give an expression such as 'the inventor of bifocals'. Let us suppose it was Benjamin Franklin who invented bifocals, and so the expression, 'the inventor of bifocals', designates or refers to a certain man, namely, Benjamin Franklin. However, we can easily imagine that the world could have been different, that under different circumstances someone else would have come upon this invention before Benjamin Franklin did, and in that case, *he* would have been the inventor of bifocals. So, in this sense, the expression 'the inventor of bifocals' is nonrigid: Under certain circumstances one man would have been the inventor of bifocals; under other circumstances, another man would have. In contrast, consider the expression 'the square root of 25'. Independently of the empirical facts, we can give an arithmetical proof that the square root of 25 is in fact the number 5, and because we have proved this mathematically, what we have proved is necessary. If we think of numbers as entities at all, and let us suppose, at least for the purpose of this lecture, that we do, then the expression 'the square root of 25' necessarily designates a certain number, namely 5. Such an expression I call 'a *rigid* designator'. Some philosophers think that anyone who even uses the notions of rigid or nonrigid designator has already shown that he has fallen into a certain confusion or has not paid attention to certain facts. What do I mean by 'rigid designator'? I mean a term that designates the same object in all possible worlds. To get rid of one confusion which certainly is not mine, I do not use "might have designated a different object" to refer to the fact that language might have been used differently. For example, the expression 'the inventor of bifocals' might have been used by inhabitants of this planet always to refer to the man who corrupted Hadleyburg. This would have been the case, if, first, the people on this planet had not spoken English, but some other language, which phonetically overlapped with English; and if, second, in that language the expression 'the inventor of bifocals' meant the 'man who corrupted Hadleyburg'. Then it would refer, of course, in their language, to whoever in fact corrupted Hadleyburg in this counterfactual situation. That is not what I mean. What I mean by saying that a description might have referred to something different, I mean that in *our* language as *we* use it in describing a counterfactual situation, there might have been a different object satisfying the descriptive conditions *we* give for reference. So, for example, we use the phrase 'the inventor of bifocals', when we are talking about another possible world or a counterfactual situation, to refer to whoever in that counterfactual situation would have invented bifocals, not to the person whom people *in* that counterfactual situation would have called 'the inventor of bifocals'. *They* might have spoken a different language which phonetically overlapped with English in which 'the inventor of bifocals' is used in some other way. I am *not* concerned with that question here. For that matter, they might have been deaf and dumb, or there might have been no people at all. (There still could have been an inventor of bifocals even if there were no people—God, or Satan, will do.)

Second, in talking about the notion of a rigid designator, I do not mean to imply that the object referred to has to exist in all possible worlds, that is, that it has to necessarily exist. Some things, perhaps mathematical entities such as the positive integers, if they exist at all, necessarily exist. Some people have held that God both exists and necessarily exists; others, that He contingently exists; others, that He contingently fails to exist; and others, that He necessarily fails to exist: [8] all four options have been tried. But at any rate, when I use the notion of rigid designator, I do not imply that the object referred to necessarily exists. All I mean is that in any possible world where the object in question *does* exist, in any situation where the object *would* exist, we use the designator in question to designate that object. In a situation where the object does not exist, then we should say that the designator has no referent and that the object in question so designated does not exist.

As I said, many philosophers would find the very notion of rigid designator objectionable per se. And the objection that people make may be stated as follows: Look, you're talking about situations which are counterfactual, that is to say, you're talking about other possible worlds. Now these worlds are completely disjoint, after all, from the actual world which is not just another possible world; it is the actual world. So, before you talk about, let us say, such an object as Richard Nixon in another possible world at all, you have to say which object in this other possible world would *be* Richard Nixon. Let us talk about a situation in which, as *you* would say, Richard Nixon would have been a member of SDS. Certainly the member of SDS you are talking about is someone very different in many of his properties from Nixon. Before we even can say whether this man would have been Richard Nixon or not, we have to set up

8. If there is no deity, and especially if the nonexistence of a diety is *necessary*, it is dubious that we can use "He" to refer to a diety. The use in the text must be taken to be non-literal.

Students for a Democratic Society

criteria of identity across possible worlds. Here are these other possible worlds. There are all kinds of objects in them with different properties from those of any actual object. Some of them resemble Nixon in some ways, some of them resemble Nixon in other ways. Well, which of these objects is Nixon? One has to give a criterion of identity. And this shows how the very notion of rigid designator runs in a circle. Suppose we designate a certain number as the number of planets. Then, if that is our favorite way, so to speak, of designating this number, then in any other possible worlds we will have to identify whatever number is the number of planets with the number 9, which in the actual world is the number of planets. So, it is argued by various philosophers, for example, implicitly by Quine, and explicitly by many others in his wake, we cannot really ask whether a designator is rigid or nonrigid because we first need a criterion of identity across possible worlds. An extreme view has even been held that, since possible worlds are so disjoint from our own, we cannot really say that any object in them is the *same* as an object existing now but only that there are some objects which resemble things in the actual world, more or less. We, therefore, should not really speak of what would have been true of Nixon in another possible world but, only of what 'counterparts' (the term which David Lewis uses [9]) of Nixon there would have been. Some people in other possible worlds have dogs whom they call 'Checkers'. Others favor the ABM but do not have any dog called Checkers. There are various people who resemble Nixon more or less, but none of them can really be said to be Nixon; they are only *counterparts* of Nixon, and you choose which one is the best counterpart by noting which resembles Nixon the most closely, according to your favorite criteria. Such views are widespread, both among the defenders of quantified modal logic and among its detractors.

All of this talk seems to me to have taken the metaphor of possible worlds much too seriously in some way. It is as if a

9. David K. Lewis, "Counterpart Theory and Quantified Modal Logic," *Journal of Philosophy*, LXV (1968), 113ff.

'possible world' were like a foreign country, or distant planet way out there. It is as if we see dimly through a telescope various actors on this distant planet. Actually David Lewis' view seems the most reasonable if one takes this picture literally. No one far away on another planet can be strictly identical with someone here. But, even if we have some marvelous methods of transportation to take one and the same person from planet to planet, we really need some epistemological criteria of identity to be able to say whether someone on this distant planet is the same person as someone here.

All of this seems to me to be a totally misguided way of looking at things. What it amounts to is the view that counterfactual situations have to be described purely qualitatively. So, we cannot say, for example, "If Nixon had only given a sufficient bribe to Senator X, he would have gotten Carswell through" because that refers to certain people, Nixon and Carswell, and talks about what things would be true of them in a counterfactual situation. We must say instead "If a man who has a hairline like such and such, and holds such and such political opinions had given a bribe to a man who was a senator and had such and such other qualities, then a man who was a judge in the South and had many other qualities resembling Carswell would have been confirmed." In other words, we must describe counterfactual situations purely qualitatively and then ask the question, "Given that the situation contains people or things with such and such qualities, which of these people is (or is a counterpart of) Nixon, which is Carswell, and so on?" This seems to me to be wrong. Who is to prevent us from saying "Nixon might have gotten Carswell through had he done certain things"? We are speaking of *Nixon* and asking what, in certain counterfactual situations, would have been true of *him*. We can say that if Nixon had done such and such, he would have lost the election to Humphrey. Those I am opposing would argue, "Yes, but how do you find out if the man you are talking about is in fact Nixon?" It would indeed be very hard to find out, if you were looking at the whole situation through a telescope, but that is not what we are doing here. Possible worlds are not something to which an epistemological question like this applies. And if the phrase 'possible worlds' is what makes anyone think some such question applies, he should just *drop* this phrase and use some other expression, say 'counterfactual situation,' which might be less misleading. If we say "If Nixon had bribed such and such a Senator, Nixon would have gotten Carswell through," what is *given* in the very description of that situation is that it is a situation in which we are speaking of Nixon, and of Carswell, and of such and such a Senator. And there seems to be no less objection to *stipulating* that we are speaking of certain *people* than there can be objection to stipulating that we are speaking of certain *qualities*. Advocates of the other view take speaking of certain qualities as unobjectionable. They do not say, "How do we know that this quality (in another possible world) is that of redness?" But they do find speaking of certain *people* objectionable. But I see no more reason to object in the one case than in the other. I think it really comes from the idea of possible worlds as existing out there, but very far off, viewable only through a special telescope. Even more objectionable is the view of David Lewis. According to Lewis, when we say "Under certain circumstances Nixon would have gotten Carswell through," we really mean "Some man, other than Nixon but closely resembling him, would have gotten some judge, other than Carswell but closely resembling him, through." Maybe that is so, that some man closely resembling Nixon could have gotten some man closely resembling Carswell through. But *that* would not comfort either Nixon or Carswell, nor would it make Nixon kick himself and say "*I* should have done such and such to get Carswell through." The question is whether under certain circumstances Nixon *himself* could have gotten *Carswell* through. And I think the objection is simply based on a misguided picture.

Instead, we can perfectly well talk about rigid and nonrigid designators. Moreover, we have a simple, intuitive test for them. We can say, for example, that the number of planets might have been a different number from the number it in fact is. For example, there might have been only seven planets. We can say that the inventor of bifocals might have been someone other than the man who *in fact* invented bifocals.[10] We cannot say, though, that the square root of 81 might have been a different number from the number it in fact is, for that number just has to be 9. If we apply this intuitive test to proper names, such as for example 'Richard Nixon', they would seem intuitively to come out to be rigid designators. First, when we talk even about the counterfactual situation in which we suppose Nixon to have done different things, we assume we are still talking about Nixon himself. We say, "If Nixon had bribed a certain Senator, he would have gotten Carswell through," and we assume that by 'Nixon' and 'Carswell' we are still referring to the very same people as in the actual world. And it seems that we cannot say "Nixon might have been a different man from the man he in fact was," unless, of course, we mean it metaphorically: He might have been a different *sort* of person (if you believe in free will and that people are not inherently corrupt). You might think the statement true in that sense, but Nixon could not have been in the other literal sense a different person from the person he, in fact, is, even though the thirty-seventh President of the United States might have been Humphrey. So the phrase "the thirty-seventh President" is nonrigid, but 'Nixon', it would seem, is rigid.

10. Some philosophers think that definite descriptions, in English, are ambiguous, that sometimes 'the inventor of bifocals' rigidly designates the man who in fact invented bifocals. I am tentatively inclined to reject this view, construed as a thesis about English (as opposed to a possible hypothetical language), but I will not argue the question here.

What I do wish to note is that, contrary to some opinions, this alleged ambiguity cannot replace the Russellian notion of the scope of a description. Consider the sentence, "The number of planets might have been necessarily even." This sentence plainly can be read so as to express a truth; had there been eight planets, the number of planets would have been necessarily even. Yet without scope distinctions, both a 'referential' (rigid) and a non-rigid reading of the description will make the statement false. (Since the number of planets is nine, the rigid reading amounts to the falsity that nine might have been necessarily even.)

The 'rigid' reading is equivalent to the Russellian primary occurrence; the non-rigid, to innermost scope—some, following Donnellan, perhaps loosely, have called this reading the 'attributive' use. The possibility of intermediate scopes is then ignored. In the present instance, the intended reading of ◇□(the number of planets is even) makes the scope of the description □(the number of planets is even), neither the largest nor the smallest possible.

P. 70

Let me make another distinction before I go back to the question of identity statements. This distinction is very fundamental and also hard to see through. In recent discussion, many philosophers who have debated the meaningfulness of various categories of truths, have regarded them as identical. Some of those who identify them are vociferous defenders of them, and others, such as Quine, say they are all identically meaningless. But usually they're not distinguished. These are categories such as 'analytic', 'necessary', 'a priori', and sometimes even 'certain'. I will not talk about all of these but only about the notions of a prioricity and necessity. Very often these are held to be synonyms. (Many philosophers probably should not be described as holding them to be synonyms; they simply *use* them interchangeably.) I wish to distinguish them. What do we mean by calling a statement *necessary*? We simply mean that the statement in question, first, is true, and, second, that it could not have been otherwise. When we say that something is *contingently* true, we mean that, though it is in fact the case, it could have been the case that things would have been otherwise. If we wish to assign this distinction to a branch of philosophy, we should assign it to metaphysics. To the contrary, there is the notion of an *a priori truth*. An a priori truth is supposed to be one which can be *known* to be true independently of all experience. Notice that this does not in and of itself say anything about all possible worlds, unless this is put into the definition. All that it says is that it can be known to be true of the actual world, independently of all experience. It may, by some philosophical argument, follow from our knowing, independently of experience, that something is true of the actual world, that it has to be known to be true also of all possible worlds. But if this is to be established, it requires some philosophical argument to establish it. Now, *this* notion, if we were to assign it to a branch of philosophy, belongs, not to metaphysics, but to epistemology. It has to do with the way we can know certain things to be in fact true. Now, it may be the case, of course, that anything which is necessary is something which *can* be known a priori. (Notice, by the way, the notion a priori truth as thus defined has in it *another* modality: it *can* be known independently of all experience. It is a little complicated because there is a double modality here.) I will not have time to explore these notions in full detail here, but one thing we can see from the outset is that these two notions are by no means trivially the same. If they are coextensive, it takes some philosophical argument to establish it. As stated, they belong to different domains of philosophy. One of them has something to do with *knowledge,* of what can be known in certain ways about the *actual* world. The other one has to do with *metaphysics,* how the world *could* have been; given that it is the way it is, could it have been otherwise, in certain ways? Now I hold, as a matter of fact, that neither class of statements is contained in the other. But, all we need to talk about here is this: Is everything that is necessary knowable a priori or known a priori? Consider the following example: the Goldbach conjecture. This says that every even number is the sum of two primes. It is a mathematical statement and if it is true at all, it has to be necessary. Certainly, one could not say that though in fact every even number is the sum of two primes, there could have been some extra number which was even and not the sum of two primes. What would that mean? On the other hand, the answer to the question whether every even number *is* in fact the sum of two primes is unknown, and we have no method at present for deciding. So we certainly do not know, a priori or even a posteriori, that every even number is the sum of two primes. (Well, perhaps we have some evidence in that no counterexample has been found.) But we certainly do not know a priori anyway, that every even number is, in fact, the sum of two primes. But, of course, the definition just says *"can* be known independently of experience," and someone might say that if it is true, we *could* know it independently of experience. It is hard to see exactly what this claim means. It might be so. One thing it might mean is that if it were true we could *prove* it. This claim is certainly wrong if it is generally applied to mathematical statements and we have to work within some fixed system. This is what Gödel proved. And even if we mean an 'intuitive proof in general' it might just be the case (at least, this view is as clear and as probable as the contrary) that though the statement is true, there is just no way the human mind could ever prove it. Of course, one way an *infinite* mind might be able to prove it is by looking through each natural number one by one and checking. In this sense, of course, it can, perhaps, be known a priori, but only by an infinite mind, and then this gets into other complicated questions. I do not want to discuss questions about the conceivability of performing an infinite number of acts like looking through each number one by one. A vast philosophical literature has been written on this: Some have declared it is logically impossible; others that it is logically possible; and some do not know. The main point is that it is not trivial that just because such a statement is necessary it can be known a priori. Some considerable clarification is required before we decide that it can be so known. And so this shows that even if everything necessary is a priori in some sense, it should not be taken as a trivial matter of definition. It is a substantive philosophical thesis which requires some work.

Another example that one might give relates to the problem of essentialism. Here is a lectern. A question which has often been raised in philosophy is: What are its essential properties? What properties, aside from trivial ones like self-identity, are such that this object has to have them if it exists at all,[11] are such that if an object did not have it, it would not be this object? [12] For example, being made of wood, and not of ice,

---

11. This definition is the usual formulation of the notion of essential property, but an exception must be made for existence itself: on the definition given, existence would be trivially essential. We should regard existence as essential to an object only if the object necessarily exists. Perhaps there are other recherché properties, involving existence, for which the definition is similarly objectionable. (I thank Michael Slote for this observation.)

12. The two clauses of the sentence footnoted give equivalent definitions of the notion of essential property, since $\Box((\exists x)(x=a) \supset Fa)$ is equivalent to $\Box(x)(\sim Fx \supset x=a)$. The second formulation, however, has served as a powerful seducer in favor of theories of 'identification across possible worlds'. For it suggests that we consider 'an object b in another possible world' and test whether it is identifiable with a by asking whether it lacks any of the essential properties of a. Let me therefore emphasize that, although an essential property is (trivially) a property without which an object cannot be a, it by no means follows that the essential, purely qualitative properties of a jointly form a sufficient condition for being a, nor that *any* purely qualitative conditions are sufficient for an object to be a. Further, even if necessary and sufficient qualitative conditions for an object to be Nixon may exist, there would still be little jus-

might be an essential property of this lectern. Let us just take the weaker statement that it is not made of ice. That will establish it as strongly as we need it, perhaps as dramatically. Supposing this lectern is in fact made of wood, could this very lectern have been made from the very beginning of its existence from ice, say frozen from water in the Thames? One has a considerable feeling that it could *not,* though in fact one certainly could have made a lectern of water from the Thames, frozen it into ice by some process, and put it right there in place of this thing. If one had done so, one would have made, of course, a *different* object. It would not have been *this very lectern,* and so one would not have a case in which this very lectern here was made of ice, or was made from water from the Thames. The question of whether it could afterward, say in a minute from now, turn into ice is something else. So, it would seem, if an example like this is correct—and this is what advocates of essentialism have held—that this lectern could not have been made of ice, that is in any counterfactual situation of which we would say that this lectern existed at all, we would have to say also that it was not made from water from the Thames frozen into ice. Some have rejected, of course, any such notion of essential property as meaningless. Usually, it is because (and I think this is what Quine, for example, would say) they have held that it depends on the notion of identity across possible worlds, and that this is itself meaningless. Since I have rejected this view already, I will not deal with it again. We can talk about *this very object,* and whether it could have had certain properties which it does not in fact have. For example, it could have been in another room from the room it in fact is in, even at this very time, but it could not have been made from the very beginning from water frozen into ice.

If the essentialist view is correct, it can only be correct if we sharply distinguish between the notions of a posteriori and a priori truth on the one hand, and contingent and necessary truth on the other hand, for although the statement that this

---

tification for the demand for a purely qualitative description of all counterfactual situations. We can ask whether Nixon might have been a Democrat without engaging in these subtleties.

table, if it exists at all, was not made of ice, is necessary, it certainly is not something that we know a priori. What we know is that first, lecterns usually are not made of ice, they are usually made of wood. This looks like wood. It does not feel cold and it probably would if it were made of ice. Therefore, I conclude, probably this is not made of ice. Here my entire judgment is a posteriori. I could find out that an ingenious trick has been played upon me and that, in fact, this lectern is made of ice; but what I am saying is, given that it is in fact not made of ice, in fact is made of wood, one cannot imagine that under certain circumstances it could have been made of ice. So we have to say that though we cannot know a priori whether this table was made of ice or not, given that it is not made of ice, it is *necessarily* not made of ice. In other words, if P is the statement that the lectern is not made of ice, one knows by a priori philosophical analysis, some conditional of the form "if P, then necessarily P." If the table is not made of ice, it is necessarily not made of ice. On the other hand, then, we know by empirical investigation that P, the antecedent of the conditional, is true—that this table is not made of ice. We can conclude by *modus ponens:*

$$P \supset \Box P$$
$$\frac{P}{\Box P}$$

The conclusion—'$\Box P$'—is that it is necessary that the table not be made of ice, and this conclusion is known a posteriori, since one of the premises on which it is based is a posteriori. So, the notion of essential properties can be maintained only by distinguishing between the notions of a priori and necessary truth, and I do maintain it.

Let us return to the question of identities. Concerning the statement 'Hesperus is Phosphorus' or the statement 'Cicero is Tully', one can find all of these out by empirical investigation, and we might turn out to be wrong in our empirical beliefs. So, it is usually argued, such statements must therefore be contingent. Some have embraced the other side of the coin and have held "Because of this argument about necessity, identity statements between names have to be knowable a priori, so, only a very special category of names, possibly, really works as names; the other things are bogus names, disguised descriptions, or something of the sort. However, a certain very narrow class of statements of identity are known a priori, and these are the ones which contain the genuine names." If one accepts the distinctions that I have made, one need not jump to either conclusion. One can hold that certain statements of identity between names, though often known a posteriori, and maybe not knowable a priori, are in fact necessary, if true. So, we have some room to hold this. But, of course, to have some room to hold it does not mean that we should hold it. So let us see what the evidence is. First, recall the remark that I made that proper names seem to be rigid designators, as when we use the name 'Nixon' to talk about a certain man, even in counterfactual situations. If we say, "If Nixon had not written the letter to Saxbe, maybe he would have gotten Carswell through," we are in this statement talking about Nixon, Saxbe, and Carswell, the very same men as in the actual world, and what would have happened to them under certain counterfactual circumstances. If names are rigid designators, then there can be no question about identities being necessary, because '*a*' and '*b*' will be rigid designators of a certain man or thing *x*. Then even in every possible world, *a* and *b* will both refer to this same object *x*, and to no other, and so there will be no situation in which *a* might not have been *b*. That would have to be a situation in which the object which we are also now calling '*x*' would not have been identical with itself. Then one could not possibly have a situation in which Cicero would not have been Tully or Hesperus would not have been Phosphorus.[13]

Aside from the identification of necessity with a priority, what has made people feel the other way? There are two things which have made people feel the other way.[14] Some people

13. I thus agree with Quine, that "Hesperus is Phosphorus" is (or can be) an empirical discovery; with Marcus, that it is necessary. Both Quine and Marcus, according to the present standpoint, err in identifying the epistemological and the metaphysical issues.

14. The two confusions alleged, especially the second, are both related to the confusion of the metaphysical question of the necessity of "Hesperus is Phos-

tend to regard identity statements as metalinguistic statements, to identify the statement "Hesperus is Phosphorus" with the metalinguistic statement, " 'Hesperus' and 'Phosphorus' are names of the same heavenly body." And that, of course, might have been false. We might have used the terms 'Hesperus' and 'Phosphorus' as names of *two* different heavenly bodies. But, of course, this has nothing to do with the necessity of identity. In the same sense "2 + 2 = 4" might have been false. The phrases "2 + 2" and "4" might have been used to refer to two different numbers. One can imagine a language, for example, in which "+", "2", and "=" were used in the standard way, but "4" was used as the name of, say, the square root of minus 1, as we should call it, "*i*." Then "2 + 2 = 4" would be false, for 2 plus 2 is not equal to the square root of minus 1. But this is not what we want. We do not want just to say that a certain statement which we in fact use to express something true could have expressed something false. We want to use the statement in *our* way and see if it could have been false. Let us do this. What is the idea people have? They say, "Look, Hesperus might not have been Phosphorus. Here a certain planet was seen in the morning, and it was seen in the evening; and it just turned out later on as a matter of empirical fact that they were one and the same planet. If things had turned out otherwise, they would have been two different planets, or two different heavenly bodies, so how can you say that such a statement is necessary?"

Now there are two things that such people can mean. First, they can mean that we do not know a priori whether Hesperus

---

phorus" with the epistemological question of its a prioricity. For if Hesperus is identified by its position in the sky in the evening, and Phosphorus by its position in the morning, an investigator may well know, in advance of empirical research, that Hesperus is Phosphorus if and only if one and the same body occupies position *x* in the evening and position *y* in the morning. The a priori material equivalence of the two statements, however, does not imply their strict (necessary) equivalence. (The same remarks apply to the case of heat and molecular motion below.) Similar remarks apply to some extent to the relationship between "Hesperus is Phosphorus" and " 'Hesperus' and 'Phosphorus' name the same thing." A confusion that also operates is, of course, the confusion between what *we* say of a counterfactual situation and how people *in* that situation would have described it; this confusion, too, is probably related to the confusion between a prioricity and necessity.

is Phosphorus. This I have already conceded. Second, they may mean that they can actually imagine circumstances that they would call circumstances in which Hesperus would not have been Phosphorus. Let us think what would be such a circumstance, using these terms here as *names* of a planet. For example, it could have been the case that Venus did indeed rise in the morning in exactly the position in which we saw it, but that on the other hand, in the position which is in fact occupied by Venus in the evening, Venus was not there, and Mars took its place. This is all counterfactual because in fact Venus is there. Now one can also imagine that in this counterfactual other possible world, the earth would have been inhabited by people and that they should have used the names 'Phosphorus' for Venus in the morning and 'Hesperus' for Mars in the evening. Now, this is all very good, but would it be a situation in which Hesperus was not Phosphorus? Of course, it is a situation in which people would have been able to *say*, truly, "Hesperus is not Phosphorus"; but we are supposed to describe things in our language, not in theirs. So let us describe it in our language. Well, how could it actually happen that Venus would not be in that position in the evening? For example, let us say that there is some comet that comes around every evening and yanks things over a little bit. (That would be a very simple scientific way of imagining it: not really too simple—that is very hard to imagine actually.) It just happens to come around every evening, and things get yanked over a bit. Mars gets yanked over to the very position where Venus is, then the comet yanks things back to their normal position in the morning. Thinking of this planet which we now call 'Phosphorus', what should we say? Well, we can say that the comet passes it and yanks Phosphorus over so that it is not in the position normally occupied by Phosphorus in the evening. If we do say this, and really use 'Phorphorus' as the name of a planet, then we have to say that, under such circumstances, Phosphorus in the evening would not be in the position where we, in fact, saw it; or alternatively, Hesperus in the evening would not be in the position in which we, in fact, saw it. We might say that under such circumstances, we would not have called Hesperus 'Hesperus' because Hesperus would have been in a different position. But that still would not make Phosphorus different from Hesperus; but what would then be the case instead is that Hesperus would have been in a different position from the position it in fact is and, perhaps, not in such a position that people would have called it 'Hesperus'. But that would not be a situation in which Phosphorus would not have been Hesperus.

Let us take another example which may be clearer. Suppose someone uses 'Tully' to refer to the Roman orator who denounced Cataline and uses the name 'Cicero' to refer to the man whose works he had to study in third-year Latin in high school. Of course, he may not know in advance that the very same man who denounced Cataline wrote these works, and that is a contingent statement. But the fact that this statement is contingent should not make us think that the statement that Cicero is Tully, if it is true, and it is in fact true, is contingent. Suppose, for example, that Cicero actually did denounce Cataline, but thought that this political achievement was so great that he should not bother writing any literary works. Would we say that these would be circumstances under which he would not have been Cicero? It seems to me that the answer is no, that instead we would say that, under such circumstances, Cicero would not have written any literary works. It is not a necessary property of Cicero—the way the shadow follows the man—that he should have written certain works; we can easily imagine a situation in which Shakespeare would not have written the works of Shakespeare, or one in which Cicero would not have written the works of Cicero. What may be the case is that we *fix the reference* of the term 'Cicero' by use of some descriptive phrase, such as 'the author of these works'. But once we have this reference fixed, we then use the name 'Cicero' *rigidly* to designate the man who in fact we have identified by his authorship of these works. We do not use it to designate whoever would have written these works in place of Cicero, if someone else wrote them. It might have been the case that the man who wrote these works was not the man who denounced Cataline. Cassius might have written these works. But we would not then say that Cicero would have been Cassius, unless we were speaking in a very loose and metaphorical way. We would say that Cicero, whom we may have identified and come to know by his works, would not have written them, and that someone else, say Cassius, would have written them in his place.

Such examples are not grounds for thinking that identity statements are contingent. To take them as such grounds is to misconstrue the relation between a *name* and a *description used to fix its reference*, to take them to be *synonyms*. Even if we fix the reference of such a name as 'Cicero' as the man who wrote such and such works, in speaking of counterfactual situations, when we speak of Cicero, we do not then speak of whoever in such counterfactual situations *would* have written such and such works, but rather of Cicero, whom we have identified by the contingent property that he is the man who in fact, that is, in the actual world, wrote certain works.[15]

I hope this is reasonably clear in a brief compass. Now, actually I have been presupposing something I do not really believe to be, in general, true. Let us suppose that we do fix the reference of a name by a description. Even if we do so, we do not then make the name *synonymous* with the description, but instead we use the name *rigidly* to refer to the object so named, even in talking about counterfactual situations where the thing named would not satisfy the description in question. Now, this is what I think in fact is true for those cases of naming where

---

15. If someone protests, regarding the lectern, that it *could* after all have *turned out* to have been made of ice, and therefore could have been made of ice, I would reply that what he really means is that *a lectern* could have looked just like this one, and have been placed in the same position as this one, and yet have been made of ice. In short, I could have been in the *same epistemological situation* in relation to *a lectern made of ice* as I actually am in relation to *this* lectern. In the main text, I have argued that the same reply should be given to protests that Hesperus could have turned out to be other than Phosphorus, or Cicero other than Tully. Here, then, the notion of 'counterpart' comes into its own. For it is not this table, but an epistemic 'counterpart', which was hewn from ice; not Hesperus-Phosphorus-Venus, but two distinct counterparts thereof, in two of the roles Venus actually plays (that of Evening Star and Morning Star), which are different. Precisely because of this fact, it is not *this table* which could have been made of ice. Statements about the modal properties of *this table* never refer to counterparts. However, if someone confuses the epistemological and the metaphysical problems, he will be well on the way to the counterpart theory Lewis and others have advocated.

the reference is fixed by description. But, in fact, I also think, contrary to most recent theorists, that the reference of names is rarely or almost never fixed by means of description. And by this I do not just mean what Searle says: "It's not a single description, but rather a cluster, a family of properties which fixes the reference." I mean that properties in this sense are not used *at all*. But I do not have the time to go into this here. So, let us suppose that at least one half of prevailing views about naming is true, that the reference is fixed by descriptions. Even were that true, the name would not be synonymous with the description, but would be used to *name* an object which we pick out by the contingent fact that it satisfies a certain description. And so, even though we can imagine a case where the man who wrote these works would not have been the man who denounced Cataline, we should not say that that would be a case in which Cicero would not have been Tully. We should say that it is a case in which Cicero did not write these works, but rather that Cassius did. And the identity of Cicero and Tully still holds.

Let me turn to the case of heat and the motion of molecules. Here surely is a case that is contingent identity! Recent philosophy has emphasized this again and again. So, if it is a case of contingent identity, then let us imagine under what circumstances it would be false. Now, concerning this statement I hold that the circumstances philosophers apparently have in mind as circumstances under which it would have been false are not in fact such circumstances. First, of course, it is argued that "Heat is the motion of molecules" is an a posteriori judgment; scientific investigation might have turned out otherwise. As I said before, this shows nothing against the view that it is necessary—at least if I am right. But here, surely, people had very specific circumstances in mind under which, so they thought, the judgment that heat is the motion of molecules would have been false. What were these circumstances? One can distill them out of the fact that we found out empirically that heat is the motion of molecules. How was this? What did we find out first when we found out that heat is the motion of molecules? There is a certain external phenomenon which we can sense by the sense of touch, and it produces a sensation which we call "the sensation of heat." We then discover that the external phenomenon which produces this sensation, which we sense, by means of our sense of touch, is in fact that of molecular agitation in the thing that we touch, a very high degree of molecular agitation. So, it might be thought, to imagine a situation in which heat would not have been the motion of molecules, we need only imagine a situation in which we would have had the very same sensation and it would have been produced by something other than the motion of molecules. Similarly, if we wanted to imagine a situation in which light was not a stream of photons, we could imagine a situation in which we were sensitive to something else in exactly the same way, producing what we call visual experiences, though not through a stream of photons. To make the case stronger, or to look at another side of the coin, we could also consider a situation in which we *are* concerned with the motion of molecules but in which such motion does not give us the sensation of heat. And it might also have happened that we, or, at least, the creatures inhabiting this planet, might have been so constituted that, let us say, an increase in the motion of molecules did not give us this sensation but that, on the contrary, a slowing down of the molecules did give us the very same sensation. This would be a situation, so it might be thought, in which heat would not be the motion of molecules, or, more precisely, in which temperature would not be mean molecular kinetic energy.

But I think it would not be so. Let us think about the situation again. First, let us think about it in the actual world. Imagine right now the world invaded by a number of Martians, who do indeed get the very sensation that we call "the sensation of heat" when they feel some ice which has slow molecular motion, and who do not get a sensation of heat—in fact, maybe just the reverse—when they put their hand near a fire which causes a lot of molecular agitation. Would we say, "Ah, this casts some doubt on heat being the motion of molecules, because there are these other people who don't get the same sensation"? Obviously not, and no one would think so. We would say instead that the Martians somehow feel the very sensation we get when we feel heat when they feel cold and that they do not get a sensation of heat when they feel heat. But now let us think of a counterfactual situation.[16] Suppose the earth had from the very beginning been inhabited by such creatures. First, imagine it inhabited by no creatures at all: then there is no one to feel any sensations of heat. But we would not say that under such circumstances it would necessarily be the case that heat did not exist; we would say that heat might have existed, for example, if there were fires that heated up the air.

Let us suppose the laws of physics were not very different: Fires do heat up the air. Then there would have been heat even though there were no creatures around to feel it. Now let us suppose evolution takes place, and life is created, and there are some creatures around. But they are not like us, they are more like the Martians. Now would we say that heat has suddenly turned to cold, because of the way the creatures of this planet sense it? No, I think we should describe this situation as a situation in which, though the creatures on this planet got our sensation of heat, they did not get it when they were exposed to heat. They got it when they were exposed to cold. And that is something we can surely well imagine. We can imagine it just as we can imagine our planet being invaded by creatures of this sort. Think of it in two steps. First there is a stage where there are no creatures at all, and one can certainly imagine the planet still having both heat and cold, though no one is around to sense it. Then the planet comes through an evolutionary process to be peopled with beings of different neural structure from ourselves. Then these creatures could be such that they were insensitive to heat; they did not feel it in the way we do; but on the other hand, they felt cold in much the same way that we feel heat. But still, heat would be heat,

16. Isn't the situation I just described also counterfactual? At least it may well be, if such Martians never in fact invade. Strictly speaking, the distinction I wish to draw compares how we *would* speak *in* a (possibly counterfactual) situation, *if* it obtained, and how we *do* speak *of* a counterfactual situation, knowing that it does not obtain—i.e., the distinction between the language we would have used in a situation and the language we *do* use to describe it. (Consider the description: "Suppose we all spoke German." This description is in English.) The former case can be made vivid by imagining the counterfactual situation to be actual.

and cold would be cold. And particularly, then, this goes in no way against saying that in this counterfactual situation heat would still *be* the molecular motion, *be* that which is produced by fires, and so on, just as it would have been if there had been no creatures on the planet at all. Similarly, we could imagine that the planet was inhabited by creatures who got visual sensations when there were sound waves in the air. We should not therefore say, "Under such circumstances, sound would have been light." Instead we should say, "The planet was inhabited by creatures who were in some sense visually sensitive to sound, and maybe even visually sensitive to light." If this is correct, it can still be and will still be a necessary truth that heat is the motion of molecules and that light is a stream of photons.

To state the view succinctly: we use both the terms 'heat' and 'the motion of molecules' as rigid designators for a certain external phenomenon. Since heat is in fact the motion of molecules, and the designators are rigid, by the argument I have given here, it is going to be *necessary* that heat is the motion of molecules. What gives us the illusion of contingency is the fact we have identified the heat by the contingent fact that there happen to be creatures on this planet—(namely, ourselves) who are sensitive to it in a certain way, that is, who are sensitive to the motion of molecules or to heat—these are one and the same thing. And this is contingent. So we use the description, 'that which causes such and such sensations, or that which we sense in such and such a way', to identify heat. But in using this fact we use a contingent property of heat, just as we use the contingent property of Cicero as having written such and such works to identify him. We then use the terms 'heat' in the one case and 'Cicero' in the other *rigidly* to designate the objects for which they stand. And of course the term 'the motion of molecules' is rigid; it always stands for the motion of molecules, never for any other phenomenon. So, as Bishop Butler said, "everything is what it is and not another thing." Therefore, "Heat is the motion of molecules" will be necessary, not contingent, and one only has the *illusion* of contingency in the way one could have the illusion of contingency in thinking that this table might have been made of ice. We might think one could imagine it, but if we try, we can see on reflection that what we are really imagining is just there being another lectern in this very position here which was in fact made of ice. The fact that we may identify this lectern by being the object we see and touch in such and such a position is something else.

Now how does this relate to the problem of mind and body? It is usually held that this is a contingent identity statement just like "Heat is the motion of molecules." That cannot be. It cannot be a contingent identity statement just like "Heat is the motion of molecules" because, if I am right, "Heat is the motion of molecules" is not a contingent identity statement. Let us look at this statement. For example, "My being in pain at such and such a time is my being in such and such a brain state at such and such a time," or, "Pain in general is such and such a neural (brain) state."

This is held to be contingent on the following grounds. First, we can imagine the brain state existing though there is no pain at all. It is only a scientific fact that whenever we are in a certain brain state we have a pain. Second, one might imagine a creature being in pain, but not being in any specified brain state at all, maybe not having a brain at all. People even think, at least prima facie, though they may be wrong, that they can imagine totally disembodied creatures, at any rate certainly not creatures with bodies anything like our own. So it seems that we can imagine definite circumstances under which this relationship would have been false. Now, if these circumstances are circumstances, notice that we cannot deal with them simply by saying that this is just an illusion, something we can apparently imagine, but in fact cannot in the way we thought erroneously that we could imagine a situation in which heat was not the motion of molecules. Because although we can say that we pick out heat contingently by the contingent property that it affects us in such and such a way, we cannot similarly say that we pick out pain contingently by the fact that it affects us in such and such a way. On such a picture there would be the brain state, and we pick it out by the contingent fact that it affects us as pain. Now that might be true of the brain state, but it cannot be true of the pain. The experience itself has to be *this experience,* and I cannot say that it is contingent property of the pain I now have that it is a pain.[17] In fact, it would seem that both the terms, 'my pain' and 'my being in such and such a brain state' are, first of all, both rigid designators. That is, whenever anything is such and such a pain, it is essentially that very object, namely, such and such a pain, and wherever anything is such and such a brain state, it is essentially that very object, namely, such and such a brain state. So both of these are rigid designators. One cannot say this pain might have been something else, some other state. These are both rigid designators.

Second, the way we would think of picking them out— namely, the pain by its being an experience of a certain sort, and the brain state by its being the state of a certain material object, being of such and such molecular configuration—both of these pick out their objects essentially and not accidentally, that is, they pick them out by essential properties. Whenever the molecules *are* in this configuration, we *do* have such and

17. The most popular identity theories advocated today explicitly fail to satisfy this simple requirement. For these theories usually hold that a mental state is a brain state, and that what makes the brain state into a mental state is its 'causal role', the fact that it tends to produce certain behavior (as intentions produce actions, or pain, pain behavior) and to be produced by certain stimuli (e.g., pain, by pinpricks). If the relations between the brain state and its causes and effects are regarded as contingent, then *being such-and-such-a-mental-state* is a contingent property of the brain state. Let X be a pain. The causal-role identity theorist holds (1) that X is a brain state, (2) that the fact that X is a pain is to be analyzed (roughly) as the fact that X is produced by certain stimuli and produces certain behavior. The fact mentioned in (2) is, of course, regarded as contingent; the brain state X might well exist and not tend to produce the appropriate behavior in the absence of other conditions. Thus (1) and (2) assert that a certain pain X might have existed, yet not have been a pain. This seems to me self-evidently absurd. Imagine any pain: is it possible that *it itself* could have existed, yet not have been a pain?

If $X = Y$, then X and Y share all properties, including modal properties. If X is a pain and Y the corresponding brain state, then *being a pain* is an essential property of X, and *being a brain state* is an essential property of Y. If the correspondence relation is, in fact, identity, then it must be *necessary* of Y that it corresponds to a pain, and *necessary* of X that it correspond to a brain state, indeed to this particular brain state, Y. Both assertions seem false; it *seems* clearly possible that X should have existed without the corresponding brain state; or that the brain state should have existed without being felt as pain. Identity theorists cannot, contrary to their almost universal present practice, accept these intuitions; they must deny them, and explain them away. This is none too easy a thing to do.

such a brain state. Whenever you feel *this*, you do have a pain. So it seems that the identity theorist is in some trouble, for, since we have two rigid designators, the identity statement in question is necessary. Because they pick out their objects essentially, we cannot say the case where you seem to imagine the identity statement false is really an illusion like the illusion one gets in the case of heat and molecular motion, because that illusion depended on the fact that we pick out heat by a certain contingent property. So there is very little room to maneuver; perhaps none.[18] The identity theorist, who holds that pain is the brain state, also has to hold that it necessarily is the brain state. He therefore cannot concede, but has to deny, that there would have been situations under which one would have had pain but not the corresponding brain state. Now usually in arguments on the identity theory, this is very far from being denied. In fact, it is conceded from the outset by the materialist as well as by his opponent. He says, "Of course, it *could* have been the case that we had pains without the brain states. It is a

18. A brief restatement of the argument may be helpful here. If "pain" and "C-fiber stimulation" are rigid designators of phenomena, one who identifies them must regard the identity as necessary. How can this necessity be reconciled with the apparent fact that C-fiber stimulation might have turned out not to be correlated with pain at all? We might try to reply by analogy to the case of heat and molecular motion; the latter identity, too, is necessary, yet someone may believe that, before scientific investigation showed otherwise, molecular motion might have turned out not to be heat. The reply is, of course, that what really is possible is that people (or some rational or sentient beings) could have been in the *same epistemic situation* as we actually are, and identify *a phenomenon* in the same way we identify heat, namely, by feeling it by the sensation we call "the sensation of heat," without the phenomenon being molecular motion. Further, the beings might not have been sensitive to molecular motion (i.e., to heat) by any neural mechanism whatsoever. It is impossible to explain the apparent possibility of C-fiber stimulations not having been pain in the same way. Here, too, we would have to suppose that we could have been in the same epistemological situation, and identify something in the same way we identify pain, without its corresponding to C-fiber stimulation. But the way we identify pain is by feeling it, and if a C-fiber stimulation could have occurred without our feeling any pain, then the C-fiber stimulation would have occurred without there *being* any pain, contrary to the necessity of the identity. The trouble is that although 'heat' is a rigid designator, heat is picked out by the contingent property of its being felt in a certain way; pain, on the other hand, is picked out by an essential (indeed necessary and sufficient) property. For a sensation to be *felt* as pain is for it to *be* pain.

contingent identity." But that cannot be. He has to hold that we are under some illusion in thinking that we can imagine that there could have been pains without brain states. And the only model I can think of for what the illusion might be, or at least the model given by the analogy the materialists themselves suggest, namely, heat and molecular motion, simply does not work in this case. So the materialist is up against a very stiff challenge. He has to show that these things we think we can see to be possible are in fact not possible. He has to show that these things which we can imagine are not in fact things we can imagine. And that requires some very different philosophical argument from the sort which has been given in the case of heat and molecular motion. And it would have to be a deeper and subtler argument than I can fathom and subtler than has ever appeared in any materialist literature that I have read. So the conclusion of this investigation would be that the analytical tools we are using go against the identity thesis and so go against the general thesis that mental states are just physical states.[19]

The next topic would be my own solution to the mind-body problem, but that I do not have.

19. All arguments against the identity theory which rely on the necessity of identity, or on the notion of essential property, are, of course, inspired by Descartes' argument for his dualism. The earlier arguments which superficially were rebutted by the analogies of heat and molecular motion, and the bifocals inventor who was also Postmaster General, had such an inspiration: and so does my argument here. R. Albritton and M. Slote have informed me that they independently have attempted to give essentialist arguments against the identity theory, and probably others have done so as well.

The simplest Cartesian argument can perhaps be restated as follows: Let 'A' be a *name* (rigid designator) of Descartes' body. Then Descartes argues that since he could exist even if A did not, $\Diamond$(Descartes $\neq A$), hence Descartes $\neq A$. Those who have accused him of a modal fallacy have forgotten that 'A' is rigid. His argument is valid, and his conclusion is correct, provided its (perhaps dubitable) premise is accepted. On the other hand, provided that Descartes is regarded as having ceased to exist upon his death, "Descartes $\neq A$" can be established without the use of a modal argument; for if so, no doubt A survived Descartes when A was a corpse. Thus A had a property (existing at a certain time) which Descartes did not. The same argument can establish that a statue is not the hunk of stone, or the congery, of molecules, of which it is composed. Mere non-identity, then, may be a weak conclusion. (See D. Wiggins, *Philosophical Review*, LXXVII [1968], 90ff.) The Cartesian modal argument, however, surely can be deployed to maintain relevant stronger conclusions as well.

3 Is Semantics Possible?

HILARY PUTNAM

Harvard University

In the last decade enormous progress seems to have been made in the syntactic theory of natural languages, largely as a result of the work of linguists influenced by Noam Chomsky and Zellig Harris. Comparable progress seems *not* to have been made in the semantic theory of natural languages, and perhaps it is time to ask why this should be the case. Why is the theory of meaning so *hard*?

The meaning of common nouns. To get some idea of the difficulties, let us look at some of the problems that come up in connection with general names. General names are of many kinds. Some, like *bachelor,* admit of an explicit definition straight off ("man who has never been married"); but the overwhelming majority do not. Some are derived by transformations from verbal forms, e.g., *hunter = one who hunts.* An important class, philosophically as well as linguistically, is the class of general names associated with *natural kinds*—that is, with classes of things that we regard as of explanatory importance; classes whose normal distinguishing characteristics are "held together" or even explained by deep-lying mechanisms. *Gold, lemon, tiger, acid,* are examples of such nouns. I want to begin this paper by suggesting that (1) *traditional* theories of meaning radically falsify the properties of such words; (2) logicians like Carnap do little more than formalize these traditional theories, inadequacies and all; (3) such semantic theories as that produced by Jer-

Reprinted from *Language, Belief, and Metaphysics,* edited by H. E. Kiefer and M. K. Munitz, pp. 50–63, by permission of the State University of New York Press. Copyright © 1970 by the State University of New York.

rold Katz and his co-workers likewise share all the defects of the traditional theory. In Austin's happy phrase, what we have been given by philosophers, logicians, and "semantic theorists" alike, is a "myth-eaten description."

On the traditional view, the meaning of, say, "lemon," is given by specifying a conjunction of *properties*. For each of these properties, the statement "lemons have the property P" is an analytic truth; and if $P_1, P_2, \ldots \ldots P_n$ are all of the properties in the conjunction, then "anything with all of the properties P_1, $\ldots, P_n$ is a lemon" is likewise an analytic truth.

In one sense, this is trivially correct. If we are allowed to invent unanalyzable properties *ad hoc*, then we can find a single property—not even a conjunction—the possession of which is a necessary and sufficient condition for being a lemon, or being gold, or whatever. Namely, we just postulate *the property of being a lemon,* or *the property of being gold,* or whatever may be needed. If we require that the properties $P_1, P_2, \ldots, P_n$ *not* be of this *ad hoc* character, however, then the situation is very different. Indeed, with any natural understanding of the term "property," it is just *false* that to say that something belongs to a natural kind is just to ascribe to it a conjunction of properties.

To see why it is false, let us look at the term "lemon." The supposed "defining characteristics" of lemons are: yellow color, tart taste, a certain kind of peel, etc. Why is the term "lemon" *not* definable by simply conjoining these "defining characteristics"?

The most obvious difficulty is that a natural kind may have *abnormal members*. A green lemon is still a lemon—even if, owing to some abnormality, it *never* turns yellow. A three-legged tiger is still a tiger. Gold in the gaseous state is still gold. It is only normal lemons that are yellow, tart, etc.; only normal tigers that are four-legged; only gold under normal conditions that is hard, white or yellow, etc.

To meet this difficulty, let us try the following definition: X is a *lemon* $= df;$ X belongs to a natural kind whose normal members have yellow peel, tart taste, etc.

There is, of course, a problem with the "etc." There is also a problem with "tart taste"—shouldn't it be *lemon* taste? But let us waive these difficulties, at least for the time being. Let us instead focus on the two notions that have come up with this attempted definition: the notions *natural kind* and *normal member*.

A natural kind *term* (to shift attention, for the moment, from natural kinds to their preferred designations) is a term that plays a special kind of role. If I describe something as a *lemon*, or as an *acid*, I indicate that it is likely to have certain characteristics (yellow peel, or sour taste in dilute water solution, as the case may be); but I also indicate that the presence of those characteristics, if they are present, is likely to be accounted for by some "essential nature" which the thing shares with other members of the natural kind. What the essential nature is is not a matter of language analysis but of scientific theory construction; today we would say it was chromosome structure, in the case of lemons, and being a proton-donor, in the case of acids. Thus it is tempting to say that a natural kind term is simply a term that plays a certain kind of role in scientific or prescientific theory: the role, roughly, of pointing to common "essential features" or "mechanisms" beyond and below the obvious "distinguishing characteristics." But this is vague, and likely to remain so. Meta-science is today in its infancy: and terms like "natural kind" and "normal member" are in the same boat as the more familiar meta-scientific terms "theory" and "explanation," as far as resisting a speedy and definitive analysis is concerned.

Even if we *could* define "natural kind"—say, "a natural kind is a class which is the extension of a term *P* which plays such-and-such a methodological role in some well-confirmed theory"— the definition would obviously embody a theory of the world, at least in part. It is not *analytic* that natural kinds are classes which play certain kinds of roles in theories; what *really* distinguishes the classes we count as natural kinds is itself a matter of (high level and very abstract) scientific investigation and not just meaning analysis.

That the proposed definition of "lemon" uses terms which themselves resist definition is not a fatal objection however. Let us pause to note, therefore, that if it is correct (and we shall soon show that even it is radically oversimplified), then the traditional idea of the force of general terms is badly mistaken. To say that something is a lemon is, on the above definition, to say that it belongs to a natural kind whose normal members have certain properties; but not to say that it necessarily has those properties itself. There are no *analytic* truths of the form *every lemon has* P. What has happened is this: the traditional theory has taken an account which is correct for the "one-criterion" concepts (i.e., for such concepts as "bachelor" and "vixen"), and made it a general account of the meaning of general names. A theory which correctly describes the behavior of perhaps three hundred words has been asserted to correctly describe the behavior of the tens of thousands of general names.

It is also important to note the following: if the above definition is correct, then knowledge of the properties that a thing has (in any natural and non "ad hoc" sense of property) is not enough to determine, in any mechanical or algorithmic way, whether or not it is a lemon (or an acid, or whatever). For even if I have a description in, say, the language of particle physics, of what are in fact the chromosomal properties of a fruit, I may not be able to tell that it is a lemon because I have not developed the theory according to which (1) those physical-chemical characteristics are the chromosomal structure-features (I may not even have the notion "chromosome"); and (2) I may not have discovered that chromosomal structure is the *essential* property of lemons. Meaning does not determine extension, in the sense that given the meaning and a list of all the "properties" of a thing (in any particular sense of "property," one can simply *read off* whether the thing is a lemon, or acid, or whatever). Even given the meaning, whether something is a lemon or not is, or at least sometimes is, or at least may sometimes be, a matter of what is the best conceptual scheme, the best theory, the best scheme of "natural kinds." (This is, of course, one reason for the failure of phenomenalistic translation schemes.)

These consequences of the proposed definition are, I believe, correct, even though the proposed definition is itself still badly oversimplified. Is it a necessary truth that the "normal" lemons, as we think of them (the tart yellow ones) are really normal members of their species? Is it logically impossible that we should have mistaken what are really very atypical lemons (perhaps diseased ones) for normal lemons? On the above definition, if there is no natural kind whose normal members are yellow, tart, etc., then even these tart, yellow, thick-peeled fruits that I make lemonade from are *not literally lemons.* But this is absurd. It is clear that they are lemons, although it is not analytic that they are *normal* lemons. Moreover, if the color of lemons changed—say, as the result of some gasses getting into the earth's atmosphere and reacting with the pigment in the peel of lemons—we would not say that lemons had ceased to exist, although a natural kind whose normal members were *yellow* and had the other characteristics of lemons *would* have ceased to exist. Thus the above definition is correct to the extent that what it says *isn't* analytic indeed isn't; but it is incorrect in that what would be analytic if it were correct isn't. We have loosened up the logic of the natural kind terms, in comparison with the "conjunction of properties" model; but we have still not loosened it up enough.

Two cases have just been considered: (1) the normal members of the natural kind in question may not really be the ones we *think* are normal; (2) the characteristics of the natural kind may change with time, possibly owing to a change in the conditions, without the "essence" changing so much that we want to stop using the same word. In the first case (normal lemons are blue, but we haven't seen any normal lemons), our theory of the natural kind is false; but at least there is a natural kind about which we have a false theory, and that is why we can still apply the term. In the second case, our theory was at least once true; but it has ceased to be true, although the natural kind has not ceased to exist, which is why we can still apply the term.

Let us attempt to cover both these kinds of cases by modifying our definition as follows:

X is a *lemon* $= df$ X belongs to a natural kind whose . . . (as before) or X belongs to a natural kind whose normal members used to . . . (as before) OR

X belongs to a natural kind whose normal
members were formerly believed to, or are
now incorrectly believed to . . . (as before).

Nontechnically, the trouble with this "definition" is that it is
slightly crazy. Even if we waive the requirement of sanity (and,
indeed, it is all too customary in philosophy to waive any such
requirement), it still doesn't work. Suppose, for example, that
some tens of thousands of years ago lemons were unknown,
but a few atypical oranges were known. Suppose these atypical
oranges had exactly the properties of peel, color, etc., that
lemons have: indeed, we may suppose that only a biologist
could tell that they were really queer oranges and not normal
lemons. Suppose that the people living at that time took them
to be normal members of a species, and thus thought that
oranges have exactly the properties that lemons in fact do have.
Then all now existing oranges would be lemons, according to
the above definition, since they belong to a species (a natural
kind) of which it was once believed that the normal members
have the characteristics of yellow peel, lemon taste, etc.

Rather than try to complicate the definition still further, in
the fashion of system-building philosophers, let us simply observe what has gone wrong. It is true—and this is what the new
definition tries to reflect—that one possible use of a natural
kind term is the following: to refer to a thing which belongs to
a natural kind which does *not* fit the "theory" associated with
the natural kind term, but which was believed to fit that theory
(and, in fact, to be *the* natural kind which fit the theory) when
the theory had not yet been falsified. Even if cats turn out to be
robots remotely controlled from Mars we will still call them
"cats"; even if it turns out that the stripes on tigers are painted
on to deceive us, we will still call them "tigers"; even if normal
lemons are blue (we have been buying and raising very atypical
lemons, but don't know it), they are still lemons (and so are the
yellow ones). Not only will we still *call* them "cats," they are
cats; not only will we still call them "tigers," they are tigers; not
only will we still call them "lemons," they are lemons. But the
fact that a term has several possible uses does not make it a dis-

junctive term; the mistake is in trying to represent the complex behavior of a natural kind word in something as simple as an analytic definition.

To say that an analytic definition is too simple a means of representation is not to say that no representation is possible. Indeed, a very simple representation is possible, *viz.:*

> *lemon:* natural kind word   associated characteristics:
> yellow peel, tart taste, etc.

To fill this out, a lot more should be said about the linguistic behavior of natural kind words; but no more need be said about *lemon.*

Katz's theory of meaning. Carnap's view of meaning in natural language is this: we divide up logical space into "logically possible worlds." (That this may be highly language-relative, and that it may presuppose the very analytic-synthetic distinction he hopes to find by his quasi-operational procedure are objections he does not discuss.) The informant is asked whether or not he would say that something is the case in each logically possible world: the assumption being that (1) each logically possible world can be described clearly enough for the informant to tell; and (2) that the informant can say that the sentence in question is *true/false/not clearly either* just on the basis of the description of the logically possible world and the meaning (or "intension") he assigns to the sentence in question. The latter assumption is false, as we have just seen, for just the reason that the traditional theory of meaning is false: even if I know the "logically possible world" you have in mind, deciding whether or not something is, for example, a lemon, may require deciding what the best *theory* is; and this is not something to be determined by asking an informant yes/no questions in a rented office. This is not to say that "lemon" has no meaning, of course: it is to say that meaning is not *that* simply connected with extension, even with "extension in logically possible worlds."

Carnap is not my main stalking-horse, however. The theory I want to focus on is the "semantic theory" recently propounded by Jerrold Katz and his co-workers. In main outlines this theory is as follows:

(1) Each word has its meaning characterized by a string of "semantic markers."

(2) These markers stand for "concepts" ("concepts" are themselves brain processes in Katz' philosophy of language; but I shall ignore this *jeu d'esprit* here). Examples of such concepts are: *unmarried, animate, seal.*

(3) Each such concept (concept for which a semantic marker is introduced) is a "linguistic universal," and stands for an *innate* notion—one in some sense-or-other "built into" the human brain.

(4) There are recursive rules—and this is the "scientific" core of Katz' "semantic theory"—whereby the "readings" of whole sentences (these being likewise strings of markers) are derived from the meanings of the individual words and the deep structure (in the sense of transformational grammar) of the sentence.

(5) The scheme as a whole is said to be justified in what is said to be the manner of a scientific theory—by its ability to explain such things as our intuitions that certain sentences have more than one meaning, or that certain sentences are queer.

(6) Analyticity relations are also supposed to be able to be read off from the theory: for example, from the fact that the markers associated with "unmarried" occur in connection with "bachelor," one can see that "all bachelors are unmarried" is analytic; and from the fact that the markers associated with "animal" occur in connection with "cat," one can see (allegedly) that "all cats are animals" is analytic.

There are internal inconsistencies in this scheme which are apparent at once. For example, "seal" is given as an example of a "linguistic universal" (at least, "seal" occurs as part of the "distinguisher" in one reading for "bachelor"—the variant reading: *young male fur seal,* in one of Katz' examples); but in no theory of human evolution is contact with seals universal. Indeed, even contact with *clothing,* or with *furniture,* or with *agriculture* is by no means universal. Thus we must take it that Katz means that whenever such terms occur they could be further analyzed into concepts which really are so primitive that a case could be made for their universality. Needless to say, this program has never been carried out, and he himself constantly ignores it in giving examples. But the point of greatest interest to us is that this scheme is an unsophisticated translation into "mathematical" language of precisely the traditional theory that it has been our concern to criticize! Indeed, as far as general names are concerned, the only change is that whereas in the traditional account each general name was associated with a list of properties, in Katz' account each general name is associated with a list of *concepts*. It follows that each counterexample to the traditional theory is at once a counterexample also to Katz' theory. For example, if Katz lists the concept "yellow" under the noun "lemon," then he will be committed to "all lemons are yellow"; if he lists the concept "striped" under the noun "tiger," then he will be committed to the analyticity of "all tigers are striped"; and so on. Indeed, although Katz denies that his "semantic markers" are themselves *words,* it is clear that they can be regarded as a kind of artificial language. Therefore, what Katz is saying is that:

(1) A mechanical scheme can be given for translating any natural language into this artificial "marker language" (and this scheme is just what Katz' "semantic theory" is).

(2) The string of markers associated with a word has exactly the meaning of the word.

If (1) and (2) were true, we would at once deduce that there exists a possible language—a "marker language"—with the property that every word that human beings have invented or could invent has an analytic definition in that language. But this is something that we have every reason to disbelieve! In fact: (1) We have just seen that if our account of "natural kind" words is correct, then none of these words has an analytic definition. In particular, a natural kind word will be analytically translatable into marker language only in the special case in which a marker happens to have been introduced with that exact meaning. (2) There are many words for which we haven't the foggiest notion what an analytic definition would even look like. What would an analytic definition of "mammoth" look like? (Would Katz say that it is analytic that mammoths are extinct? Or that they have a certain kind of molar? These are the items mentioned in the dictionary!) To say that a word is the name of an extinct species of elephant is to exactly communicate the use of that word; but it certainly isn't an analytic definition (i.e., an analytical necessary and sufficient condition). (3) *Theoretical terms* in science have no analytic definitions, for reasons familiar to every reader of recent philosophy of science; yet these are surely items (and not atypical items) in the vocabulary of natural languages.

We have now seen, I believe, one reason for the recent lack of progress in semantic theory: you may dress up traditional mistakes in modern dress by talking of "recursive rules" and "linguistic universals," but they remain the traditional mistakes. The problem in semantic theory is to get away from the picture of the meaning of a word as something like a *list of concepts;* not to formalize that misguided picture.

Quine's pessimism. Quine has long expressed a profound pessimism about the very possibility of such a subject as "semantic theory." Certainly we cannot assume that *there is* a scientific subject to be constructed here just because ordinary people have occasion to use the word "meaning" from time to time; that would be like concluding that there must be a scientific subject to be constructed which will deal with "causation" just because ordinary people have occasion to use the word "cause" from time to time. In one sense, *all* of science is a theory of causation; but not in the sense that it uses the word *cause.* Similarly, any successful and developed theory of language-use will in one sense be a theory of meaning; but not necessarily in the sense that it will employ any such notion as the "meaning" of a word or of an utterance. Elementary as this point is, it seems to be constantly overlooked in the social sciences, and people seem constantly to expect that psychology, for example, must talk of "dislike," "attraction," "belief," etc., simply because ordinary men use these words in psychological description.

Quine's pessimism cannot, then, be simply dismissed; and as far as the utility of the traditional notion of "meaning" is concerned, Quine may well turn out to be right. But we are still left with the task of trying to say what are the real problems in the area of language-use, and of trying to erect a conceptual framework within which we can begin to try to solve them.

Let us return to our example of the natural kind words. It is a fact, and one whose importance to this subject I want to bring out, that the use of words can be taught. If someone does not know the meaning of "lemon," I can somehow convey it to him. I am going to suggest that in this simple phenomenon lies the problem, and hence the *raison d'être,* of "semantic theory."

How do I convey the meaning of the word "lemon"? Very likely, I show the man a lemon. Very well, let us change the example. How do I convey the meaning of the word "tiger"? *I tell him what a tiger is.*

It is easy to see that Quine's own theoretical scheme (in *Word and Object*) will not handle this case very well. Quine's basic notion is the notion of *stimulus meaning* (roughly this is the set of nerve-ending stimulations which will "prompt assent" to *tiger*). But: (1) it is very unlikely that I convey exactly the stimulus-meaning that "tiger" has in my idiolect; and (2) in any case I don't convey it directly, i.e., by describing it. In fact, I couldn't describe it. Quine also works with the idea of *accepted sentences;* thus he might try to handle this case somewhat as follows: "the hearer, in your example already shares a great deal of language with you; otherwise you couldn't tell him what a tiger is. When you 'tell him what a tiger is,' you simply tell him certain sentences that you accept. Once he knows what sentences you accept, naturally he is able to use the word, at least observation words."

Let us, however, refine this last counter somewhat. If conveying the meaning of the word "tiger" involved conveying the totality of accepted scientific theory about tigers, or even the totality of what I believe about tigers, then it would be an impossible task. It is true that when I tell someone what a tiger is I "simply tell him certain sentences"—though not necessarily sentences I *accept,* except as descriptions of linguistically stereotypical tigers. But the point is, *which* sentences?

In the special case of such words as "tiger" and "lemon," we proposed an answer earlier in this paper. The answer runs as follows: there is somehow associated with the word "tiger" a *theory;* not the actual theory we believe about tigers, which is very complex, but an oversimplified theory which describes a, so to speak, tiger *stereotype.* It describes, in the language we used earlier, a *normal member* of the natural kind. It is not necessary that we believe this theory, though in the case of "tiger" we do. But it is necessary that we be aware that *this* theory is associated with the word: if our stereotype of a tiger ever changes, then the word "tiger" will have changed its meaning. If, to change the example, lemons all turn blue, the word "lemon" will not immediately change its meaning. When I first say, with surprise, "lemons have all turned blue," lemon will still mean what it means now—which is to say that "lemon" will still be associated with the stereotype *yellow lemon,* even though I will be using the word to deny that lemons (even normal lemons) are in fact yellow. I can refer to a natural kind by a term which is "loaded" with a theory which is known not to be any longer true of that natural kind, just because it will be clear to everyone that what I intend is to refer to *that* kind, and not to assert the theory. But, of course, if lemons really did turn blue (and stayed that way) then in time "lemon" would come to have a meaning with the following representation:

lemon: natural kind word   associated characteristics:
                              blue peel, tart taste, etc.

Then "lemon" would have changed its meaning.

To sum this up: there are a few facts about "lemon" or "tiger" (I shall refer to them as *core facts*) such that one can convey the use of "lemon" or "tiger" by simply conveying those facts. More precisely, one can frequently convey the approximate use; and still more precisely, one cannot convey the approximate use *unless* one gets the core facts across.

Let me emphasize that this has the status of an empirical hypothesis. The hypothesis is that there are, in connection with almost any word (not just "natural kind" words), certain core facts such that (1) one cannot convey the normal use of the word (to the satisfaction of native speakers) without conveying those core facts, and (2) in the case of many words and many speakers, conveying those core facts is sufficient to convey at least an approximation to the normal use. In the case of a natural kind word, the core facts are that a normal member of the kind has certain characteristics, or that this idea is at least the stereotype associated with the word.

If this hypothesis is false, then I think that Quine's pessimism is probably justified. But if this hypothesis is right, then I think it is clear what the problem of the theory of meaning is, regardless of whether or not one chooses to call it "theory of *meaning":* the question is to explore and explain this empirical phenomenon. Questions which naturally arise are: What different kinds of words are associated with what different kinds of core facts? and By what mechanism does it happen that just conveying a small set of core facts brings it about that the hearer is able to imitate the normal use of a word?

Wittgensteinians, whose fondness for the expression "form of life" appears to be directly proportional to its degree of preposterousness in a given context, say that acquiring the customary use of such a word as "tiger" is coming to share a form of life. What they miss, or at any rate fail to emphasize, is that while the acquired disposition may be sufficiently complex and sufficiently interlinked with other complex dispositions to warrant special mention (though hardly the overblown phrase "form of life"), what *triggers* the disposition is often highly discrete—e.g., a simple lexical definition frequently succeeds in conveying a pretty good idea of how a word is used. To be sure, as Wittgenstein emphasizes, this is only possible because we have a shared human nature, and because we have shared an acculturation process—there has to be a great deal of stage-setting before one can read a lexical definition and guess how a word is used. But in the process of "debunking" this fact—the fact that something as simple as a lexical definition *can* convey the use of a word—they forget to be impressed by it. To be sure there is a great deal of stage-setting, but it is rarely stage-setting specifically designed to enable one to learn the use of *this* word. The fact that one *can* acquire the use of an indefinite number of new words, and on the basis of simple "statements of what they mean," is an amazing fact: it is *the* fact, I repeat, on which semantic theory rests.

Sometimes it is said that the key problem in semantics is: how

do we come to understand a new sentence? I would suggest
that this is a far simpler (though not unimportant) problem.
How logical words, for example, can be used to build up complex sentences out of simpler ones is easy to describe, at least in
principle (of course, natural language analogues of logical
words are far less tidy than the logical words of the mathematical logician), and it is also easy to say how the truth-conditions,
etc., of the complex sentences are related to the truth-conditions of the sentences from which they were derived. This
much *is* a matter of finding a structure of recursive rules with a
suitable relation to the transformational grammar of the language in question. I would suggest that the question, How do
we come to understand a new *word*? has far more to do with
the whole phenomenon of giving definitions and writing dictionaries than the former question. And it is this phenomenon—the phenomenon of writing (and needing) dictionaries—
that gives rise to the whole idea of "semantic theory."

Kinds of core facts. Let us now look a little more closely at the
kind of information that one conveys when one conveys the
meaning of a word. I have said that in the case of a "natural
kind" word one conveys the associated *stereotype:* the associated
idea of the characteristics of a normal member of the kind. But
this is not, in general, enough; one must also convey the extension, one must indicate *which* kind the stereotype is supposed to
"fit."

From the point of view of any traditional meaning theory, be
it Plato's or Frege's or Carnap's or Katz', this is just nonsense.
How can I "convey" the extension of, say, "tiger"? Am I supposed to give you all the tigers in the world (heaven forfend!)?
I can convey the extension of a term only by giving a description of that extension; and then that description must be a
"part of the meaning," or else my definition will not be a
meaning-statement at all. To say: "I gave him certain conditions associated with the word, *and* I gave him the extension"
(as if that weren't just giving *further* conditions) can only be
nonsense.

The mistake of the traditional theorist lies in his attachment
to the word "meaning." If giving the meaning is *giving* the

meaning, then it is giving a definite thing; but giving the meaning isn't, as we shall see in a moment, giving some one definite thing. To drop the word "meaning," which is here extremely misleading: there is no *one* set of facts which has to be conveyed to convey the normal use of a word; and taking account of this requires a complication in our notion of "core facts."

That the same stereotype might be associated with different kinds seems odd if the kind word one has in mind is "tiger"; but change the example to, say, "aluminum" and it will not seem odd at all. About all *I* know about aluminum is that it is a light metal, that it makes durable pots and pans, and that it doesn't appear to rust (although it does occasionally discolor). For all I know, every one of these characteristics may also fit molybdenum.

Suppose now that a colony of English-speaking Earthlings is leaving in a spaceship for a distant planet. When they arrive on their distant planet, they discover that no one remembers the atomic weight (or any other defining characteristic) of aluminum, nor the atomic weight (or any other characteristic) of molybdenum. There is some aluminum in the spacecraft, and some molybdenum. Let us suppose that they guess which is which, and they guess wrong. Henceforth, they use "aluminum" as the name for molybdenum, and "molybdenum" as the name for aluminum. It is clear that "aluminum" has a different meaning in this community than in ours: in fact, it means *molybdenum.* Yet how can this be? Didn't they possess the normal "linguistic competence"? Didn't they all "know the meaing of the word 'aluminum' "?

Let us duck this question for a moment. If I want to make sure that the word "aluminum" will continue to be used in what counts as a "normal" way by the colonists in my example, it will suffice to give them some test for aluminum (or just to give them a carefully labelled sample, and let them discover a test, if they are clever enough). Once they know how to *tell* aluminum from other metals, they will go on using the word with the correct extension as well as the correct "intension" (i.e., the correct stereotype). But notice: it does not matter *which* test we give the colonists. The test isn't part of the meaning; but what there be some test or other (or something, e.g., a sample, from which one might be derived), is necessary to preservation of "the normal usage." Meaning indeed determines extension; but only because extension (fixed by *some* test or other) is, in some cases, "part of the meaning."

There are two further refinements here: if we give them a test, they mustn't make it part of the stereotype—that would be a change of meaning. (Thus it's better if they don't all *know* the test; as long as only experts do, and the average speaker "asks an expert" in case of doubt, the criteria mentioned in the test can't infect the stereotype.) Asking an expert is enough of a test for the normal speaker; that's why we don't give a test in an ordinary context.

We can now modify our account of the "core facts" in the case of a natural kind word as follows: (1) The core facts are the stereotype *and the extension.* (2) Nothing normally need be said about the extension, however, since the hearer knows that he can always consult an expert if any question comes up. (3) In special cases—such as the case of colonists—there may be danger that the word will get attached to the wrong natural kind, even though the right stereotype is associated with it. In such cases, one must give some way of getting the extension right, but no one *particular* way is necessary.

In the case of "lemon" or "tiger" a similar problem comes up. It is logically possible (although empirically unlikely, perhaps) that a species of fruit biologically unrelated to lemons might be indistinguishable from lemons in taste and appearance. In such a case, there would be two possibilities: (1) to call them *lemons,* and thus let "lemon" be a word for any one of a number of natural kinds; or (2) to say that they are not lemons (which is what, I suspect, biologists would decide to do). In the latter case, the problems are exactly the same as with *aluminum:* to be sure one has the "normal usage" or "customary meaning" or whatever, one has to be sure one has the right extension.

The problem: that giving the extension is part of giving the meaning arises also in the case of names of sensible qualities, e.g., colors. Here, however, it is normal to give the extension by giving a sample, so that the person learning the word learns to recognize the quality in the normal way. Frequently it has been regarded as a defect of *dictionaries* that they are "cluttered up" with color samples, and with stray pieces of empirical information (e.g., the atomic weight of aluminum), not sharply distinguished from "purely linguistic" information. The burden of the present discussion is that this is no defect at all, but essential to the function of conveying the core facts in each case.

Still other kinds of words may be mentioned in passing. In the case of "one-criterion" words (words which possess an analytical necessary and sufficient condition) it is obvious why the core fact is just the analytical necessary and sufficient condition (e.g. "man who has never been married," in the case of "bachelor"). In the case of "cluster" words (e.g., the name of a disease which is known not to have any one underlying cause), it is obvious why the core facts are just the typical symptoms or elements of the cluster; and so on. Given the *function* of a kind of word, it is not difficult to explain why certain facts function as core facts for conveying the use of words of that kind.

The possibility of semantics. Why, then, is semantics so hard? In terms of the foregoing, I want to suggest that semantics is a typical social science. The sloppiness, the lack of precise theories and laws, the lack of mathematical rigor, are all characteristic of the social sciences today. A general and precise theory which answers the questions (1) why do words have the different sorts of functions they do? and (2) exactly how does conveying core facts enable one to learn the use of a word? is not to be expected until one has a general and precise model of a language-user; and that is still a long way off. But the fact that Utopia is a long way off does not mean that daily life should come to a screeching halt. There is plenty for us to investigate, in our sloppy and impressionistic fashion, and there are plenty of real results to be obtained. The first step is to free ourselves from the oversimplifications foisted upon us by the tradition, and to see where the real problems lie. I hope this paper has been a contribution to that first step.

4 Meaning and Reference

HILARY PUTNAM

Unclear as it is, the traditional doctrine that the notion "meaning" possesses the extension/intension ambiguity has certain typical consequences. The doctrine that the meaning of a term is a concept carried the implication that meanings are mental entities. Frege, however, rebelled against this "psychologism." Feeling that meanings are *public* property—that the *same* meaning can be "grasped" by more than one person and by persons at different times—he identified concepts (and hence "intensions" or meanings) with abstract entities rather than mental entities. However, "grasping" these abstract entities was still an individual psychological act. None of these philosophers doubted that understanding a word (knowing its intension) was just a matter of being in a certain psychological state (somewhat in the way in which knowing how to factor numbers in one's head is just a matter of being in a certain very complex psychological state).

Secondly, the timeworn example of the two terms 'creature with a kidney' and 'creature with a heart' does show that two terms can have the same extension and yet differ in intension. But it was taken to be obvious that the reverse is impossible: two terms cannot differ in extension and have the same intension. Interestingly, no argument for this impossibility was ever offered. Probably it reflects the tradition of the ancient and medieval philosophers, who assumed that the concept corresponding to a term was just a conjunction of predicates, and

Reprinted from *The Journal of Philosophy*, LXX (November 8, 1973), 699–711, by permission of the author and editor.

219

hence that the concept/corresponding to a term must *always* provide a necessary and sufficient condition for falling into the extension of the term. For philosophers like Carnap, who accepted the verifiability theory of meaning, the concept corresponding to a term provided (in the ideal case, where the term had "complete meaning") a *criterion* for belonging to the extension (not just in the sense of "necessary and sufficient condition," but in the strong sense of *way of recognizing* whether a given thing falls into the extension or not). So theory of meaning came to rest on two unchallenged assumptions:

(1) That knowing the meaning of a term is just a matter of being in a certain psychological state (in the sense of "psychological state," in which states of memory and belief are "psychological states"; no one thought that knowing the meaning of a word was a continuous state of consciousness, of course).

(2) That the meaning of a term determines its extension (in the sense that sameness of intension entails sameness of extension).

I shall argue that these two assumptions are not jointly satisfied by *any* notion, let alone any notion of meaning. The traditional concept of meaning is a concept which rests on a false theory.

[handwritten: Section: 'Psychological state' and methodological solipsism]

Are Meanings in the Head? *[handwritten: That psychological state does not determine extension will now be shown]*

223

For the purpose of the following science-fiction examples, we shall suppose that somewhere there is a planet we shall call Twin Earth. Twin Earth is very much like Earth: in fact, people on Twin Earth even speak *English*. In fact, apart from the differences we shall specify in our science-fiction examples, the reader may suppose that Twin Earth is *exactly* like Earth. He may even suppose that he has a *Doppelgänger*—an identical copy—on Twin Earth, if he wishes, although my stories will not depend on this.

Although some of the people on Twin Earth (say, those who call themselves "Americans" and those who call themselves "Canadians" and those who call themselves "Englishmen," etc.) speak English, there are, not surprisingly, a few tiny dif-

[handwritten at bottom: "D" is spelt correctly in the longer paper]

ferences between the dialects of English spoken on Twin Earth and standard English.

One of the peculiarities of Twin Earth is that the liquid called "water" is not H_2O but a different liquid whose chemical formula is very long and complicated. I shall abbreviate this chemical formula simply as XYZ. I shall suppose that XYZ is indistinguishable from water at normal temperatures and pressures. Also, I shall suppose that the oceans and lakes and seas of Twin Earth contain XYZ and not water, that it rains XYZ on Twin Earth and not water, etc.

If a space ship from Earth ever visits Twin Earth, then the supposition at first will be that 'water' has the same meaning on Earth and on Twin Earth. This supposition will be corrected when it is discovered that "water" on Twin Earth is XYZ, and the Earthian space ship will report somewhat as follows.

"On Twin Earth the word 'water' means XYZ."

Symmetrically, if a space ship from Twin Earth ever visits Earth, then the supposition at first will be that the word 'water' has the same meaning on Twin Earth and on Earth. This supposition will be corrected when it is discovered that "water" on Earth is H_2O, and the Twin Earthian space ship will report:

"On Earth the word 'water' means H_2O."

Note that there is no problem about the extension of the term 'water': the word simply has two different meanings (as we say); in the sense in which it is used on Twin Earth, the sense of water$_{TE}$, what *we* call "water" simply isn't water, while in the sense in which it is used on Earth, the sense of water$_E$, what the Twin Earthians call "water" simply isn't water. The extension of 'water' in the sense of water$_E$ is the set of all wholes consisting of H_2O molecules, or something like that; the extension of water in the sense of water$_{TE}$ is the set of all wholes consisting of XYZ molecules, or something like that.

Now let us roll the time back to about 1750. The typical Earthian speaker of English did not know that water consisted of hydrogen and oxygen, and the typical Twin Earthian speaker of English did not know that "water" consisted of XYZ. Let Oscar$_1$ be such a typical Earthian English speaker, and let Oscar$_2$ be his counterpart on Twin Earth. You may suppose that there is no belief that Oscar$_1$ had about water that Oscar$_2$ did not have about "water." If you like, you may even suppose that Oscar$_1$ and Oscar$_2$ were exact duplicates in appearance, feelings, thoughts, interior monologue, etc. Yet the extension of the term 'water' was just as much H$_2$O on Earth in 1750 as in 1950; and the extension of the term 'water' was just as much XYZ on Twin Earth in 1750 as in 1950. Oscar$_1$ and Oscar$_2$ understood the term 'water' differently in 1750 *although they were in the same psychological state,* and although, given the state of science at the time, it would have taken their scientific communities about fifty years to discover that they understood the term 'water' differently. Thus the extension of the term 'water' (and, in fact, its "meaning" in the intuitive preanalytical usage of that term) is *not* a function of the psychological state of the speaker by itself.[1]

But, it might be objected, why should we accept it that the term 'water' had the same extension in 1750 and in 1950 (on both Earths)? Suppose I point to a glass of water and say "this liquid is called water." My "ostensive definition" of water has the following empirical presupposition: that the body of liquid I am pointing to bears a certain sameness relation (say, *x is the same liquid as y,* or *x is the same$_L$ as y*) to most of the stuff I and other speakers in my linguistic community have on other occasions called "water." If this presupposition is false because, say, I am—unknown to me—pointing to a glass of gin and not a glass of water, then I do not intend my ostensive definition to be accepted. Thus the ostensive definition conveys what might be called a "defeasible" necessary and sufficient condition: the necessary and sufficient condition for being water is bearing the relation *same$_L$* to the stuff in the glass; but this is the necessary and sufficient condition only if the empirical presupposition is satisfied. If it is not satisfied, then one of a series of, so to speak, "fallback" conditions becomes activated.

The key point is that the relation *same$_L$* is a *theoretical* relation: whether something is or is not the same liquid as *this* may take an indeterminate amount of scientific investigation to determine. Thus, the fact that an English speaker in 1750 might

1. See fn. 2, p. 132 below, and the corresponding text.

have called XYZ "water," whereas he or his successors would not have called XYZ water in 1800 or 1850 does not mean that the "meaning" of 'water' changed for the average speaker in the interval. In 1750 or in 1850 or in 1950 one might have pointed to, say, the liquid in Lake Michigan as an example of "water." What changed was that in 1750 we would have mistakenly thought that XYZ bore the relation $same_L$ to the liquid in Lake Michigan, whereas in 1800 or 1850 we would have known that it did not.

Let us now modify our science-fiction story. I shall suppose that molybdenum pots and pans *can't* be distinguished from aluminum pots and pans save by an expert. (This could be true for all I know, and, a fortiori, it could be true for all I know by virtue of "knowing the meaning" of the words *aluminum* and *molybdenum*.) We will now suppose that molybdenum is as common on Twin Earth as aluminum is on Earth, and that aluminum is as rare on Twin Earth as molybdenum is on Earth. In particular, we shall assume that "aluminum" pots and pans are made of molybdenum on Twin Earth. Finally, we shall assume that the words 'aluminum' and 'molybdenum' are *switched* on Twin Earth: 'aluminum' is the name of *molybdenum,* and 'molybdenum' is the name of *aluminum.* If a space ship from Earth visited Twin Earth, the visitors from Earth probably would not suspect that the "aluminum" pots and pans on Twin Earth were not made of aluminum, especially when the Twin Earthians *said* they were. But there is one important difference between the two cases. An Earthian metallurgist could tell very easily that "aluminum" was molybdenum, and a Twin Earthian metallurgist could tell equally easily that aluminum was "molybdenum." (The shudder quotes in the preceding sentence indicate Twin Earthian usages.) Whereas in 1750 no one on either Earth or Twin Earth could have distinguished water from "water," the confusion of aluminum with "aluminum" involves only a part of the linguistic communities involved.

This example makes the same point as the preceding example. If Oscar$_1$ and Oscar$_2$ are standard speakers of Earthian English and Twin Earthian English, respectively, and neither is chemically or metallurgically sophisticated, then there may be no difference at all in their psychological states when they use

226

the word 'aluminum'; nevertheless, we have to say that 'aluminum' has the extension *aluminum* in the idiolect of Oscar₁ and the extension *molybdenum* in the idiolect of Oscar₂. (Also we have to say that Oscar₁ and Oscar₂ mean different things by 'aluminum'; that 'aluminum' has a different meaning on Earth than it does on Twin Earth, etc.) Again we see that the psychological state of the speaker does *not* determine the extension (*or* the "meaning," speaking preanalytically) of the word.

Before discussing this example further, let me introduce a *non*-science-fiction example. Suppose you are like me and cannot tell an elm from a beech tree. We still say that the extension of 'elm' in my idiolect is the same as the extension of 'elm' in anyone else's, viz., the set of all elm trees, and that the set of all beech trees is the extension of 'beech' in *both* of our idiolects. Thus 'elm' in my idiolect has a different extension from 'beech' in your idiolect (as it should). Is it really credible that this difference in extension is brought about by some difference in our *concepts?* My *concept* of an elm tree is exactly the same as my concept of a beech tree (I blush to confess). If someone heroically attempts to maintain that the difference/between the extension of 'elm' and the extension of 'beech' in *my* idiolect is explained by a difference in my psychological state, then we can always refute him by constructing a "Twin Earth" example—just let the words 'elm' and 'beech' be switched on Twin Earth (the way 'aluminum' and "molybdenum" were in the previous example). Moreover, suppose I have a *Doppelgänger* on Twin Earth who is molecule for molecule "identical" with me. If you are a dualist, then also suppose my *Dopplegänger* thinks the same verbalized thoughts I do, has the same sense data, the same dispositions, etc. It is absurd to think *his* psychological state is one bit different from mine: yet he "means" *beech* when he says "elm," and *I* "mean" *elm* when I say "elm." Cut the pie any way you like, "meanings" just ain't in the *head!*

A Sociolinguistic Hypothesis

The last two examples depend upon a fact about language that seems, surprisingly, never to have been pointed out: that there is *division of linguistic labor*. We could hardly use such words as 'elm' and 'aluminum' if no one possessed a way of recognizing elm trees and aluminum metal; but not everyone to whom the distinction is important has to be able to make the distinction. Let us shift the example; consider *gold*. Gold is important for many reasons: it is a precious metal; it is a monetary metal; it has symbolic value (it is important to most people that the "gold" wedding ring they wear *really* consist of gold and not just *look* gold); etc. Consider our community as a "factory": in this "factory" some people have the "job" of *wearing gold wedding rings;* other people have the "job" of selling gold wedding rings; still other people have the job of *telling whether or not something is really gold*. It is not at all necessary or efficient that everyone who wears a gold ring (or a gold cufflink, etc.), or discusses the "gold standard," etc., engage in buying and selling gold. Nor is it necessary or efficient that everyone who buys and sells gold be able to tell whether or not something is really gold in a society where this form of dishonesty is uncommon (selling fake gold) and in which one can easily consult an expert in case of doubt. And it is *certainly* not necessary or efficient that everyone who has occasion to buy or wear gold be able to tell with any reliability whether or not something is really gold.

The foregoing facts are just examples of mundane division of labor (in a wide sense). But they engender a division of linguistic labor: everyone to whom gold is important for any reason has to *acquire* the word 'gold'; but he does not have to acquire the *method of recognizing* whether something is or is not gold. He can rely on a special subclass of speakers. The features that are generally thought to be present in connection with a general name—necessary and sufficient conditions for membership in the extension, ways of recognizing whether something is in the extension, etc.—are all present in the linguistic community *considered as a collective body;* but that collective body divides the "labor" of knowing and employing these various parts of the "meaning" of 'gold'.

This division of linguistic labor rests upon and presupposes the division of *non*linguistic labor, of course. If only the people who know how to tell whether some metal is really gold or not have any reason to have the word 'gold' in their vocabulary, then the word 'gold' will be as the word 'water' was in 1750 with respect to that subclass of speakers, and the other speakers just won't acquire it at all. And some words do not exhibit any division of linguistic labor: 'chair', for example. But with the increase of division of labor in the society and the rise of science, more and more words begin to exhibit this kind of division of labor. 'Water', for example, did not exhibit it at all before the rise of chemistry. Today it is obviously necessary for every speaker to be able to recognize water (reliably under normal conditions), and probably most adult speakers even know the necessary and sufficient condition "water is H_2O," but only a few adult speakers could distinguish water from liquids that superficially resembled water. In case of doubt, other speakers would rely on the judgment of these "expert" speakers. Thus the way of recognizing possessed by these "expert" speakers is also, through them, possessed by the collective linguistic body, even though it is not possessed by each individual member of the body, and in this way the most *recherché* fact about water may become part of the *social* meaning of the word although unknown to almost all speakers who acquire the word.

It seems to me that this phenomenon of division of linguistic labor is one that it will be very important for sociolinguistics to investigate. In connection with it, I should like to propose the following hypothesis:

HYPOTHESIS OF THE UNIVERSALITY OF THE DIVISION OF LINGUISTIC LABOR: Every linguistic community exemplifies the sort of division of linguistic labor just described; that is, it possesses at least some terms whose associated "criteria" are known only to a subset of the speakers who acquire the terms, and whose use by the other speakers depends upon a structured cooperation between them and the speakers in the relevant subsets.

It is easy to see how this phenomenon accounts for some of the examples given above of the failure of the assumptions (1 and 2). When a term is subject to the division of linguistic labor, the "average" speaker who acquires it does not acquire anything that fixes its extension. In particular, his individual psychological state *certainly* does not fix its extension; it is only the sociolinguistic state of the collective linguistic body to which the speaker belongs that fixes the extension.

We may summarize this discussion by pointing out that there are two sorts of tools in the world: there are tools like a hammer or a screwdriver which can be used by one person; and there are tools like a steamship which require the cooperative activity of a number of persons to use. Words have been thought of too much on the model of the first sort of tool.

Indexicality and Rigidity

The first of our science-fiction examples—'water' on Earth and on Twin Earth in 1750—does not involve division of linguistic labor, or at least does not involve it in the same way the examples of 'aluminum' and 'elm' do. There were not (in our story, anyway) any "experts" on water on Earth in 1750, nor any experts on "water" on Twin Earth. The example *does* involve things which are of fundamental importance to the theory of reference and also to the theory of necessary truth, which we shall now discuss.

Let W_1 and W_2 be two possible worlds in which I exist and in which this glass exists and in which I am giving a meaning explanation by pointing to this glass and saying "This is water." Let us suppose that in W_1 the glass is full of H_2O and in W_2 the glass is full of XYZ. We shall also suppose that W_1 is the *actual* world, and that XYZ is the stuff typically called "water" in the world W_2 (so that the relation between English speakers in W_1 and English speakers in W_2 is exactly the same as the relation between English speakers on Earth and English speakers on Twin Earth). Then there are two theories one might have concerning the meaning of 'water':

(1) One might hold that 'water' was *world-relative* but *constant* in meaning (i.e., the word has a constant relative meaning). On this theory, 'water' means the same in W_1 and W_2; it's just that water is H_2O in W_1, and water is XYZ in W_2.

(2) One might hold that water is H_2O in all worlds (the stuff called "water" in W_2 isn't water), but 'water' doesn't have the same meaning in W_1 and W_2.

If what was said before about the Twin Earth case was correct, then (2) is clearly the correct theory. When I say "*this* (liquid) is water," the "this" is, so to speak, a *de re* "this"—i.e., the force of my explanation is that "water" is whatever bears a certain equivalence relation (the relation we called "*same_L*" above) to the piece of liquid referred to as "this" *in the actual world*.

We might symbolize the difference between the two theories as a "scope" difference in the following way. On theory (1), the following is true:

(1') (For every world W) (For every x in W) (x is water $\equiv x$ bears *same_L* to the entity referred to as "this" in W)

while on theory (2):

(2') (For every world W) (For every x in W) (x is water $\equiv x$ bears *same_L* to the entity referred to as "this" *in the actual world W_1*)

I call this a "scope" difference because in (1') 'the entity referred to as "this"' is within the scope of 'For every world W'—as the qualifying phrase 'in W' makes explicit—whereas in (2') 'the entity referred to as "this"' means "the entity referred to as 'this' *in the actual world*," and has thus a reference *independent* of the bound variable 'W'.

Kripke calls a designator "rigid" (in a given sentence) if (in that sentence) it refers to the same individual in every possible world in which the designator designates. If we extend this notion of rigidity to substance names, then we may express Kripke's theory and mine by saying that the term 'water' is *rigid*.

The rigidity of the term 'water' follows from the fact that when I give the "ostensive definition": "*this* (liquid) is water," I intend (2') and not (1').

We may also say, following Kripke, that when I give the ostensive definition "*this* (liquid) is water," the demonstrative 'this' is *rigid*.

What Kripke was the first to observe is that this theory of the meaning (or "use," or whatever) of the word 'water' (and other natural kind terms as well) has startling consequences for the theory of necessary truth.

To explain this, let me introduce the notion of a *cross-world relation*. A two-term relation R will be called *cross-world* when it is understood in such a way that its extension is a set of ordered pairs of individuals *not all in the same possible world*. For example, it is easy to understand the relation *same height as* as a cross-world relation: just understand it so that, e.g., if x is an individual in a world W_1 who is 5 feet tall (in W_1) and y is an individual in W_2 who is 5 feet tall (in W_2), then the ordered pair x,y belongs to the extension of *same height as*. (Since an individual may have different heights in different possible worlds in which that same individual exists, strictly speaking, it is not the ordered pair x,y that constitutes an element of the extension of *same height as*, but rather the ordered pair x-*in-world-*W_1, y-*in-world-*W_2.)

Similarly, we can understand the relation $same_L$ (same liquid as) as a cross-world relation by understanding it so that a liquid in world W_1 which has the same important physical properties (in W_1) that a liquid in W_2 possesses (in W_2) bears $same_L$ to the latter liquid.

Then the theory we have been presenting may be summarized by saying that an entity x, in an arbitrary possible world, is *water* if and only if it bears the relation $same_L$ (construed as a cross-world relation) to the stuff *we* call "water" in the actual world.

Suppose, now, that I have not yet discovered what the important physical properties of water are (in the actual world)—i.e., I don't yet know that water is H_2O. I may have ways of *recognizing* water that are successful (of course, I may make a small number of mistakes that I won't be able to detect until a later stage in our scientific development), but not know the microstructure of water. If I agree that a liquid with the superficial properties of "water" but a different microstructure *isn't really water*, then my ways of recognizing water cannot be regarded as an analytical specification of what *it is to be* water. Rather, the operational definition, like the ostensive one, is simply a way of pointing out a standard—pointing out the stuff *in the actual world* such that, for x to be water, in *any* world, is for x to bear the relation *same*$_L$ to the *normal* members of the class of *local* entities that satisfy the operational definition. "Water" on Twin Earth is not water, even if it satisfies the operational definition, because it doesn't bear *same*$_L$ to the *local* stuff that satisfies the operational definition, and local stuff that satisfies the operational definition but has a microstructure different from the rest of the local stuff that satisfies the/operational definition isn't water either, because it doesn't bear *same*$_L$ to the *normal* examples of the local "water."

Suppose, now, that I discover the microstructure of water— that water is H_2O. At this point I will be able to say that the stuff on Twin Earth that I earlier *mistook* for water isn't really water. In the same way, if you describe, not another planet in the actual universe, but another possible universe in which there is stuff with the chemical formula XYZ which passes the "operational test" for *water,* we shall have to say that that stuff isn't water but merely XYZ. You will not have described a possible world in which "water is XYZ," but merely a possible world in which there are lakes of XYZ, people drink XYZ (and not water), or whatever. In fact, once we have discovered the nature of water, nothing counts as a possible world in which water doesn't have that nature. Once we have discovered that water (in the actual world) is H_2O, *nothing counts as a possible world in which water isn't H_2O.*

On the other hand, we can perfectly well imagine having experiences that would convince us (and that would make it rational to believe that) water *isn't* H_2O. In that sense, it is conceivable that water isn't H_2O. It is conceivable but it isn't possible! Conceivability is no proof of possibility.

Kripke refers to statements that are rationally unrevisable (assuming there are such) as *epistemically necessary.* Statements that are true in all possible worlds he refers to simply as necessary (or sometimes as "metaphysically necessary"). In this terminology, the point just made can be restated as: a statement can be (metaphysically) necessary and epistemically contingent.

Human intuition has no privileged access to metaphysical necessity.

In this paper, our interest is in theory of meaning, however, and not in theory of necessary truth. Words like 'now', 'this', 'here' have long been recognized to be *indexical,* or *token-reflexive*—i.e., to have an extension which varies from context to context or token to token. For these words, no one has ever suggested the traditional theory that "intension determines extension." To take our Twin Earth example: if I have a *Doppelgänger* on Twin Earth, then when I think "I have a headache," *he* thinks "I have a headache." But the extension of the particular token of 'I' in his verbalized thought is himself (or his unit class, to be precise), while the extension of the token of 'I' in *my* verbalized thought is *me* (or my unit class, to be precise). So the same word, 'I', has two different extensions in two different idiolects; but it does not follow that the concept I have of myself is in any way different from the concept my *Dopplegänger* has of himself.

Now then, we have maintained that indexicality extends beyond the *obviously* indexical words and morphemes (e.g., the tenses of verbs). Our theory can be summarized as saying that words like 'water' have an unnoticed indexical component: "water" is stuff that bears a certain similarity relation to the water *around here.* Water at another time or in another place or even in another possible world has to bear the relation $same_L$ to *our* "water" *in order to be water.* Thus the theory that (1) words have "intensions," which are something like concepts associated with the words by speakers; and (2) intension determines extension—cannot be true of natural kind words like 'water' for the same reason it cannot be true of obviously indexical words like 'I'.

The theory that natural kind words like 'water' are indexical leaves it open, however, whether to say that 'water' in the Twin Earth dialect of English has the same *meaning* as 'water' in the Earth dialect and a different extension—which is what we normally say about 'I' in different idiolects—thereby giving up the doctrine that "meaning (intension) determines extension," or to say, as we have chosen to do, that difference in extension is *ipso facto* a difference in meaning for natural kind words, thereby giving up the doctrine that meanings are concepts, or, indeed, mental entities of *any* kind.[2]

It should be clear, however, that Kripke's doctrine that natural kind words are rigid designators and our doctrine that they are indexical are but two ways of making the same point. We have now seen that the extension of a term is not fixed by a concept that the individual speaker has in his head, and this is true both because extension is, in general, determined *socially*— there is division of linguistic labor as much as of "real" labor— and because extension is, in part, determined *indexically*. The extension of our terms depends upon the actual nature of the particular things that serve as paradigms, and this actual nature is not, in general, fully known to the speaker. Traditional semantic theory leaves out two contributions to the determination of reference—the contribution of society and the contribution of the real world; a better semantic theory must encompass both.

> 2. Our reasons for rejecting the first option—to say that 'water' has the same meaning on Earth and on Twin Earth, while giving up the doctrine that meaning determines references—are presented in "The Meaning of 'Meaning'." They may be illustrated thus: Suppose 'water' has the same meaning on Earth and on Twin Earth. Now, let the word 'water' become phonemically different on Twin Earth—say, it becomes 'quaxel'. Presumably, this is not a change in meaning per se, on any view. So 'water' and 'quaxel' have the same meaning (although they refer to different liquids). But this is highly counterintuitive. Why not say, then, that 'elm' in my idiolect has the same meaning as 'beech' in your idiolect, although they refer to different trees?

[handwritten margin notes: "quot. from Kripke", "245", "p. 711", "pp 235–271 not covered"]

5 Underlying Trait Terms

WILLIAM K. GOOSENS

University of Virginia

Programs for the Analysis of Concepts. There are many terms that seem to lack logically necessary and sufficient conditions. Nevertheless, persons use and understand such terms. As Ziff puts it, while they do not have a meaning, they have meaning.[1] In this paper we are concerned with the analysis of some of these terms, such as "tiger," "acid," "copper"—terms which, for reasons that will become clear only later, we call underlying trait terms. Given that logically necessary and sufficient conditions do not seem to provide a promising approach to such terms, what does?

In *Concepts of Science* Peter Achinstein provides an alternative program. Referring to such terms as part of his "list A," he writes, "If the relationship between a property of an item on list A and being an item of that sort is, in general, not one of logical necessity or sufficiency, how can it be described?" [2] What follows is his introduction of the concepts of relevance and semantical relevance. *Relevant* properties for a term are those such that having the property counts, to some degree, for or against the term applying to an object. *Semantically relevant* properties for a term are those which are relevant to a term in and of themselves. Achinstein's program is inclusive of logically necessary and sufficient conditions, for whenever such condi-

Previously unpublished. Published by permission of the author.

1. Paul Ziff, *Semantic Analysis* (Ithaca, N.Y.: Cornell University Press, 1960), chap. 5.
2. Peter Achinstein, *Concepts of Science* (Baltimore: Johns Hopkins University Press, 1968), p. 6.

tions exist, ipso facto there will be semantically relevant conditions.[3] For many terms, such as "quadruped" and "density," such conditions can be provided.

In this essay I wish to use Achinstein as a dialectical foil for developing and defending an alternative program—one related to the work of Hilary Putnam [4] and one that approaches meaning through reference. Achinstein's program, I believe, represents the best hope of classical intensionalist semantics for giving an account of such terms, and its failure indicates the need for a radically different approach.

Reducibility and Semantical Relevance. What makes a property relevant "in and of itself"? Basically, a relevant property gives us information about whether or not a term applies to objects that have the property. That information may be relevant because it gives information about other relevant properties. If so, the original is relevant not in and of itself, but rather through other properties. For example, "mined in Chile" is relevant for "copper," and "used in margarine" is relevant for "soybean oil," but neither is relevant in and of itself. Instead, the information merely increases the probability that an object is composed of a certain chemical substance. Let us say that a property A relevant for a term T is irreducible if and only if there are no other properties C relevant for T such that the reason A is relevant to T is that A gives us information about C. In the case where we can specify the properties C in terms of which A is reducible, let us say that A is *reduced*. The possibility that properties are reducible but not reduced is more than academic. Consider the following example, suggested by Putnam [5]

3. It does not follow that just because C is logically necessary and sufficient, C is semantically relevant. Triangles are closed figures with straight sides, the interior angles summing to 180°, yet the semantically relevant conditions are being closed, having straight sides, and having three sides.

4. See the following works by Putnam: "Dreaming and 'Depth Grammar'," in *Analytical Philosophy,* ed. by R. J. Butler (Oxford: Blackwell, 1962); "Explanation and Reference," in *Conceptual Change,* ed. by G. Pearce and P. Maynard (Dordrecht: D. Reidel, 1973); "Is Semantics Possible?" (in this volume); "The Meaning of 'Meaning'," in *Language, Mind, and Knowledge,* ed. by K. Gunderson (Minneapolis: University of Minnesota Press, 1976).

5. "Dreaming and 'Depth Grammar'," p. 218.

and in turn discussed by Achinstein.[6] Currently we do not know the cause of multiple sclerosis. We identify cases by relevant symptoms. Suppose that we in fact discover that the cause is a certain virus. We then discover that the cause is lacking in some cases where the symptoms are present. Putnam suggests that we could say that the person didn't have the disease, and moreover that this claim in no way reflects a semantical shift in the concept of multiple sclerosis.

Putnam's reason for his claim is that all along the cause, known or unknown, is our conception of the disease, so that the symptoms never formed our conception. While I agree that symptoms never formed our conception, it is not correct that cause is the general semantical category for diseases. Many— perhaps most—diseases are bodily states or conditions independent of the causes by which these conditions are produced. Jaundice, for example, refers to a condition that has many causes. Nor, contrary to a general suggestion of Putnam,[7] would it be correct to regard jaundice as its symptoms. The symptoms of jaundice are yellowness of the skin, eyes, and urine. Jaundice, though, is an excess of bile pigments in the blood and tissues. (The term "nausea," however, probably does refer to symptoms.) Even when we associate a disease with a unique causal mechanism, the disease is often not the cause but the effect. Scurvy, it is often said, is a vitamin deficiency disease. Vitamin deficiency is the cause, but scurvy is a bodily condition whose symptoms include spongy gums and general debility.[8] Arteriosclerosis, cirrhosis (of the liver), and (sugar) diabetes are likewise conditions to be in no way confused with their causes. If multiple sclerosis as a disease were a resultant condition, the discovery of a cause would in no way alter our

6. *Concepts of Science*, pp. 22–23.

7. "In the case of 'cluster' words (e.g., the name of a disease which is known not to have one underlying cause), it is obvious why the core facts are just the typical symptoms or elements of the cluster" (Putnam, "Is Semantics Possible?" p. 118, above). The core facts are here the stereotype.

8. To see this, consider that the resultant condition of all of the following states of affairs would still be scurvy. Vitamin C is ingested but not digested (due to some disorder in digestion). Vitamin C is digested, but cannot be utilized due to the lack of some protein in the diet. A chemical taken (possibly a

conception of the disease. It is not at all clear that our conception of multiple sclerosis is the presence of some organism (including viruses) now unknown.

Nor is it clear that, even if a disease is uniquely associated with the presence of some organism, the presence of the organism is semantically relevant. It might be suggested that tuberculosis is not just caused by an organism, but *is* the presence of an organism. Now, suppose an insecticide sprayed on tobacco caused the symptoms and damage of tuberculosis, without an organism being present. Is this condition tuberculosis? Suppose, further, we discover that the disease organism secretes the same chemical compound, and moreover, is harmless without it. Is the insecticide-caused condition tuberculosis? Suppose, further, that the same cures work. Now, this illustration is not purely fictional. The isolation of chemical toxins responsible for disease effects shows that the fundamental causes of many diseases are chemical as opposed to biological.

Nevertheless, Putnam's example shows that the role of unknown properties has to be considered in the analysis of concepts. The symptoms of multiple sclerosis are not now reduced to causes. Accepting (wrongly) that cause is the semantically relevant category, we would believe the symptoms to be reducible, though we cannot specify the cause they are to be reduced to. The symptoms are reducible but not reduced. Obviously, then, the defense of Putnam's position that no semantical shift was involved requires that irreducibility be necessary for semantical relevance. Two considerations back up Putnam's position. First, there is the widespread use of identifying tests that clearly do not enter into the concept. Obviously, the outcome of a pregnancy test does not in and of itself count toward a person's being pregnant. Symptoms of diseases seem to be of the same kind. Empirical correlations with the development of multiple sclerosis allow doctors to detect the disease. The fact that the nature of a disease is known or unknown in no way seems to af-

---

medicine for some other disease) blocks the utilization of vitamin C by interfering with a metabolic process. And a person would not have scurvy if he lacked vitamin C, yet another chemical substituted for it and resulted in a normal, healthy state.

fect the status of a test for it. Assuming cause is the semantically relevant category, this does seem to argue against the
semantic relevancy of symptoms. More important, as long as we
do believe that a property is reducible, then we do not believe
that it is relevant in and of itself. Even though we may not
know how to effect a reduction, nevertheless, as we use the
term, its relevance is derivative.

Achinstein himself seems to allow that reducibility can rule
out semantical relevance. He considers the question, also raised
by Putnam,[9] whether Bronsted's theory of acids, based upon
"inner structure," reflects a change from the eighteenth-century notions of acids, according to which the only known relevant properties were observational. Achinstein says that aside
from possible changes in centrality of relevance, the answer
depends upon "whether, as the term was once used, and still is
by many, having a common 'inner structure' (though unknown)
would have been considered semantically relevant."[10] He
allows that granting continued centrality, the observational
properties were possibly (but not probably) always nonseman-
tically relevant, and that the use changed only in being more
specific.

The difficulty for Achinstein is double. Reducibility comes
into play two ways for underlying trait terms, one relative and
one absolute. Success in reducing specific properties to others is
not coupled with the belief that other properties are themselves
ultimately irreducible. Future inquiry may yet reveal more fundamental properties. In the analysis of natures, we believe ourselves not to be able to ascribe absolute irreducibility to any specific property. Second, even if we were to discover specific
properties that were irreducible parts of a nature, the reason
we would associate these properties with the term would still be
that these properties are a part of the nature. The problem
then comes to a head with this question. Properties associated
with underlying trait terms are reducible on both epistemological and semantical grounds. But can a property which
is reducible, i.e., one that has reasons for its relevance, be rele-

9. "Dreaming and 'Depth Grammar'," p. 220.
10. *Concepts of Science*, p. 51.

vant "in and of itself," i.e., semantically relevant? If irreducibility is required for semantical relevance, terms like "oxygen" and "metal," as used, do not have properties which are relevant in and of themselves. Put another way, just as it is not part of our conceptioῐ of the terms that the properties we associate with them are logically necessary or logically sufficient, it is no part of our conception that these properties are relevant in and of themselves. Achinstein's program for analyzing concepts without necessary and sufficient conditions amounts, for underlying trait terms, to the notion of relevance and degrees of relevance.

This argument that semantical relevance collapses to relevance, however, hangs on the crucial thread that semantical relevance requires irreducibility. But this premise is not always true. We sharply distinguish underlying trait terms—which *mean* an underlying trait—from terms *with* (or that *have*) an underlying trait. The latter notion is not semantical, but empirical. If the previous argument were correct, the altogether too strong conclusion would follow that terms with underlying traits never have semantically relevant conditions. There are two ways a property can be reducible and remain semantically relevant. First, the property may be reducible to properties not in the meaning of the term. This situation is characteristic, I hold, of disposition terms, which should be semantically distinguished from underlying trait terms. Consider three disposition terms: "fragile," "malleable," and "(electrical) conductor." (I would also include perception terms like "blue" and "sour.") In a fully legitimate sense of "reason," we can discover the reason why something is fragile, malleable, or a conductor. Nevertheless, though the properties of having these dispositions are reducible, the reduction does not affect the semantic status of properties associated with the terms, because it is not a part of the meaning of these terms that things with the underlying trait are in the extension. We mean by "conductor" a substance capable of transmitting electricity. In general, disposition terms mean the disposition, and not any possible trait underlying them. Here I part company from Kripke and Putnam, who are inclined to extend the empiricist account to disposition terms as a class of natural kind terms. My intuitions are that a different semantical account is needed.

Second, reducibility need not entail nonsemantical relevance when not all the properties in the meaning are independent. Here a property may be reducible to properties in the meaning, and yet itself be in the meaning. For example, the term "earthquake" may mean the nature of things in an extension and still require semantically that earthquakes shake the ground. The underlying trait provides the reason for some of the properties that nonetheless are included in the meaning. A real possibility is that parts of the meaning of a term may serve as reasons for other parts. In the case of underlying trait terms, that properties are connected to the nature of the extension provides a standing reason for their relevance or association. When we mean by a term things sharing a nature more or less unknown, even if properties are a part of meaning we still have recourse to a reason for their inclusion. Asked repeatedly why things to which the term applies have a given property, we are not left ultimately with the answer that we mean by the term *just* things with that property. The question remains open, then, if any associated properties are part of the meaning of underlying trait terms. To answer that, we must face the question of the relationship between meaning and revisability.

Need Terms Have Properties Associated Linguistically with Them? Let us ask Achinstein's question again: what is the relationship between being an X and the properties Xs have? His answer is that some properties are relevant to being an X, and some of these relevant properties are semantically relevant. This answer is in keeping with the following more general position, which I wish to contest.

Among relevant properties, two classes are to be distinguished. The association of some properties with a term is more than just factual. Some properties are in addition *linguistically* associated with a term. The association reflects a linguistic fact, a fact by convention. One learns the association merely in virtue of understanding the term. The association reflects linguistic competence, a semantical aspect of use. Only through such linguistically associated properties can nonlinguistically associated properties ever become associated with the term. Some terms fit this approach well: what I call property terms like "red" (a color) "golden" (made of the metal), and "malleable." The association of a property with these terms reflects linguistic conventions, and the property is semantically relevant. But a large class of noun terms, covering some natural kind terms and some quantitative concepts in ordinary language and science, such as "table salt," "base," and "electricity," do not have semantically relevant properties associated with them.

What I shall argue is that the essential function in use that such words have is reference and characterization, but not the semantic characterization of the things they refer to.. (These words, of course, have linguistic associations governing contextural use. Without such linguistic associations, we would not have a sense of well-formed sentences. This is not, however, the association of properties with the term.) Philosophers of language who hold that meaning has a logical priority over reference must disagree with the position just espoused. How is it, they ask, that one could be in a position to ascribe a noun to an object without some understanding of properties in virtue of which the noun would apply? But ascription shows only the need for relevant properties, not for semantically relevant ones. But that is no escape, such philosophers add, for how is it that one could be in a position to justify that a property is relevant to a term apart from a knowledge of the properties in virtue of which we have a case of the term in question? And so the circle of priorities closes on meanings (intensions).

First of all, reference can be initiated without such meanings by the use of ostension and enumeration. Needing to refer to objects, one can stipulate that a term refers to them. Once reference is established, properties can be associated with a term by the discovery of similarities and differences among things included and excluded. More typically, reference can be introduced in relationship to causes, effects, and processes. Substances can be introduced as products of processes generating them (e.g., olive oil, oxygen). Electricity could be known as a thing that a procedure generates. In such cases does the introducing event characterize a term by linguistically associating properties with it? Not at all! From the very beginning the process generating a thing need not be viewed as characterizing it. A description may be associated with a term, but the function of it is to secure reference. Initially, what is linguistically associated with such terms are references. From the beginning, oxygen and X-rays were whatever accounts for the nature of the things. A referent has discoverable properties: some are causally important, some determine other properties and relations, some properties true of it hold in virtue of others. Empirical investigation reveals the nature of the thing. Properties are associated with terms, but it is investigation that does the associating. A third way in which references can be introduced is via associated properties. But these associated properties nevertheless are not part of meaning. Introduction via associated properties occurs when a complex of properties is thought or discovered to be significant, and an underlying trait term is introduced for the complex. The introducing properties are, however, seen as theoretical and tentative. This tends to be so, I conjecture, for more abstract natural kinds, such as "mammal." With organisms like flies, tigers, and toads, it is possible to tie reference to representative samples. As Putnam suggests, to ensure that space settlers will continue to use certain words as we do, they might well take along labeled samples.[11] But for a term like "mammal" with a wide diversity of forms, there is no good representative. The notion of mammal is considerably more abstract than these other biological categories, and it seems correspondingly implausible that the idea developed as an underlying trait term from some readily identifiable reference. More likely, the term was proposed only after considerable observation, analysis, and theorizing, in which case its introduction was probably simultaneous with the realization that a complex of properties was significant. Unlike the term "shoat," which is just a name for pigs in a certain stage of development, the term "mammal" is meant to be open to the advance of knowledge about mammals. The properties used to introduce the term may not all prove to be significant. The

11. "Is Semantics Possible?" p. 116.

function of the introducing properties is simultaneously to characterize theoretically and to secure reference, not to determine meaning.

No wonder, then, that such terms lack logically necessary and sufficient conditions. Nor is it the case that a property in and of itself is associated with such a term. Properties are associated with these terms, as are extensions. But the relationship of term, extension, and associated properties is not that the associated properties determine the extension of the term. The three interact in a more flexible way. Associated properties can be generated from extensions. The discovery of things similar to the extension but lacking associated properties can weaken the association of a property with the term, as can the discovery of things different from the extension but having the associated properties.

But, it might be objected, at any time are there not fixed degrees of association for unreduced properties, and wouldn't this be the semantical use of the term at that time? Perhaps there are such fixed degrees of association, but those associations are not linguistic facts. At any time, the status of the associations is flexible and empirical. At any time, the empirical forces concerning properties and relations of things influence the associations. At no time are these associations features of the language except insofar as knowledge of the world is embodied in language use. Consider the properties associated centrally with "copper": color, malleability, conductivity of heat and electricity, specific gravity, atomic number. None of these is per se linguistically associated with copper. Individually and collectively they embody knowledge of copper.

Not all nouns are like this. The terms "shoat," "grandfather," and "square knot" have properties linguistically associated with them. The difference between these terms and the others is revealing. Such terms refer to objects or relationships which not only are relatively stable and recurrent in human experience, but upon which the advance of knowledge has little potential effect. Advance in knowledge has great potential, however, for realignment of our conceptions of terms like "blood," "scurvy," and "copper." We need associated properties for these latter terms, but not linguistically associated properties. The business of discovery is not only open-ended but backbiting: our conceptions which serve this process are molded by it.

Achinstein sees that the properties associated with "copper" and company are empirical discoveries, and yet he holds that the association of such a property is defensible on linguistic grounds alone.[12] How could this be? One temporarily withdraws an associated property, and ascertains whether things with the other semantically relevant properties generally have this property.[13] No such "now you see it, now you don't" maneuver is required on our account: for such terms we are never in a position to defend the association on linguistic grounds. If one means by "linguistic association" merely the association of something with a linguistic entity, then properties are linguistically associated with the terms I am discussing. But more is usually meant: that the association is a fact of language, that it is not just an empirical contingency but, given use, an analytical truth that the property is associated with a term.

Hilary Putnam, whose views have much influenced mine, nevertheless maintains the idea of linguistic association:

I said before that different speakers use the word 'electricity' without there being a discernible "intension" they all share. If an "intension" is anything like a necessary and sufficient condition, then I think that this is right. But it does not follow that there are no ideas about electricity which are in some way linguistically associated with the word. Just as the idea that tigers are striped is linguistically associated with the word 'tiger', so it seems that some idea that "electricity" (i.e., electric charge or charges) is capable of flow or motion is linguistically associated with 'electricity'. And perhaps this is all—apart from being a physical magnitude or quantity in the sense described before—that is linguistically associated with the world.[14]

First of all, that electricity is capable of motion need not have been, and probably was not, intimately connected with the introduction of the term, simply because static electricity, not currents of electricity, could have been the introductory phenome-

---

12. *Concepts of Science*, p. 39f.   13. *Ibid.*, pp. 41–42.
14. "Explanation and Reference," p. 204.

non. Nor need electricity have been conceived of as a quantity, so that "more" and "less" could apply to it. One might have come to suspect this with the discovery that electric effects (e.g., attraction of light materials) varied in strength. Putnam rightly emphasizes the importance of introductory events to terms, but the essential function is securing reference. With electricity present, we discover it is capable of flow and is a quantity.

The reason Putnam is inclined to call the association of some properties with a term linguistic is that he believes that the association is important for linguistic competence. Part of what it is for a person to have linguistic competence with a term is to associate the right properties with it.[15] The properties form what Putnam calls a stereotype, and discoveries of similarity with the stereotype enable a person to apply the term in novel situations. The stereotype of "lemon" includes yellow color, tart taste, thick peel. As Putnam shows,[16] it is not analytically true that all, or even most, of the extension has these properties. But likewise, on Putnam's own grounds, given the use of the term, it is not analytically true that "lemon" is associated with these properties. As Putnam notes, the yellow color of lemons may be due to some impurity in the air, or some fungus, so that their natural color is blue.[17] With a change in the world or our knowledge of it, the stereotype would change. Hence, that certain properties are associated with a term has to do with the world and our knowledge of it—the associations, even if they are linguistic, remain empirical.

As argued earlier, there are in-kind differences among terms that have associated properties. It is an analytical (and linguistic) truth that, in the context of their use, the term "vermillion" is associated with a certain red color, that "square" is associated with having sides. The function of such terms is to allow us to ascribe fixed properties. But properties are associated with "hydrogen bond," "buffalo," and "subspecies" in a quite different way, with a very different status. Given their use, it is not an analytical truth that certain properties are associated with them.

15. *Ibid.*, p. 208.
16. In "Explanation and Reference," and "Is Semantics Possible?"
17. "Is Semantics Possible?" p. 106.

A key question is how the fact that a property is linguistically associated with a term is to bear on the defensibility of that association. The implication is usually that the association can be defended at least as a fact of language—that linguistic grounds alone provide some reason for the association. This implication is an explicit commitment in Achinstein, who intends that if property P is a part of the meaning of term T, then the assertion that Ts have P can be defended on linguistic grounds alone, and he is clear that his linguistic grounds are nonempirical.[18] Once we realize that the reason for associating properties with underlying trait terms is their connection to the nature of the extension, then we see that inclusion in the meaning does not augment or change the defensibility in the way that Achinstein thinks it does. With underlying trait terms we are never in a position to defend the association on linguistic grounds, except in the epiphenomenalist sense that the linguistic grounds are nothing but the empirical grounds. Of course, for terms that are not underlying trait terms, the inclusion of properties in the meaning can constitute a linguistic and nonempirical ground for the association. What I am claiming is that the grounds for inclusion of properties in the meaning of underlying trait terms will have to allow that the defensibility of the association remains empirical and is unchanged by inclusion in meaning.

The discovery of underlying traits may make our knowledge of stars and acids more specific, but if we choose to call that specific knowledge our conception of a thing, then the properties are associated with the term in a way that, in our very conception, could be mistaken. Properties are associated with these terms on other than linguistic grounds, and without intrinsically relevant conditions.

The Meaning of Underlying Trait Terms. In this section I wish to question views of Achinstein and (especially) Putnam concerning the meaning of underlying trait terms. My main destructive thesis is that the properties associated with underlying trait terms are almost never a part of their meaning. Constructively, the only general constituents of their meaning are reference, plus the fact that a term is an underlying trait term.

18. *Concepts of Science,* pp. 42–43.

Let us call the plenary theory of meaning the thesis that all of the following are part of the meaning of an underlying trait term: (1) the well-formedness of the term in the context of sentences, (2) the association of the term with some more general terms, (3) the association of properties with the term apart from those in (2), and (4) an extension. Putnam has come to such a view of meaning.[19] He treats (1) in terms of syntactic markers such as "noun" and "mass noun." If this is what explains well-formedness, well and good. He treats (2) in terms of category indicators, such as "animal" for "tiger," "color" for "red," and "period of time" for "hour," and calls these indicators semantic markers (in general these categories seem to approach necessary conditions). In (3) would be things like "sour" for "lemon" and "striped" for "tiger." The extension (4) appears to be a characterization of the underlying trait ("H_2O" for "water").

Putnam's expositions fail to emphasize the crucial factor of the *status* of the properties associated with the term in (2) and (3). To see the importance and distinctiveness of this factor, let us consider a hypothetical subject S and the term "toad." Let us suppose that S has a knowledge of (1), so that he knows how to use "toad" in sentences (e.g., he doesn't say "Toad one the tennis racket"), plus a knowledge of (2), so that knowing the sorts of things toads are, he does not make extremely odd statements (e.g., "This square is a toad"). Moreover, he associates the right specific properties with "toad"—let us say "warty-looking skin, eats insects, lays eggs in water, awkward." S then has an understanding of "toad" that includes general beliefs we have about toads, and these allow him to identify toads, to use the term well in most circumstances, including novel ones, and to treat some assertions as more central than others. What more is there to understanding the meaning of "toad"?

Suppose the following circumstances arise. We discover that the warty-looking skin of toads is caused by a disease which not only debilitates toads but makes them lethargic and awkward. Moreover, we discover that only in the last thousand years have

19. See "The Meaning of 'Meaning'."

toads been struck by this disease. Moreover, for the first time, a gene arises carrying resistance to the disease. These resistant toads not only are sleek in appearance but have an agility and grace approaching that of otters. The question is what S says of these new animals that look and behave differently.

Suppose S responds as follows: For better or worse, it is just a part of the meaning of "toad" that toads are awkward and have warty-looking skin. These new animals do not fit the concept of "toad" as well as previous ones. S may still call these animals toads because he realizes that "warty-looking skin" and "awkward" were never logically necessary, and because the animals still have the other properties associated with "toad." But we could easily augment the story to argue against the other associated properties in (3). S would then eventually have to treat these new animals as non-toads. What I claim is that S's understanding of the meaning of the term is crucially flawed. S has misconstrued the relationship of the term with its associated properties. He treats these properties literally as "linguistically associated," as "intrinsically toad-making properties," as "relevant in and of themselves," as "part of the meaning." To put the problem in a nutshell, S thinks that the properties associated with the term have a nonempirical status.

In the circumstances described, the properties associated with "toad" change. *But why?* Putnam suggests that the properties we associate represent our theory of what a normal toad is like.[20] While I do not agree with this particular answer, nevertheless it is the right sort of answer. The properties we associate do collectively represent a theory, and we discover that our theory is mistaken. This is exactly what our hypothetical person does not understand, and why he cannot make the transition. The animals for him are less toadlike, perhaps even non-toads. He does not understand the status and character of the properties associated with "toad." Although Putnam sees the empirical status of the associated properties, he nevertheless includes associated properties in the meaning of the term.[21] To see how this is wrongheaded, let us again consider S. S would find that

20. "Is Semantics Possible?" pp. 112–113.
21. *Ibid.* See also "The Meaning of 'Meaning'."

others around him use the term "toad" in ways that go counter to what he takes to be its meaning. These uses are to him mystifying. *S* is in the same position as he would be if he were transported back to Shakespeare's time, and "foolish" were used where we would say "fond."

What position is Putnam forced to with respect to the changed use of "toad"? Although he understands the status of the associated properties, this is of no real help in explaining the transition. There are the old properties associated with "toad"—call them *M*. Now "toad" is used with different associated properties *M'*. This change follows on the heels of empirical discoveries. *M'* is preferable to *M* because *M'* includes a better theory of toads than *M*. This explains the replacement of *M* by *M'*. But the replacement is then just that—a replacement, a jump, *not a transition*. *M'* is not an outgrowth of *M*, but an incompatible alternative which supplants it. Now, what happens if *M* and *M'* are treated as part of meaning? That something does not satisfy *M* would have counted against it being a toad. We would have to call these new animals toads *in spite of* some properties. Yet in the case described, that we associate "warty-looking skin" and "awkward" with "toad" argues not at all against calling the new animals toads. The properties associated with "toad" change with the advance in knowledge not in spite of our conception but *because* of it. To shift the usage of "foolish" to "fond" is a shift of meaning. To shift the usage of "tiger" to any ferocious animal would almost always be a change in meaning. To associate "graceful" and "smooth-skinned" with "toad" would be a shift in meaning *only if* we then said that those animals that we used to call toads were now *merely* a lot like toads. Unless our beliefs about tigers or toads are radically wrong, only a change in meaning would allow tigers to be toads. That the properties associated with "toad" change under the impact of the new knowledge is *completely predictable, based on merely a knowledge of current usage*. But this predictability is exactly a criterion of constancy in meaning. To use the same argument Putnam himself once used against Malcolm,[22] speakers of English would apply "toad" to the old and

22. "Dreaming and 'Depth Grammar'," pp. 223–224.

the new animals. Constancy in meaning is what makes the usage in novel circumstances predictable. Again, that the term "toad" would be applied in the modified way is in no way *at odds* with its former meaning, but is *required* by it.

It is constancy of meaning that explains the systematic change in properties associated with underlying trait terms. The kind of revision that is possible, however, extends even to the general properties we associate with these terms. Tigers may not be animals, diamonds may be viruses. Thus we are led to deny not just that (3) is a part of meaning, but (2) also. Underlying trait terms thus combine constancy in meaning with radical revisability in associated properties. Putnam and Achinstein both include some associated properties in meaning. This is often enough true, but not for underlying trait terms. Central to the meaning of underlying trait terms is that they are underlying trait terms. In virtue of this they are permeable to the advance of knowledge, and the properties associated with them have an empirical status. I suggest that underying trait terms form a distinctive semantic kind—a kind that does not seem to be a syntactic marker or a general property, and that therefore does not fit into either (1) or (2) in the plenary theory of meaning. To expropriate for our purposes a term Putnam, in "The Meaning of 'Meaning'," expropriated from Katz, we might call "underlying trait term" a semantic marker, indicating that a distinct kind of semantic analysis is appropriate.

What then differentiates the underlying trait terms? The answer is simple: the underlying trait terms themselves! In order to associate properties with the terms, we need some way of securing reference. The way of determining reference is not then part of the meaning, but rather the underlying trait we happen to latch onto. That the term is an underlying trait term is what makes the underlying trait part of what we mean by the term. To employ a fictional example, we may call the product of a certain plant "sandalwood oil", which, it turns out, is the same as "oil of vitriol" produced by a laboratory reaction from inert chemicals. On my view, the terms mean the same. The reason that people think they mean something different is that they incorrectly believe these terms not to be underlying trait terms. They think that "being sandalwood oil" means "produced from the plant." The term would then be a property term, not an underlying trait term. "Sandalwood oil," however, refers to the product, not the process of production. As I understood him in "The Meaning of 'Meaning'," this point constitutes condition (4) in Putnam's theory of meaning, and I strongly concur (for underlying trait terms—but as a general theory of meaning, it seems to me to be quite mistaken).

Notice that if I am right about the meaning of underlying trait terms, it follows that a knowledge of the meaning of such terms provides very little linguistic competence. A mere knowledge of meaning provides little basis for using the term in context, nor much knowledge at all about the sort of thing a term refers to. What a knowledge of meaning does provide is part of a basis for building up such knowledge. Putnam in "The Meaning of 'Meaning' " explicitly includes what one needs to know in order to have linguistic competence as a part of meaning. In the case of many terms, such as "square," "promise," and "shoat," I concur. But underlying trait terms represent an extreme case where linguistic competence requires much more than knowledge of meaning.[23]

What is the Relation Between a Term and its Associated Properties? Let us try to answer Achinstein's question about the nature of the association between a team and its properties, in view of our analysis. First of all, there is no single answer. For what I call property terms, the association of some properties largely constitutes the meaning. For what I call underlying trait terms, it is important to understand that subsets of associated properties are not part of meaning, contrary to Achinstein and Putnam. Instead the associations constitute empirical knowledge.

23. If one insists, as a condition of adequacy for any theory of meaning, that knowledge of meaning explain individual competency, then with qualifications Putnam is right to include properties in the meaning of underlying trait terms. Then my point is as follows. One part of the meaning (properties) must be subjugant to another part (underlying trait account). While speakers may be linguistically obligated to associate properties in order to be competent, this obligation is conditional on the state of knowledge. For underlying trait terms, it is a part of their meaning that the properties associated with them alter with the advance of knowledge—even for properties in the meaning. Properties can be included in the meaning of underlying trait terms only if the concept of meaning is loosened up to allow parts of meaning to remain empirical.

However, there are interesting subsets of associated properties for underlying trait terms. Foremost of all, there are those properties that are more fundamental. I do not say "fundamental" because that suggests finality. Without pursuing the details, what makes a property here more fundamental is that it causally determines others. Such properties constitute our best answer to the question "What is X?" and I suggest we call them the basis of our *characterizing theory* (of X). Equally significant are those properties which we believe to be the "surface" of underlying traits. They are those properties which underlying traits underlie—properties which, if we could just explain, we would get at underlying traits. These properties are particularly important in that they guide the formation of theories of underlying traits, and when theories fail, they give us a basic knowledge to fall back upon. These properties evolve with both change in theories and the advance of empirical knowledge. I suggest we call them the basis of our *phenomenal conception* (of X). Here "phenomenal" has nothing per se to do with "observational." Other significant subsets are the observational properties, and properties useful for identification. These properties are important because they aid us in connecting terms to reference. Like the previously mentioned properties, they give us a nexus of connections which can guide investigation.

Finally, there are those properties which—while they do reflect knowledge of the world—are largely based on associations of language users on a group or societal level. Characteristically, there is a small group of properties which "come to mind" as distinguishing properties. Mules are stubborn, tigers are striped, acids are sour, aluminum is lightweight. These associations tend to be standardized images or ideas, and following Putnam, I suggest we call them *stereotypes*. Stereotypes embody a kind of information (which can be inaccurate), which is often recounted when a person with no knowledge of a term asks about it. Tigers, one might say, are catlike, have a certain fairly large size, are yellow with black stripes, and are meat-eating hunters. The stereotype forms a basic knowledge expected of language users. Sometimes very little is expected—for molybdenum, perhaps only that it is a metal; for spruces, perhaps only that they are evergreen trees. Markings may be important for tigers and zebras, unimportant for pronghorn antelope and cheetahs. Taste may be crucial for lemons and mints, negligible for rose hips and honeysuckle.

Of these subsets of associated properties, the stereotype seems to be the least important. Putnam, however, hangs considerable weight upon the notion. He claims at least four things of the stereotype: it is a simplification of our knowledge, it is basically a theory of what a normal member is like,[24] the stereotypic properties are likely to be explicable by a theory about the essential nature of the thing,[25] and the stereotype forms a general feature of meaning.[26] I concur only with the first claim.

Let us begin with the third. There is little reason to expect that what I call a characterizing theory will explain the stereotype. The reason is simple. The properties in the stereotype are not selected for their causal importance or importance in nature. Stripes may be important for the life and adaptability of tigers, but then they may not be. The sour taste of lemons probably is unimportant. Accidental and less important properties will not connect to essential ones.

More important, is the stereotype a theory about a normal member of the kind? Many properties of normal members are not included in the stereotype. Why not? The only answer Putnam can give is that certain things are just singled out in a culture and society. This lack of explanatory power is indicative of a failure to capture the true rationale behind the stereotype. Our stereotype, as a species of "ordinary conception," is indeed highly socially conditioned. But the properties in the stereotype generally reflect the thing *in relationship to man.* One very important factor is usefulness. Were lemons not used for culinary purposes, taste would be unimportant. If man did not need long-lasting metals, the rust resistance of aluminum and chromium would not be noteworthy. The reason that properties which distinguish among evergreens do not figure in the common conception is that we have so little need to distinguish evergreens. The nature of our experiential encounter with ob-

24. "Is Semantics Possible?" pp. 112–113. 25. *Ibid.*, p. 104.
26. "The Meaning of 'Meaning'." Also "Is Semantics Possible?" p. 113.

jects often determines the associated properties—hence a rat-
tlesnake is just a poisonous snake with a rattle on its tail, and
the stereotype of a tiger includes nothing about mating habits,
diseases, and anatomy. Sometimes traits are included because
they are striking or unusual—hence a giraffe has a long neck
and stiltlike legs, and a zebra is striped. The sensory and aes-
thetic experience of man distinguishes grapes (as plants) for
the taste of their fruit, and flowers for their fragrance and the
color of their bloom (not for root structure or reproductive
mechanisms or evolutionary potential). Some associations, such
as the manes of lions, even have symbolic significance in the
lore of men.

What is the cash value of knowledge of stereotypes? A knowledge of a background of common associations aids one in getting around linguistically in man's world. When a term is ordinarily used, it carries its sterotypic associations with it. But it
does not follow that these are part of what the term means. For
the speakers themselves, these associations are open to modification by the advance of knowledge. Even if an association is
linguistic in the sense of being required for a person to have
acquired the word, the association derives from the needs of
communication and does not become more than empirical.

For underlying trait terms, then, the associated properties
serve a variety of functions, but none are included in meaning,
and none are relevant in and of themselves. Underlying trait
terms are coordinated by a core conception—reference plus the
fact that the term is an underlying trait term—so that our conception lies in knowledge of the world, not language. For such
terms, conceptual change is not a change of meaning—the
meaning, rather, explains the change (of course, these terms
could change in meaning).

Philosophers have long viewed what is called "conceptual
analysis" as central to their enterprise. Conventions have fig-
ured large in conceptual analysis in two ways. First, there are
rules of use in language, and secondly, for speech acts (such as
affirming, promising) it is only in virtue of certain conventions
that certain events count as the acts they are. For a large
number of terms, the association of properties with them is a

significant additional feature of understanding them. Here the assumption is widespread that these associations must have a core of conventionality—that, in explaining why properties are associated with a term, we must eventually end with "Well, those properties are just what we mean by the term." For underlying trait terms, which are a part of ordinary language but which are especially prominent in science, it is exactly this additional element of conventionality that is missing, and because of this the analysis of underlying trait terms is different. How these terms can develop, function, and have meaning without having linguistically associated properties is, indeed, the central point of this paper.

6 Natural Kinds

W . V . Q U I N E

Harvard University

What tends to confirm an induction? This question has been aggravated on the one hand by Hempel's puzzle of the non-black non-ravens,[1] and exacerbated on the other by Goodman's puzzle of the grue emeralds.[2] I shall begin my remarks by relating the one puzzle to the other, and the other to an innate flair that we have for natural kinds. Then I shall devote the rest of the paper to reflections on the nature of this notion of natural kinds and its relation to science.

Hempel's puzzle is that just as each black raven tends to confirm the law that all ravens are black, so each green leaf, being a non-black non-raven, should tend to confirm the law that all non-black things are non-ravens, that is, again, that all ravens are black. What is paradoxical is that a green leaf should count toward the law that all ravens are black.

Goodman propounds his puzzle by requiring us to imagine that emeralds, having been identified by some criterion other than color, are now being examined one after another and all up to now are found to be green. Then he proposes to call anything *grue* that is examined today or earlier and found to be green or is not examined before tomorrow and is blue. Should

Reprinted from *Essays in Honor of Carl G. Hempel,* edited by Nicholas Rescher et al., pp. 5–23, by permission of D. Reidel Publishing Co.

1. C. G. Hempel, *Aspects of Scientific Explanation and Other Essays* (New York: Free Press, 1965), p. 15.

2. Nelson Goodman, *Fact, Fiction, and Forecast* (Cambridge, Mass.: Harvard University Press, 1955, or New York: Bobbs-Merrill, 1965), p. 74. I am indebted to Goodman and to Burton Dreben for helpful criticisms of earlier drafts of the present paper.

we expect the first one examined tomorrow to be green, because all examined up to now were green? But all examined up to now were also grue; so why not expect the first one tomorrow to be grue, and therefore blue?

The predicate "green," Goodman says,[3] is *projectible;* "grue" is not. He says this by way of putting a name to the problem. His step toward solution is his doctrine of what he calls entrenchment,[4] which I shall touch on later. Meanwhile the terminological point is simply that projectible predicates are predicates ζ and η whose shared instances all do count, for whatever reason, toward confirmation of ⌜All ζ are η⌝.

Now I propose assimilating Hempel's puzzle to Goodman's by inferring from Hempel's that the complement of a projectible predicate need not be projectible. "Raven" and "black" are projectible; a black raven does count toward "All ravens are black." Hence a black raven counts also, indirectly, toward "No non-black things are non-ravens," since this says the same thing. But a green leaf does not count toward "All non-black things are non-ravens," nor, therefore, toward "All ravens are black"; "non-black" and "non-raven" are not projectible. "Green" and "leaf" are projectible, and the green leaf counts toward "All leaves are green" and "All green things are leaves"; but only a black raven can confirm "All ravens are black," the complements not being projectible.

If we see the matter in this way, we must guard against saying that a statement ⌜All ζ are η⌝ is lawlike only if ζ and η are projectible. "All non-black things are non-ravens" is a law despite its non-projectible terms, since it is equivalent to "All ravens are black." Any statement is lawlike that is logically *equivalent* to ⌜All ζ and η⌝ for some projectible ζ and η.[5]

Having concluded that the complement of a projectible predicate need not be projectible, we may ask further whether there is *any* projectible predicate whose complement is projectible. I can conceive that there is not, when complements are taken strictly. We must not be misled by limited or relative comple-

3. Goodman, *Fact,* pp. 82f.   4. *Ibid.,* pp. 95ff.
5. I mean this only as a sufficient condition of lawlikeness. See Donald Davidson, "Emeroses by other names," *Journal of Philosophy,* 63 (1966), 778–780.

mentation; "male human" and "non-male human" are indeed both projectible.

To get back now to the emeralds, why do we expect the next one to be green rather than grue? The intuitive answer lies in similarity, however subjective. Two green emeralds are more similar than two grue ones would be if only one of the grue ones were green. Green things, or at least green emeralds, are a kind.[6] A projectible predicate is one that is true of all and only the things of a kind. What makes Goodman's example a puzzle, however, is the dubious scientific standing of a general notion of similarity, or of kind.

The dubiousness of this notion is itself a remarkable fact. For surely there is nothing more basic to thought and language than our sense of similarity; our sorting of things into kinds The usual general term, whether a common noun or a verb or an adjective, owes its generality to some resemblance among the things referred to. Indeed, learning to use a word depends on a double resemblance: first, a resemblance between the present circumstances and past circumstances in which the word was used, and second, a phonetic resemblance between the present utterance of the word and past utterances of it. And every reasonable expectation depends on resemblance of circumstances, together with our tendency to expect similar causes to have similar effects.

The notion of a kind and the notion of similarity or resemblance seem to be variants or adaptations of a single notion. Similarity is immediately definable in terms of kind; for, things are similar when they are two of a kind. The very words for "kind" and "similar" tend to run in etymologically cognate pairs. Cognate with "kind" we have "akin" and "kindred." Cognate with "like" we have "ilk." Cognate with "similar" and "same" and "resemble" there are "*sammeln*" and "assemble," suggesting a gathering into kinds.

We cannot easily imagine a more familiar or fundamental notion than this, or a notion more ubiquitous in its applications. On this score it is like the notions of logic: like identity,

6. This relevance of kind is noted by Goodman, *Fact*, first edition, pp. 119f; second edition, pp. 121f.

negation, alternation, and the rest. And yet, strangely, there is
something logically repugnant about it. For we are baffled
when we try to relate the general notion of similarity significantly to logical terms. One's first hasty suggestion might be to
say that things are similar when they have all or most or many
properties in common. Or, trying to be less vague, one might
try defining comparative similarity—"*a* is more similar to *b*
than to *c*"—as meaning that *a* shares more properties with *b*
than with *c*. But any such course only reduces our problem to
the unpromising task of settling what to count as a property.

The nature of the problem of what to count as a property
can be seen by turning for a moment to set theory. Things are
viewed as going together into sets in any and every combination, describable and indescribable. Any two things are joint
members of any number of sets. Certainly then we cannot define "*a* is more similar to *b* than to *c*" to mean that *a* and *b*
belong jointly to more sets than *a* and *c* do. If properties are to
support this line of definition where sets do not, it must be
because properties do not, like sets, take things in every random combination. It must be that properties are shared only by
things that are significantly similar. But properties in such a
sense are no clearer than kinds. To start with such a notion of
property, and define similarity on that basis, is no better than
accepting similarity as undefined.

The contrast between properties and sets which I suggested
just now must not be confused with the more basic and familiar
contrast between properties, as intensional, and sets as exten-
sional. Properties are intensional in that they may be counted
as distinct properties even though wholly coinciding in respect
of the things that have them. There is no call to reckon kinds as
intensional. Kinds can be seen as sets, determined by their
members. It is just that not all sets are kinds.

If similarity is taken simple-mindedly as a yes-or-no affair,
with no degrees, then there is no containing of kinds within
broader kinds. For, as remarked, similarity now simply means
belonging to some one same kind. If all colored things comprise a kind, then all colored things count as similar, and the
set of all red things is too narrow to count as a kind. If on the

other hand the set of all red things counts as a kind, then colored things do not all count as similar, and the set of all colored things is too broad to count as a kind. We cannot have it both ways. Kinds can, however, overlap; the red things can comprise one kind, the round another.

When we move up from the simple dyadic relation of similarity to the more serious and useful triadic relation of comparative similarity, a correlative change takes place in the notion of kind. Kinds come to admit now not only of overlapping but also of containment one in another. The set of all red things and the set of all colored things can now both count as kinds; for all colored things can now be counted as resembling one another more than some things do, even though less, on the whole, than red ones do.

At this point, of course, our trivial definition of similarity as sameness of kind breaks down; for almost any two things could count now as common members of some broad kind or other, and anyway we now want to define comparative or triadic similarity. A definition that suggests itself is this: *a* is more similar to *b* than to *c* when *a* and *b* belong jointly to more kinds than *a* and *c* do. But even this works only for finite systems of kinds.

The notion of kind and the notion of similarity seemed to be substantially one notion. We observed further that they resist reduction to less dubious notions, as of logic or set theory. That they at any rate be definable each in terms of the other seems little enough to ask. We just saw a somewhat limping definition of comparative similarity in terms of kinds. What now of the converse project, definition of kind in terms of similarity?

One may be tempted to picture a kind, suitable to a comparative similarity relation, as any set which is "qualitatively spherical" in this sense: it takes in exactly the things that differ less than so-and-so much from some central norm. If without serious loss of accuracy we can assume that there are one or more actual things (*paradigm cases*) that nicely exemplify the desired norm, and one or more actual things (*foils*) that deviate just barely too much to be counted into the desired kind at all, then our definition is easy: *the kind with paradigm a and foil b* is the set of all the things to which *a* is more similar than *a* is to *b*.

More generally, then, a set may be said to be a *kind* if and only if there are *a* and *b*, known or unknown, such that the set is the kind with paradigm *a* and foil *b*.

If we consider examples, however, we see that this definition does not give us what we want as kinds. Thus take red. Let us grant that a central shade of red can be picked as norm. The trouble is that the paradigm cases, objects in just that shade of red, can come in all sorts of shapes, weights, sizes, and smells. Mere degree of overall similarity to any one such paradigm case will afford little evidence of degree of redness, since it will depend also on shape, weight, and the rest. If our assumed relation of comparative similarity were just comparative chromatic similarity, then our paradigm-and-foil definition of kind would indeed accommodate redkind. What the definition will not do is distill purely chromatic kinds from mixed similarity.

A different attempt, adapted from Carnap, is this: a set is a kind if all its members are more similar to one another than they all are to any one thing outside the set. In other words, each non-member differs more from some member than that member differs from any member. However, as Goodman showed in a criticism of Carnap,[7] this construction succumbs to what Goodman calls the difficulty of imperfect community. Thus consider the set of all red round things, red wooden things, and round wooden things. Each member of this set resembles each other member somehow: at least in being red, or in being round, or in being wooden, and perhaps in two or all three of these respects or others. Conceivably, moreover, there is no one thing outside the set that resembles every member of the set to even the least of these degrees. The set then meets the proposed definition of kind. Yet surely it is not what anyone means by a kind. It admits yellow croquet balls and red rubber balls while excluding yellow rubber balls.

The relation between similarity and kind, then, is less clear and neat than could be wished. Definition of similarity in terms of kind is halting, and definition of kind in terms of similarity is unknown. Still the two notions are in an important sense cor-

---

7. Nelson Goodman, *The Structure of Appearance*, 2d ed. (New York: Bobbs-Merrill, 1966), pp. 163f.

relative. They vary together. If we reassess something *a* as less similar to *b* than to *c*, where it had counted as more similar to *b* than to *c*, surely we will correspondingly permute *a*, *b*, and *c* in respect of their assignment to kinds; and conversely.

I have stressed how fundamental the notion of similarity or of kind is to our thinking, and how alien to logic and set theory. I want to go on now to say more about how fundamental these notions are to our thinking, and something also about their non-logical roots. Afterward I want to bring out how the notion of similarity or of kind changes as science progresses. I shall suggest that it is a mark of maturity of a branch of science that the notion of similarity or kind finally dissolves, so far as it is relevant to that branch of science. That is, it ultimately submits to analysis in the special terms of that branch of science and logic.

For deeper appreciation of how fundamental similarity is, let us observe more closely how it figures in the learning of language. One learns by *ostension* what presentations to call yellow; that is, one learns by hearing the word applied to samples. All he has to go on, of course, is the similarity of further cases to the samples. Similarity being a matter of degree, one has to learn by trial and error how reddish or brownish or greenish a thing can be and still be counted yellow. When he finds he has applied the word too far out, he can use the false cases as samples to the contrary; and then he can proceed to guess whether further cases are yellow or not by considering whether they are more similar to the in-group or the out-group. What one thus uses, even at this primitive stage of learning, is a fully functioning sense of similarity, and relative similarity at that: *a* is more similar to *b* than to *c*.

All these delicate comparisons and shrewd inferences about what to call yellow are, in Sherlock Holmes's terminology, elementary. Mostly the process is unconscious. It is the same process by which an animal learns to respond in distincitve ways to his master's commands or other discriminated stimulations.

The primitive sense of similarity that underlies such learning has, we saw, a certain complexity of structure: *a* is more similar to *b* than to *c*. Some people have thought that it has to be much more complex still: that it depends irreducibly on *respects,* thus similarity in color, similarity in shape, and so on. According to this view, our learning of yellow by ostension would have depended on our first having been told or somehow apprised that it was going to be a question of color. Now hints of this kind are a great help, and in our learning we often do depend on them. Still one would like to be able to show that a single general standard of similarity, but of course comparative similarity, is all we need, and that respects can be abstracted afterward. For instance, suppose the child has learned of a yellow ball and block that they count as yellow, and of a red ball and block that they do not, and now he has to decide about a yellow cloth. Presumably he will find the cloth more similar to the yellow ball and to the yellow block then to the red ball or red block; and he will not have needed any prior schooling in colors and respects. Carnap undertook to show long ago how some respects, such as color, could by an ingenious construction be derived from a general similarity notion; [8] however, this development is challenged, again, by Goodman's difficulty of imperfect community.

A standard of similarity is in some sense innate. This point is not against empiricism; it is a commonplace of behavioral psychology. A response to a red circle, if it is rewarded, will be elicited again by a pink ellipse more readily than by a blue triangle; the red circle resembles the pink ellipse more than the blue triangle. Without some such prior spacing of qualities, we could never acquire a habit; all stimuli would be equally alike and equally different. These spacings of qualities, on the part of men and other animals, can be explored and mapped in the laboratory by experiments in conditioning and extinction.[9] Needed as they are for all learning, these distinctive spacings cannot themselves all be learned; some must be innate.

If then I say that there is an innate standard of similarity, I am making a condensed statement that can be interpreted, and

8. Rudolf Carnap, *The Logical Structure of the World* (Berkeley: University of California Press, 1967), pp. 141–147 (German edition, 1928).

9. See my *Word and Object* (Boston: MIT Press, 1960), pp. 83f, for further discussion and references.

truly interpreted, in behavioral terms. Moreover, in this behavioral sense it can be said equally of other animals that they have an innate standard of similarity too. It is part of our animal birthright. And, interestingly enough, it is characteristically animal in its lack of intellectual status. At any rate we noticed earlier how alien the notion is to mathematics and logic.

This innate qualitative spacing of stimulations was seen to have one of its human uses in the ostensive learning of words like "yellow." I should add as a cautionary remark that this is not the only way of learning words, nor the commonest; it is merely the most rudimentary way. It works when the question of the reference of a word is a simple question of spread: how much of our surroundings counts as yellow, how much counts as water, and so on. Learning a word like "apple" or "square" is more complicated, because here we have to learn also where to say that one apple or square leaves off and another begins. The complication is that apples do not add up to an apple, nor squares, generally, to a square. "Yellow" and "water" are mass terms, concerned only with spread; "apple" and "square" are terms of divided reference, concerned with both spread and individuation. Ostension figures in the learning of terms of this latter kind too, but the process is more complex.[10] And then there are all the other sorts of words, all those abstract and neutral connectives and adverbs and all the recondite terms of scientific theory; and there are also the grammatical constructions themselves to be mastered. The learning of these things is less direct and more complex still. There are deep problems in this domain, but they lie aside from the present topic.

Our way of learning "yellow," then, gives less than a full picture of how we learn language. Yet more emphatically, it gives less than a full picture of the human use of an innate standard of similarity, or innate spacing of qualities. For, as remarked, every reasonable expectation depends on similarity. Again on this score, other animals are like man. Their expectations, if we choose so to conceptualize their avoidance movements and salivation and pressing of levers and the like, are clearly depen-

---

10. See *Word and Object*, pp. 90–95.

dent on their appreciation of similarity. Or, to put matters in their methodological order, these avoidance movements and salivation and pressing of levers and the like are typical of what we have to go on in mapping the animals' appreciation of similarity, their spacing of qualities.

Induction itself is essentially only more of the same: animal expectation or habit formation. And the ostensive learning of words is an implicit case of induction. Implicitly the learner of "yellow" is working inductively toward a general law of English verbal behavior, though a law that he will never try to state; he is working up to where he can in general judge when an English speaker would assent to "yellow" and when not.

Not only is ostensive learning a case of induction; it is a curiously comfortable case of induction, a game of chance with loaded dice. At any rate this is so if, as seems plausible, each man's spacing of qualities is enough like his neighbor's. For the learner is generalizing on his yellow samples by similarity considerations, and his neighbors have themselves acquired the use of the word "yellow," in their day, by the same similarity considerations. The learner of "yellow" is thus making his induction in a friendly world. Always, induction expresses our hope that similar causes will have similar effects; but when the induction is the ostensive learning of a word, that pious hope blossoms into a foregone conclusion. The uniformity of people's quality spaces virtually assures that similar presentations will elicit similar verdicts.

It makes one wonder the more about other inductions, where what is sought is a generalization not about our neighbor's verbal behavior but about the harsh impersonal world. It is reasonable that our quality space should match our neighbor's, we being birds of a feather; and so the general trustworthiness of induction in the ostensive learning of words was a put-up job. To trust induction as a way of access to the truths of nature, on the other hand, is to suppose, more nearly, that our quality space matches that of the cosmos. The brute irrationality of our sense of similarity, its irrelevance to anything in logic and mathematics, offers little reason to expect that this sense is somehow in tune with the world—a world which, unlike language, we never made. Why induction should be trusted, apart from special cases such as the ostensive learning of words, is the perennial philosophical problem of induction.

One part of the problem of induction, the part that asks why there should be regularities in nature at all, can, I think, be dismissed. *That* there are or have been regularities, for whatever reason, is an established fact of science; and we cannot ask better than that. *Why* there have been regularities is an obscure question, for it is hard to see what would count as an answer. What does make clear sense is this other part of the problem of induction: why does our innate subjective spacing of qualities accord so well with the functionally relevant groupings in nature as to make our inductions tend to come out right? Why should our subjective spacing of qualities have a special purchase on nature and a lien on the future?

There is some encouragement in Darwin. If people's innate spacing of qualities is a gene-linked trait, then the spacing that has made for the most successful inductions will have tended to predominate through natural selection.[11] Creatures inveterately wrong in their inductions have a pathetic but praiseworthy tendency to die before reproducing their kind.

At this point let me say that I shall not be impressed by protests that I am using inductive generalizations, Darwin's and others, to justify induction, and thus reasoning in a circle. The reason I shall not be impressed by this is that my position is a naturalistic one; I see philosophy not as an a priori propaedeutic or groundwork for science, but as continuous with science. I see philosophy and science as in the same boat—a boat which, to revert to Neurath's figure as I so often do, we can rebuild only at sea while staying afloat in it. There is no external vantage point, no first philosophy. All scientific findings, all scientific conjectures that are at present plausible, are therefore in my view as welcome for use in philosophy as elsewhere. For me then the problem of induction is a problem about the world: a problem of how we, as we now are (by our present scientific

11. This was noted by S. Watanabe on the second page of his paper "Une explication mathematique du classement d'objets," in *Information and Prediction in Science,* ed. by S. Dockx and P. Bernays (New York: Academic Press, 1965).

lights), in a world we never made, should stand better than random or coin-tossing chances of coming out right when we predict by inductions which are based on our innate, scientifically unjustified similarity standard. Darwin's natural selection is a plausible partial explanation.

It may, in view of a consideration to which I next turn, be almost explanation enough. This consideration is that induction, after all, has its conspicuous failures. Thus take color. Nothing in experience, surely, is more vivid and conspicuous than color and its contrasts. And the remarkable fact, which has impressed scientists and philosophers as far back at least as Galileo and Descartes, is that the distinctions that matter for basic physical theory are mostly independent of color contrasts. Color impresses man; raven black impresses Hempel; emerald green impresses Goodman. But color is cosmically secondary. Even slight differences in sensory mechanisms from species to species, Smart remarks,[12] can make overwhelming differences in the grouping of things by color. Color is king in our innate quality space, but undistinguished in cosmic circles. Cosmically, colors would not qualify as kinds.

Color is helpful at the food-gathering level. Here it behaves well under induction, and here, no doubt, has been the survival value of our color-slanted quality space. It is just that contrasts that are crucial for such activities can be insignificant for broader and more theoretical science. If man were to live by basic science alone, natural selection would shift its support to the color-blind mutation.

Living as he does by bread and basic science both, man is torn. Things about his innate similarity sense that are helpful in the one sphere can be a hindrance in the other. Credit is due man's inveterate ingenuity, or human sapience, for having worked around the blinding dazzle of color vision and found the more significant regularities elsewhere. Evidently natural selection has dealt with the conflict by endowing man doubly: with both a color-slanted quality space and the ingenuity to rise above it.

12. J. J. C. Smart, *Philosophy and Scientific Realism* (New York: Humanities, 1963), pp. 68–72.

He has risen above it by developing modified systems of kinds, hence modified similarity standards for scientific purposes. By the trial-and-error process of theorizing he has regrouped things into new kinds which prove to lend themselves to many inductions better than the old.

A crude example is the modification of the notion of fish by excluding whales and porpoises. Another taxonomic example is the grouping of kangaroos, opossums, and marsupial mice in a single kind, marsupials, while excluding ordinary mice. By primitive standards the marsupial mouse is more similar to the ordinary mouse than to the kangaroo; by theoretical standards the reverse is true.

A theoretical kind need not be a modification of an intuitive one. It may issue from theory full-blown, without antecedents; for instance the kind which comprises positively charged particles.

We revise our standards of similarity or of natural kinds on the strength, as Goodman remarks,[13] of second-order inductions. New groupings, hypothetically adopted at the suggestion of a growing theory, prove favorable to inductions and so become "entrenched." We newly establish the projectibility of some predicate, to our satisfaction, by successfully trying to project it. In induction nothing succeeds like success.

Between an innate similarity notion or spacing of qualities and a scientifically sophisticated one, there are all gradations. Science, after all, differs from common sense only in degree of methodological sophistication. Our experiences from earliest infancy are bound to have overlaid our innate spacing of qualities by modifying and supplementing our grouping habits little by little, inclining us more and more to an appreciation of theoretical kinds and similarities, long before we reach the point of studying science systematically as such. Moreover, the later phases do not wholly supersede the earlier; we retain different similarity standards, different systems of kinds, for use in different contexts. We all still say that a marsupial mouse is more like an ordinary mouse than a kangaroo, except when we are concerned with genetic matters. Something like our innate

13. Goodman, *Fact,* pp. 95ff.

quality space continued to function alongside the more sophisticated regroupings that have been found by scientific experience to facilitate induction.

We have seen that a sense of similarity or of kinds is fundamental to learning in the widest sense—to language learning, to induction, to expectation. Toward a further appreciation of how utterly this notion permeates our thought, I want now to point out a number of other very familiar and central notions which seem to depend squarely on this one. They are notions that are definable in terms of similarity, or kinds, and further irreducible.

A notable domain of examples is the domain of dispositions, such as Carnap's example of solubility in water. To say of some individual object that it is soluble in water is not to say merely that it always dissolves when in water, because this would be true by default of any object, however insoluble, if it merely happened to be destined never to get into water. It is to say rather that it *would* dissolve if it were in water; but this account brings small comfort, since the device of a subjunctive conditional involves all the perplexities of disposition terms and more. Thus far I simply repeat Carnap.[14] But now I want to point out what could be done in this connection with the notion of kind. Intuitively, what qualifies a thing as soluble though it never gets into water is that it is of the same kind as the things that actually did or will dissolve; it is similar to them. Strictly we can't simply say "*the* same kind," nor simply "similar," when we have wider and narrower kinds, less and more similarity. Let us then mend our definition by saying that the soluble things are the common members of *all* such kinds. A thing is soluble if *each* kind that is broad enough to embrace all actual victims of solution embraces it too.

Graphically the idea is this: we make a set of all the sometime victims, all the things that actually did or will dissolve in water, and then we add just enough other things to round the set out into a kind. This is the water-soluble kind.

If this definition covers just the desired things, the things

14. Carnap, "Testability and Meaning," *Philosophy of Science*, 3 (1936), 419–471; 4 (1937), 1–40.

that are really soluble in water, it owes its success to a circumstance that could be otherwise. The needed circumstance is that a sufficient variety of things actually get dissolved in water to assure their not all falling under any one kind narrower than the desired water-soluble kind itself. But it is a plausible circumstance, and I am not sure that its accidental character is a drawback. If the trend of events had been otherwise, perhaps the solubility concept would not have been wanted.

However, if I seem to be defending this definition, I must now hasten to add that of course it has much the same fault as the definition which used the subjunctive conditional. This definition uses the unreduced notion of kind, which is certainly not a notion we want to rest with either; neither theoretical kind nor intuitive kind. My purpose in giving the definition is only to show the link between the problem of dispositions and the problem of kinds.

As between theoretical and intuitive kinds, certainly the theoretical ones are the ones wanted for purposes of defining solubility and other dispositions of scientific concern. Perhaps "amiable" and "reprehensible" are disposition terms whose definitions should draw rather on intuitive kinds.

Another dim notion, which has intimate connections with dispositions and subjunctive conditionals, is the notion of cause; and we shall see that it too turns on the notion of kinds. Hume explained cause as invariable succession, and this makes sense as long as the cause and effect are referred to by general terms. We can say that fire causes heat, and we can mean thereby, as Hume would have it, that each event classifiable under the head of fire is followed by an event classifiable under the head of heat, or heating up. But this account, whatever its virtues for these general causal statements, leaves singular causal statements unexplained.

What does it mean to say that the kicking over of a lamp in Mrs. O'Leary's barn caused the Chicago fire? It cannot mean merely that the event at Mrs. O'Leary's belongs to a set, and the Chicago fire belongs to a set, such that there is invariable succession between the two sets: every member of the one set is followed by a member of the other. This paraphrase is trivially true and too weak. Always, if one event happens to be followed by another, the two belong to *certain* sets between which there is invariable succession. We can rig the sets arbitrarily. Just put any arbitrary events in the first set, including the first of the two events we are interested in; and then in the other set put the second of those two events, together with other events that happen to have occurred just after the other members of the first set.

Because of this way of trivialization, a singular causal statement says no more than that the one event was followed by the other. That is, it says no more if we use the definition just now contemplated; which, therefore, we must not. The trouble with that definition is clear enough: it is the familiar old trouble of the promiscuity of sets. Here, as usual, kinds, being more discriminate, enable us to draw distinctions where sets do not. To say that one event caused another is to say that the two events are of *kinds* between which there is invariable succession. If this correction does not yet take care of Mrs. O'Leary's cow, the fault is only with invariable succession itself, as affording too simple a definition of general causal statements; we need to hedge it around with provisions for partial or contributing causes and a good deal else. That aspect of the causality problem is not my concern. What I wanted to bring out is just the relevance of the notion of kinds, as the needed link between singular and general causal statements.

We have noticed that the notion of kind, or similarity, is crucially relevant to the notion of disposition, to the subjunctive conditional, and to singular causal statements. From a scientific point of view these are a pretty disreputable lot. The notion of kind, or similarity, is equally disreputable. Yet some such notion, some similarity sense, was seen to be crucial to all learning, and central in particular to the processes of inductive generalization and prediction which are the very life of science. It appears that science is rotten to the core.

Yet there may be claimed for this rot a certain undeniable fecundity. Science reveals hidden mysteries, predicts successfully, and works technological wonders. If this is the way of rot, then rot is rather to be prized and praised than patronized.

Rot, actually, is not the best model here. A better model is human progress. A sense of comparative similarity, I remarked earlier, is one of man's animal endowments. Insofar as it fits in with regularities of nature, so as to afford us reasonable success in our primitive inductions and expectations, it is presumably an evolutionary product of natural selection. Secondly, as remarked, one's sense of similarity or one's system of kinds develops and changes and even turns multiple as one matures, making perhaps for increasingly dependable prediction. And at length standards of similarity set in which are geared to theoretical science. This development is a development away from the immediate, subjective, animal sense of similarity to the remoter objectivity of a similarity determined by scientific hypotheses and posits and constructs. Things are similar in the later or theoretical sense to the degree that they are interchangeable parts of the cosmic machine revealed by science.

This progress of similarity standards, in the course of each individual's maturing years, is a sort of recapitulation in the individual of the race's progress from muddy savagery. But the similarity notion even in its theoretical phase is itself a muddy notion still. We have offered no definition of it in satisfactory scientific terms. We of course have a behavioral definition of what counts, for a given individual, as similar to what, or as more similar to what than to what; we have this for similarity old and new, human and animal. But it is no definition of what it means really for *a* to be more similar to *b* than to *c;* really, and quite apart from this or that psychological subject.

Did I already suggest a definition to this purpose, metaphorically, when I said that things are similar to the extent that they are interchangeable parts of the cosmic machine? More literally, could things be said to be similar in proportion to how much of scientific theory would remain true on interchanging those things as objects of reference in the theory? This only hints a direction; consider for instance the dimness of "how much theory." Anyway the direction itself is not a good one; for it would make similarity depend in the wrong way on theory. A man's judgments of similarity do and should depend on his theory, on his beliefs; but similarity itself, what the man's judgments purport to be judgments of, purports to be an objective relation in the world. It belongs in the subject matter not of our theory of theorizing about the world, but of our theory of the world itself. Such would be the acceptable and reputable sort of similarity concept, if it could be defined.

It does get defined in bits: bits suited to special branches of science. In this way, on many limited fronts, man continues his rise from savagery, sloughing off the muddy old notion of kind or similarity piecemeal, a vestige here and a vestige there. Chemistry, the home science of water-solubility itself, is one branch that has reached this stage. Comparative similarity of the sort that matters for chemistry can be stated outright in chemical terms, that is, in terms of chemical composition. Molecules will be said to *match* if they contain atoms of the same elements in the same topological combinations. Then, in principle, we might get at the comparative similarity of objects a and b by considering how many pairs of matching molecules there are, one molecule from a and one from b each time, and how many unmatching pairs. The ratio gives even a theoretical measure of relative similarity, and thus abundantly explains what it is for a to be more similar to b than to c. Or we might prefer to complicate our definition by allowing also for degrees in the matching of molecules; molecules having almost equally many atoms, or having atoms whose atomic numbers or atomic weights are almost equal, could be reckoned as matching better than others. At any rate a lusty chemical similarity concept is assured.

From it, moreover, an equally acceptable concept of kinds is derivable, by the paradigm-and-foil definition noted early in this paper. For it is a question now only of distilling purely chemical kinds from purely chemical similarity; no admixture of other respects of similarity interferes. We thus exonerate water-solubility, which, the last time around, we had reduced no further than to an unexplained notion of kind. Therewith also the associated subjunctive conditional, "If this were in water it would dissolve," gets its bill of health.

The same scientific advances that have thus provided a solid underpinning for the definition of solubility in terms of kinds,

have also, ironically enough, made that line of definition point-
less by providing a full understanding of the mechanism of
solution. One can redefine water-solubility by simply describing
the structural conditions of that mechanism. This embarrass-
ment of riches is, I suspect, a characteristic outcome. That is,
once we can legitimize a disposition term by defining the relevant similarity standard, we are apt to know the mechanism of
the disposition, and so by-pass the similarity. Not but that the
similarity standard is worth clarifying too, for its own sake or
for other purposes.

Philosophical or broadly scientific motives can impel us to
seek still a basic and absolute concept of similarity, along with
such fragmentary similarity concepts as suit special branches of
science. This drive for a cosmic similarity concept is perhaps
identifiable with the age-old drive to reduce things to their elements. It epitomizes the scientific spirit, though dating back to
the pre-Socratics: to Empedocles with his theory of four elements, and above all to Democritus with his atoms. The modern physics of elementary particles, or of hills in space-time, is a
more notable effort in this direction.

This idea of rationalizing a single notion of relative similarity, throughout its cosmic sweep, has its metaphysical attrac-
tions. But there would remain still need also to rationalize the
similarity notion more locally and superficially, so as to capture
only such similarity as is relevant to some special science. Our
chemistry example is already a case of this, since it stops short
of full analysis into neutrons, electrons, and the other elementary particles.

A more striking example of superficiality, in this good sense,
is afforded by taxonomy, say in zoology. Since learning about
the evolution of species, we are in a position to define comparative similarity suitably for this science by consideration of family
trees. For a theoretical measure of the degree of similarity of
two individual animals we can devise some suitable function
that depends on proximity and frequency of their common an-
cestors. Or a more significant concept of degree of similarity
might be devised in terms of genes. When kind is construed in
terms of any such similarity concept, fishes in the corrected,

whale-free sense of the word qualify as a kind while fishes in the more inclusive sense do not.

Different similarity measures, or relative similarity notions, best suit different branches of science; for there are wasteful complications in providing for finer gradations of relative similarity than matter for the phenomena with which the particular science is concerned. Perhaps the branches of science could be revealingly classified by looking to the relative similarity notion that is appropriate to each. Such a plan is reminiscent of Felix Klein's so-called *Erlangerprogramm* in geometry, which involved characterizing the various branches of geometry by what transformations were irrelevant to each. But a branch of science would only qualify for recognition and classification under such a plan when it had matured to the point of clearing up its similarity notion. Such branches of science would qualify further as unified, or integrated into our inclusive systematization of nature, only insofar as their several similarity concepts were *compatible;* capable of meshing, that is, and differing only in the fineness of their discriminations.

Disposition terms and subjunctive conditionals in these areas, where suitable senses of similarity and kind are forthcoming, suddenly turn respectable; respectable and, in principle, superfluous. In other domains they remain disreputable and practically indispensable. They may be seen perhaps as unredeemed notes; the theory that would clear up the unanalyzed underlying similarity notion in such cases is still to come. An example is the disposition called intelligence—the ability, vaguely speaking, to learn quickly and to solve problems. Sometime, whether in terms of proteins or colloids or nerve nets or overt behavior, the relevant branch of science may reach the stage where a similarity notion can be constructed capable of making even the notion of intelligence respectable. And superfluous.

In general we can take it as a very special mark of the maturity of a branch of science that it no longer needs an irreducible notion of similarity and kind. It is that final stage where the animal vestige is wholly absorbed into the theory. In this career of the similarity notion, starting in its innate phase, developing over the years in the light of accumulated experience, passing then from the intuitive phase into theoretical similarity, and finally disappearing altogether, we have a paradigm of the evolution of unreason into science.

7 Essence and Accident

IRVING M. COPI

University of Hawaii

The notions of essence and accident play important and unobjectionable roles in pre-analytic or pre-philosophical thought and discourse. These roles are familiar, and need no elaboration here. Philosophers cannot ignore them, but must either explain them or (somehow) explain them away. My interest is in explaining them.

If they are taken seriously, the notions of essence and accident seem to me most appropriately discussed within the framework of a metaphysic of substance, which I shall accordingly assume. The account of essence and accident that I wish to set forth and argue for derives very largely from Aristotle, although it is not strictly Aristotelian. Where it differs from Aristotle's account it does so in order to accommodate some of the insights formulated by Locke in his discussion of "real" and "nominal" essences. My discussion is to be located, then, against the background of a substance metaphysic and a realist epistemology. The theory of essence and accident to be proposed seems to me not only to fit the demands of the general philosophical position mentioned, but also to be consistent with the apparent requirements of contemporary scientific development. I wish to begin my discussion with some historical remarks.

The earliest Western philosophers were much concerned with change and permanence, taking positions so sharply opposed that the issue appeared to be more paradox than prob-

Reprinted from *The Journal of Philosophy*, LI (November 11, 1954), 706–719, by permission of the author and editor.

lem. If an object which changes really changes, then it cannot literally be one and the same object which undergoes the change. But if the changing thing retains its identity, then it cannot really have changed. Small wonder that early cosmologists divided into warring factions, each embracing a separate horn of their common dilemma, the one denying permanence of any sort, the other denying the very possibility of change.

Aristotle discussed this problem in several of his treatises, bringing to bear on it not only his superb dialectical skill but an admirable, common-sense, dogged insistence that some things do maintain their identity while undergoing change. To explain the observed facts he was led to distinguish different kinds of change. A man does retain his identity though his complexion may change from ruddy to pale, or though he may move from one place to another. He is the same man though he become corpulent in middle life or his sinews shrink with age. In these types of change, called *alteration, locomotion, growth,* and *diminution,* the changing thing remains substantially or essentially what it was before changing.

Another type of change, however, was admitted to be more thoroughgoing. To take, for example, an artificial substance, we can say that if a wooden table is not just painted or moved, but destroyed by fire, we have neither alteration, locomotion, growth, nor diminution alone, but *substantial* change. The characteristic mark of substantial change is that the object undergoing the change does not survive that change or persist through it, but is destroyed in the process. The ashes (and gas and radiant energy) that appear in place of the burned table are not an altered, moved, or larger or smaller table, but no table at all. In substantial change its essential property of being a table disappears.

It seems clear that distinguishing these different kinds of change involves distinguishing different kinds of attributes. The basic dichotomy between substantial change and other kinds of change is parallel to that between essential attributes or *essences,* and other kinds of attributes, which may be lumped together as accidental attributes or *accidents.* (Here we diverge rather sharply from at least one moment of Aristotle's own terminology, in ignoring the intermediate category of "property" or "proprium.")

Of the various bases that have been proposed for distinguishing between essence and accident, two stand out as most reasonable. The first has already been implied. If we can distinguish the different kinds of change, then we can say that a given attribute is essential to an object if its loss would result in the destruction of that object, whereas an attribute is a mere accident if the object would remain identifiably and substantially the same without it. This basis for distinguishing between essence and accident, although helpful heuristically, is not adequate philosophically, for it seems to me that the distinctions among these kinds of change presuppose those among the different kinds of attributes.

The other, more satisfactory basis for distinguishing essence from accident is an epistemological or methodological one. Knowledge of the essence of a thing is said to be more important than knowledge of its other attributes. In the *Metaphysics* Aristotle wrote: " . . . we know each thing most fully, when we know what it is, e.g. what man is or what fire is, rather than when we know its quality, its quantity, or its place. . . ." [1] It is the essence that is intended here, for a subsequent passage explains that: ". . . the essence is precisely what something *is*. . . ." [2] It is perhaps an understatement to say that Aristotle held knowledge of essence to be "more important" than knowledge of accidents, for he later says explicitly that: ". . . to *know* each thing . . . is just to know its essence. . . ." [3] And if we confine our attention to scientific knowledge, Aristotle repeatedly assures us that there is no knowledge of accidents at all,[4] but only of essences.[5]

Aristotle was led to draw an ontological conclusion from the foregoing epistemological doctrine. If some attributes of ob-

---

1. 1028a37–1028b2. Quotations are from the Oxford translation.
2. 1030a1.   3. 1031b20.
4. 1026b4; 1027a20, 28; 1064b30; 1065a4. Cf. also *Posterior Analytics* 75a18–22.
5. 75a28–30.

jects are epistemologically significant and others are not, the implication is that the former constitute the real natures of those objects, whereas the latter can be relegated to some less ultimate category. I must confess that I am in sympathy with the realist position which underlies and justifies such an inference, but to expound it in detail would take us too far afield.

As a biologist Aristotle was led to classify things into genera and species, holding that things belong to the same species if and only if they share a common essence. In remarking this fact we need not commit ourselves to any position with respect to the systematic or genetic priority of either logic or biology in Aristotle's thought. He apparently believed these species to be fixed and limited, and tended to ignore whatever could not be conveniently classified within them, holding, for example, that "the production of a mule by a horse" was "contrary to nature," [6] a curious phrase. Some modern writers have tended to regard this shortcoming as fatal to the Aristotelian system. Thus Susan Stebbing wrote: "Modern theories of organic evolution have combined with modern theories of mathematics to destroy the basis of the Aristotelian conception of essence. . . ." [7] It seems to me, however, that the fixity of species is a casual rather than an integral part of the Aristotelian system, which in its broad outlines as a metaphysical framework can be retained and rendered adequate to the most contemporary of scientific developments. A not dissimilar objection was made by Dewey, who wrote that: "In Aristotelian cosmology, ontology and logic . . . all quantitative determinations were relegated to the state of *accidents,* so that apprehension of them had no scientific standing. . . . Observe by contrast the place occupied by measuring in modern knowledge. Is it then credible that the logic of Greek knowledge has relevance to the logic of modern knowledge?" [8] But the Aristotelian notion of essence *can* admit of quantitative determination, as is suggested by Aristotle himself in admitting ratio as essence.[9] Hence I do not think that

6. 1033b33. But cf. 770b9–13.
7. *A Modern Introduction to Logic* (London: Methuen, 1961), p. 433.
8. *Logic: The Theory of Inquiry* (New York: Holt, 1938), pp. 89–90.
9. 993a17–20.

this criticism of Dewey's can be regarded as any more decisive than that of Miss Stebbing.

Having set forth in outline an Aristotelian philosophy of essence and accident, I propose next to examine what I consider to be the most serious objection that has been raised against it. According to this criticism, the distinction between essence and accident is not an objective or intrinsic one between genuinely different types of attributes. Attributes are really all of the same basic kind, it is said, and the alleged distinction between essence and accident is simply a projection of differences in human interests or a reflection of peculiarities of vocabulary. Let us try to understand this criticism in as sympathetic a fashion as we can.

The distinction between different kinds of change, on this view, is subjective rather than objective. We happen to be interested, usually, in some attributes of a thing more than in others. When the thing changes, we say that it persists through the change provided that it does not lose those attributes by whose possession it satisfies our interests. For example, our interest in tables is for the most part independent of their colors. Hence that interest remains satisfiable by a given table regardless of any alteration it may suffer with respect to color. Paint a brown table green, and it remains substantially or essentially the same; the change was only an accidental one. If our interests were different, the same objective fact would be classified quite differently. Were our interest to lie in *brown* tables exclusively, then the application of green paint would destroy the object of our interest, would change it substantially or essentially from something which satisfied our interest to something which did not. The implication is that attributes are neither essential nor accidental in themselves, but can be so classified only on the basis of our subjective interests in them. Dewey stated this point of view very succinctly, writing: "As far as present logical texts still continue to talk about essences, properties and accidents as something inherently different from one another, they are repeating distinctions that once had an ontological meaning and that no longer have it. Anything is 'essential' which is indispensable in a given inquiry and anything is 'accidental' which is superfluous." [10]

The present criticism lends itself easily to reformulation in more language-oriented terms. That we regard a table as essentially the same despite alteration in color or movement from place to place is a consequence of the peculiar nature and limitations of our vocabulary, which has a single word for tables, regardless of color, but lacks special words for tables of different colors. Suppose that our language contained no word for tables in general, but had instead—say—the word "towble" for brown table and the word "teeble" for green table. Then the application of green paint to a towble would be said to change it essentially, it might be argued, for no towble would remain; in its place would appear a teeble. Or if there were a single word which applied indiscriminately to tables and heaps of ashes, say "tashble," with no special substantive denoting either of them univocally, then perhaps the destruction of a table by fire would not be regarded as an essential change. That which appeared at the end of the process would admittedly be in a different state from what was there at the start, but it would still be identifiably the same tashble. C. I. Lewis regards the difference between essence and accident to be strictly relative to vocabulary, writing: "Traditionally any attribute required for application of a term is said to be of the essence of the thing named. It is, of course, meaningless to speak of the essence of a thing except relative to its being named by a particular term." [11]

I think that for our purpose these two criticisms can be regarded as variants of a single basic one, for the connection between human interests and human vocabulary is a very intimate one. It is an anthropological and linguistic commonplace that the concern of a culture with a given phenomenon is reflected in the vocabulary of that culture, as in the several Eskimo words which denote subtly different kinds of snow. In

10. *Logic*, p. 138.
11. *An Analysis of Knowledge and Valuation* (La Salle, Ill.: Open Court, 1946), p. 41.

our own culture new interests lead continually to innovations in vocabulary; and surely it is the decline of interest in certain things that leads to the obsolescence of words used to refer to them.

Both variants of this criticism were formulated long ago by Locke, and developed at considerable length in his *Essay*. Locke paid comparatively little attention to the problem of change, but where he did discuss it his treatment was very similar to Aristotle's. Thus we are assured in the *Essay* that: ". . . an oak growing from a plant to a great tree, and then lopped, is still the same oak; and a colt grown up to a horse, sometimes fat, sometimes lean, is all the while the same horse. . . ." [12] The oak ". . . continues to be the same plant as long as it partakes of the same life . . ." [13] and the identity of animals is explained in similar terms. Personal identity is explained in terms of sameness of consciousness.[14] If we ignore the Cartesian dualism implicit in that last case, and if we are not too critical of the reappearance of the term "same" in the explanation of *sameness,* we can recognize these answers to be the Aristotelian ones, for according to Aristotle the soul is the principle of life,[15] the life of a plant is the nutritive soul,[16] that of an animal its sensitive soul,[17] and that of man his rational soul,[18] these souls constituting the substantial forms or essences of the respective substances.[19] On the other hand, in his brief discussion of identity as applied to non-living things, Locke construes it very strictly to apply only to things which ". . . vary not at all. . . ." [20] But the following passage has a characteristically Aristotelian flavor: "Thus that which was grass to-day, is to-morrow the flesh of a sheep; and within a few days after becomes part of a man: in all which, and the like changes, it is evident their real essence, i.e. that constitution, whereon the properties of these several things depended, is destroyed, and perishes with them." [21]

12. Bk. 2, ch. 27, §3.   13. *Ibid.*
14. Bk. 2, ch. 27, §8, §9, §10, §16, §17, §23.
15. *De Anima* 402a6, 415b8.
16. 432a29, 434a22–26; cf. also *De Plantis* 815b28–34.   17. 432a30.
18. *Politics* 1332b5.   19. *De Anima* 412a20, 412b13, 415b10.
20. Bk. 2, ch. 27, §1.   21. Bk. 3, ch. 4, §19. But cf. Bk. 3, ch. 6, §4, §5.

Despite this partial similarity of their views, the bases for distinguishing between the essential properties and other properties of a thing are very different for Locke than for Aristotle. For Aristotle, the distinction is twofold: first, the essential properties of an object are those which are retained by it during any change through which the object remains identifiably the same object; and second, the essential properties of an object are most important in our scientific knowledge of it. For Locke, on the other hand, the *real* essence of a thing is a set of properties which *determine* all the other properties of that thing.[22] Since all other properties depend on its real essence, *any* change in an object entails a change in its real essence. Hence for Locke the essential properties of an object are *not* retained by it during any change. This view is very different from Aristotle's, on which the accidents of a thing are not bound to its essence but can change independently of it. The epistemological difference is equally striking. Whereas for Aristotle all scientific knowledge is knowledge of the essence, for Locke there is *no* knowledge of the real essences of things.[23]

Locke was more interested in what he called "nominal essences," which are more nearly analogous to the Aristotelian notion of essence. Our idea of a particular substance, according to Locke, is a complex idea composed of a number of simple ideas which are noticed to "go constantly together," plus the notion of a substratum "wherein they do subsist." [24] A general or abstract idea of a sort or species of substance is made out of our complex ideas of various particular substances that resemble each other by leaving out "that which is peculiar to each" and retaining "only what is common to all." [25] Such an abstract idea *determines* a sort or species,[26] and is called a "nominal essence," [27] for "everything contained in that idea is essential to that sort." [28]

The properties contained in the nominal essence of a thing

22. Bk. 3, ch. 3, §15.
23. Bk. 3, ch. 3, §15, §17, §18; ch. 6, §3, §6, §9, §12, §18, §49; ch. 9, §12; ch. 10, §18.
24. Bk. 2, ch. 23, §1.   25. Bk. 3, ch. 3, §7.   26. Bk. 3, ch. 3, §12.
27. Bk. 3, ch. 3, §15.   28. Bk. 3, ch. 6, §2.

can be distinguished from the other properties of that thing on the same basis as that on which the Aristotelian essence is distinguished from accidents. In the first place, a particular substance of a given species can change with respect to some property whose idea is *not* included in the nominal essence of that species, and will continue to be recognizably the same thing; whereas it must be regarded as a quite different thing if it changes with respect to some property whose idea *is* included in the nominal essence.[29] And in the second place, the nominal essence is more important in knowledge than other properties. To have knowledge of a thing is to know what *sort* of thing it is, and to know the nominal essence is to know the sort. Locke says, moreover, that the leading qualities of a thing, that is, the most observable and hence, for Locke, the most knowable, are ingredients in the nominal essence.[30] Finally, it is argued in the *Essay* that knowledge of nominal essences is required if we are ever to be certain of the truth of any general proposition.[31] Since Locke's nominal essences play so similar a role to that of Aristotle's essences, Locke's arguments intended to prove their subjectivity and relativity to human interests and vocabulary can be interpreted as applying to Aristotle's notion as well as his own.

One fairly minor difference should be noted before going on. Since Locke's nominal essences are abstract *ideas,* they are immediately subjective in a way that Aristotle's essences are not. But that difference is not decisive, for substances may well have objective properties that nominal essences are ideas *of,* or objective *powers* that correspond to them exactly.[32]

Locke urges that essences are subjective in a less trivial sense. Since they are "inventions" [33] or the "workmanship" [34] of the understanding, different persons in fashioning abstract ideas which they signify by the same term can and do incorporate different simple ideas into them. Acts of choice or selection are involved here, and people do make different choices, as proved

29. Bk. 2, ch. 27, §28.   30. Bk. 3, ch. 11, §20.
31. Bk. 4, ch. 6, §4.   32. Bk. 2, ch. 23, §7.   33. Bk. 3, ch. 3, §11.
34. Bk. 3, ch. 3, §12, §13, §14.

by the disputes that so frequently arise over whether particular bodies are of certain species or not.[35]

That essences are relative to vocabulary is argued by Locke in terms of an example: "A silent and a striking watch are but one species to those who have but one name for them: but he that has the name watch for one, and clock for the other, and distinct complex ideas, to which those names belong, to him they are different species." [36]

That the ". . . boundaries of species are as men, and not as nature, makes them . . . ," [37] proved by the verbal disputes already referred to, is explained by the fact that since we have ". . . need of general names for present use . . ." [38] we ". . . stay not for a perfect discovery of all those qualities which would best show us their most material differences and agreements; but we ourselves divide them, by certain obvious appearances, into species. . . ." [39] Nominal essences are made for *use,* and different intended uses or interests will determine different essences. Even the *noticing* of similarities between distinct particulars is relative to our interest in them, so our selection of simple ideas for inclusion in a nominal essence is relative to such interests. These determining interests are not scientific, for as Locke observed, ". . . languages, in all countries, have been established long before sciences." [40] The situation is rather that the terms of ordinary discourse ". . . have for the most part, in all languages, received their birth and signification from ignorant and illiterate people. . . ." [41] And for the purposes or interests of those practical people, the properties selected by them as essential to the objects they deal with are adequate enough. For "Vulgar notions suit vulgar discourses; and both, though confused enough, yet serve pretty well the market and the wake." [42]

Now do these arguments succeed in establishing that the distinction between essence and accident is subjective rather than

35. Bk. 3, ch. 3, §14; ch. 6, §26, §27; ch. 9, §16; ch. 10, §22; ch. 11, §6, §7.
36. Bk. 3, ch. 6, §39.   37. Bk. 3, ch. 6, §30.   38. *Ibid.*
39. *Ibid.*   40. Bk. 3, ch. 6, §25.   41. *Ibid.*
42. Bk. 3, ch. 11, §10.

objective, that is, relative to human interests and vocabulary?

I think that the objections are not utterly destructive of the Aristotelian doctrine, although they do call attention to needed modifications of it. Locke's case, it seems to me, depends upon his distinction between real and nominal essences, and his belief that real essences are unknowable. But his doctrine that real essences cannot be known flows from two peculiarities of his philosophy, which I see no reason to accept. One of the bases for his belief that real essences are unknowable is his view that the only objects of our knowledge are the ideas that we have in our minds.[43] Locke's other basis for his belief that real essences are unknowable is his doctrine that experiment and observation yield only ". . . judgment and opinion, not knowledge. . . ."[44] Here the term "knowledge" is reserved for what is *certain*.

I would reject these two doctrines on the following grounds. The first of them, that knowledge is only of ideas, is the germ of scepticism. Locke's premises lead necessarily to Hume's conclusions, and the partial scepticism we find explicitly set forth in Locke is but a fragment of the complete scepticism that Hume later showed to be implicitly contained there. It seems to me that if a philosophy denies the very possibility of scientific knowledge, then so much the worse for that philosophy. As for reserving the term "knowledge" for what is certain, that usage has but little to commend it. It seems more reasonable to accept the results of experiment and observation, although probable rather than demonstrative, as knowledge nonetheless.

It must be admitted that the doctrine of the unknowability of real essences was not an unreasonable conclusion to draw from the relatively undeveloped state of science in Locke's day. For chemistry, at least, if we can believe what is said of it in the *Essay*, was in a very bad way in the seventeenth century. Locke tells us of the "sad experience" of chemists ". . . when they, sometimes in vain, seek for the same qualities in one parcel of sulphur, antimony or vitriol, which they have found in others. For though they are bodies of the same species, having the

43. Bk. 2, ch. 1, §1.   44. Bk. 4, ch. 12, §10; cf. also Bk. 4, ch. 3, §28.

same nominal essence, under the same name; yet do they often, upon severe ways of examination, betray qualities so different one from another, as to frustrate the expectations of very wary chemists." [45]

Contemporary science, however, presents a quite different picture. Locke characterized the (allegedly unknowable) real essences of things as the ". . . constitution of their insensible parts; from which flow those sensible qualities, which serve us to distinguish them one from another. . . ." [46] Now modern atomic theory is directly concerned with the insensible parts of things. Through the use of his Periodic Table, interpreted as dealing with atomic number and valency, ". . . Mendeléev was enabled to predict the existence *and properties* . . ." of half a dozen elements whose existence had not been previously known or even suspected.[47] And other scientists have subsequently been able to make similar predictions. Modern science seeks to know the *real* essences of things, and its increasing successes seem to be bringing it progressively nearer to that goal.

It must be granted that Locke's distinction between real and nominal essence is a helpful one, even though it is not absolute. The construction of nominal essences is usually relative to practical interests, and the ordinary notion of the essence of a thing is relative to the words used in referring to it. I think that Locke (and Dewey and Lewis) are correct in that contention. Surely different interests lead different people to classify or sort things in different ways, and thus to adopt different nominal essences, the more permanently useful of which receive separate names in ordinary language. Thus it is that: "Merchants and lovers, cooks and taylors, have words wherewithal to dispatch their ordinary affairs. . . ." [48]

The distinction, however, is not absolute. Not every interest is narrowly practical. The interest of the scientist is in knowledge and understanding. The scientist desires to know how

45. Bk. 3, ch. 6, §8.   46. Bk. 3, ch. 3, §17.
47. J. D. Main Smith, in the *Encyclopaedia Britannica* (14th ed.; 1947), Vol. 17, p. 520 (my italics).
48. Bk. 3, ch. 11, §10.

things behave, and to account for their behavior by means of explanatory hypotheses or theories which permit him to predict what will occur under specified conditions. He is interested in discovering general laws to which objects conform, and the causal relations which obtain among them. The scientist's sorting or classifying of objects is relative to this interest, which is not well served by classifying things on the basis of properties which are either most obvious or most immediately practical. It is better served by classifying things in terms of properties which are relevant to the framing of a maximum number of causal laws and the formulation of explanatory theories. Thus a foodstuff and a mineral source of aluminum, common salt and cryolite, are both classified by the chemist as sodium compounds, because in the context of modern chemical theory it is this common characteristic which is most significant for predicting and understanding the behavior of these substances. In the sphere of scientific inquiry, the distinction between real and nominal essence tends to disappear. The scientist's classification of things is intended to be in terms of their *real* essences. And here, too, the process is reflected in vocabulary, not necessarily or even usually in that of the man in the street, but rather in the technical jargon of the specialist.

The essences which science seeks to discover, then, are real essences rather than nominal ones. Since the arguments for subjectivity or relativity to interest or vocabulary were concerned with nominal rather than real essences, they simply do not apply to real essences as either Locke or Aristotle conceived them.

In one passage of his *Essay*, though, Locke does make the further claim that even a real essence relates to a sort and supposes a species.[49] But on Locke's own account of real essence, the real essence of a particular must be that set of its properties on which all of its other properties depend. And that can be investigated independently of any sorting or classifying we may do—although once its real essence is discovered, that will deter-

49. Bk. 3, ch. 6, §6.

mine how we should classify it scientifically if the occasion for doing so arises.

At this point let me indicate the direction in which I think the Aristotelian doctrine of essence and accident might well be modified. Aristotle definitely held that there could be no scientific knowledge of accidents,[50] but contemporary science would admit no such limitation. It seems to me that both Locke's and Aristotle's views about unknowability should be rejected. Contrary to Locke, I should hold that real essences are in principle knowable, and contrary to Aristotle, I should hold that non-essential or accidental properties can also be objects of scientific knowledge.

It seems to me also that neither Locke nor Aristotle gives a satisfactory account of the relationship between essence and accident. For Locke, all (other) properties of a thing depend on its "real constitution" or real essence [51]; but it is not clear whether the dependence is supposed to be causal or logico-deductive. The former is obviously the more acceptable doctrine. Aristotle, on the other hand, held that some properties of a thing, namely, its accidents, do not in any way depend upon its essence. I think that Locke's view, understood as asserting a causal dependence of accident on essence, is the more plausible one, and that the Aristotelian doctrine ought to be so modified as to accord with that of Locke in this respect.

Now if both essences and accidents are scientifically knowable, on what basis are they to be distinguished from each other? I suggest that the epistemological or methodological distinction is still valid. For example, common salt has many properties, some more obvious than others, and some more important than others relative to different practical interests. The scientist singles out its being a compound of equal parts of sodium and chlorine as its essential nature. In doing so he surely does not mean to imply that its chemical constitution is more easily observed than its other properties, or more important to either cook, tailor, merchant, or lover. He classifies it as sodium

50. 1064b30–1065a25.   51. Bk. 3, ch. 3, §18.

chloride because, within the context of his theory, that property is fundamental. From its chemical formula more of its properties can be inferred than could be from any other. Since the connection is causal rather than logical, the inference from essence to accident must make use of causal law premises or modes of inference as well as strictly logical ones. Hence to derive conclusions about *all* accidental properties of a substance, we should need to know both its real essence and all relevant causal laws. That is an ideal towards which science strives, rather than its present achievement, of course. To the extent to which one small group of properties of a substance can serve as a basis from which its other properties can be causally derived, to that extent we can be justified in identifying that group of properties as its real essence. This view, it should be noted, is in agreement with Aristotle's doctrine that the definition of a thing should state its essence,[52] and that definition is a scientific process.[53]

There is a certain relativity implied in this account, although it is quite different from those previously discussed. Our *notion* of what constitutes the real essence of a thing is relative to the science of our day. Centuries hence, wiser men will have radically different and more adequate theories, and their notions will be closer approximations than ours to the real essences of things. But it will still be the real essences of things that are destined to be known by Pierce's ultimate community of knowers.

There is one other and more radical sense of accident that I would agree to be relative. Each separate science is concerned with only some of the properties or aspects of things which it studies. Those left out will be accidental relative to the special science which ignores them. They will not be derivable from what that science considers to be the real essences of those things, although a different special science might be much concerned with them, and even include them in *its* notion of the thing's real essence. But as (and if) the sciences become more unified, no properties of a thing will be wholly accidental in this sense, and all will be causally derivable from the real essence.

52. 91a1, 101b21, 38.   53. 1039b32.

In closing, I should like to refer once again to the topic of change. If all of a thing's properties depend on its real essence, then it would seem to follow that every change is an essential one. In my opinion, that unwelcome conclusion can be evaded in two ways. In the first place, with respect to common-sense, practical usage, our ordinary sortings will continue to be based on nominal rather than real essences, so that changes can continue to be classified as accidental or essential in the traditional way. And in the second place, with respect to scientific usage, we can say the following. The real essence of a thing will consist very largely of powers or, in modern terms, dispositional properties. An essential change in a thing will involve the replacement of some of its dispositions or powers by other dispositions or powers. But a change which is non-essential or accidental would involve no such replacement; it would rather consist in differently actualized manifestations of the same dispositional property or power. Unfortunately, lack of space prevents an adequate development of this suggestion.

8 The Causal Theory of Names

GARETH EVANS

Oxford University

I

1. In a paper which provides the starting point of this enquiry Saul Kripke opposes what he calls the Description Theory of Names and makes a counter-proposal of what I shall call the Causal Theory.[1] To be clear about what is at stake and what should be the outcome in the debate he initiated seems to me important for our understanding of talk and thought about the world in general as well as for our understanding of the functioning of proper names. I am anxious therefore that we identify the profound bases and likely generalizations of the opposing positions and do not content ourselves with counter-examples.

I should say that Kripke deliberately held back from presenting his ideas as a theory. I shall have to tighten them up, and I may suggest perhaps unintended directions of generalization; therefore his paper should be checked before the Causal Theory I consider is attributed to him.

There are two related but distinguishable questions concerning proper names. The first is about what the name denotes upon a particular occasion of its use when this is understood as

Reprinted from *Aristotelian Society Supplementary Volume* XLVII, 187–208, by courtesy of the Editor of the Aristotelian Society. © 1973 The Aristotelian Society.

1. S. A. Kripke, "Naming and Necessity" (and Addenda), in *Semantics of Natural Languages,* ed. by D. Davidson and G. Harman (Dordrecht: D. Reidel, 1972), pp. 253–355, 763–769.

being partly determinative of what the speaker strictly and literally said. I shall use the faintly barbarous coinage: *what the speaker denotes* (upon an occasion) for this notion. The second is about *what the name denotes;* we want to know what conditions have to be satisfied by an expression and an item for the first to be the, or a, name of the second. There is an entirely parallel pair of questions concerning general terms. In both cases it is ambiguity which prevents an easy answer of the first in terms of the second; to denote x it is not sufficient merely to utter something which is x's name.

Consequently there are two Description Theories, not distinguished by Kripke.[2] The Description Theory of speaker's denotation holds that a name 'N.N.' denotes x upon a particular occasion of its use by a speaker S just in case x is uniquely that which satisfies all or most of the descriptions ϕ such that S would assent to 'N.N. is ϕ' (or '*That* N.N. is ϕ'). Crudely: the cluster of information S has associated with the name determines its denotation upon a particular occasion by *fit*. If the speaker has no individuating information he will denote nothing.

The Description Theory of what a name denotes holds that, associated with each name as used by a group of speakers who believe and intend that they are using the name with the same denotation, is a description or set of descriptions cullable from their beliefs which an item has to satisfy to be the bearer of the name. This description is used to explain the rôle of the name in existential, identity and opaque contexts. The theory is by no means committed to the thesis that every user of the name must be in possession of the description; just as Kripke is not committed to holding that every user of the expression 'one metre' knows about the metre rod in Paris by saying that its reference is fixed by the description 'Length of stick S in Paris'. Indeed if the description is arrived at in the manner of Straw-

2. This can be seen in the way the list of theses defining the Description Theory alternate between those mentioning a speaker and those that don't, culminating in the uneasy idea of an idiolect of one. The Description Theorists of course do not themselves distinguish them clearly either, and many espouse both.

son [3]—averaging out the different beliefs of different speakers—it is most unlikely that the description will figure in every user's name-associated cluster.

The direct attack in Kripke's paper passes this latter theory by; most conspicuously the charge that the Description Theory ignores the social character of naming. I shall not discuss it explicitly either, though it will surface from time to time and the extent to which it is right should be clear by the end of the paper.

Kripke's direct attacks are unquestionably against the first Description Theory. He argues:

(a) An ordinary man in the street can denote the physicist Feynman by using the name 'Feynman' and say something true or false of him even though there is no description uniquely true of the physicist which he can fashion. (The conditions aren't necessary.)

(b) A person who associated with the name 'Gödel' merely the description 'prover of the incompleteness of Arithmetic' would nonetheless be denoting Gödel and saying something false of him in uttering 'Gödel proved the incompleteness of Arithmetic' even if an unknown Viennese by the name of Schmidt had in fact constructed the proof which Gödel had subsequently broadcast as his own. (If it is agreed that the speaker does not denote Schmidt the conditions aren't sufficient; if it is also agreed that he denotes Gödel, again they are not necessary.)

The strong thesis (that the Description Theorist's conditions are sufficient) is outrageous. What the speaker denotes in the sense we are concerned with is connected with saying in that strict sense which logicians so rightly prize, and the theory's deliverances of strict truth conditions are quite unacceptable. They would have the consequence, for example, that if I was previously innocent of knowledge or belief regarding Mr. Y, and X is wrongly introduced to me as Mr. Y, then I must speak the truth in uttering 'Mr. Y is here' since X satisfies the overwhelming majority of descriptions I would associate with the

---

3. P. F. Strawson, *Individuals* (London: Methuen, 1965), p. 191.

name and X is there. I have grave doubts as to whether anyone has ever seriously held this thesis.

It is the weaker thesis—that some descriptive identification is necessary for a speaker to denote something—that it is important to understand. Strictly, Kripke's examples do not show it to be false since he nowhere provides a convincing reason for not taking into account speakers' possession of descriptions like 'man bearing such-and-such a name'; but I too think it is false. It can be seen as the fusion of two thoughts. First: that in order to be saying something by uttering an expression one must utter the sentence with certain intentions; this is felt to require, in the case of sentences containing names, that one be aiming at something with one's use of the name. Secondly—and this is where the underpinning from a certain Philosophy of Mind becomes apparent—to have an intention or belief concerning some item (which one is not in a position to demonstratively identify) one must be in possession of a description uniquely true of it. Both strands deserve at least momentary scrutiny.

We are prone to pass too quickly from the observation that neither parrots nor the wind *say* things to the conclusion that to say that p requires that one must intend to say that p and therefore, so to speak, be able to identify p independently of one's sentence. But the most we are entitled to conclude is that to say something one must intend to say something by uttering one's sentence (one normally will intend to say what it says). The application of the stricter requirement would lead us to relegate too much of our discourse to the status of mere mouthing. We constantly use general terms of whose satisfaction conditions we have but the dimmest idea. 'Microbiologist', 'chlorine' (the stuff in swimming pools), 'nicotine' (the stuff in cigarettes); these (and countless other words) we cannot define nor offer remarks which would distinguish their meaning from that of closely related words. It is wrong to say that we say nothing by uttering sentences containing these expressions, even if we recoil from the strong thesis, from saying that what we do say is determined by those hazy ideas and half-identifications we would offer if pressed.

The Philosophy of Mind is curiously popular but rarely

made perfectly explicit.[4] It is held by anyone who holds that S believes that a is F if and only if

$$\exists\phi[(S \text{ believes } \exists x(\phi x \ \& \ (\forall y) \ (\phi y \rightarrow x = y) \ \& \ Fx)) \ \& \ \phi a \& \ (\forall y)$$
$$(\phi y \rightarrow y = a)]$$

Obvious alterations would accommodate the other psychological attitudes. The range of the property quantifier must be restricted to exclude such properties as 'being identical with a'; otherwise the criterion is trivial.[5] The situation in which a thinking, planning or wanting human has some item which is the object of his thought, plan or desire is represented as a species of essentially the same situation as that which holds when there is no object and the thought, plan or desire is, as we might say, purely general. There are thoughts, such as the thought that there are 11-fingered men, for whose expression general terms of the language suffice. The idea is that when the psychological state involves an object, a general term believed to be uniquely instantiated and in fact uniquely instantiated by the item which is the object of the state will figure in its specification. This idea may be coupled with a concession that there are certain privileged objects to which one may be more directly related; indeed such a concession appears to be needed if the theory is to be able to allow what appears an evident possibility: object-directed thoughts in a perfectly symmetrical or cyclical universe.

This idea about the nature of object-directed psychological attitudes obviously owes much to the feeling that there must be something we can say about what is believed or wanted even when there is no appropriate object actually to be found in the world. But it can also be seen as deriving support from a Principle of Charity: so attribute objects to beliefs that true belief is maximized. (I do not think this is an acceptable principle; the acceptable principle enjoins minimizing the attribution of *inex-*

---

4. For example, see J. R. Searle, *Speech Acts* (Cambridge: Cambridge University Press, 1969), p. 87; E. Gellner, "Ethics and Logic," *Proceedings of the Aristotelian Society* 1954–55; B. Russell, *Problems of Philosophy* (Oxford: Oxford University Press, 1912), p. 29. E. Sosa criticizes it in "Quantifiers Belief and Sellars" in *Philosophical Logic*, ed. by Davis, Hockney, and Wilson (Dordrecht: D. Reidel, 1969), p. 69.

5. I owe this observation to G. Harman.

plicable error and therefore cannot be operated without a theory of the causation of belief for the creatures under investigation.)

We cannot deal comprehensively with this Philosophy of Mind here. My objections to it are essentially those of Wittgenstein. For an item to be the object of some psychological attitude of yours may be simply for you to be placed in a context which relates you to that thing. What makes it one rather than the other of a pair of identical twins that you are in love with? Certainly not some specification blueprinted in your mind; it may be no more than this: it was one of them and not the other that you have met. The theorist may gesture to the description 'the one I have met' but can give no explanation for the impossibility of its being outweighed by other descriptions which may have been acquired as a result of error and which may in fact happen to fit the other, unmet, twin. If God had looked into your mind, he would not have seen there with whom you were in love, and of whom you were thinking.

With that I propose to begin considering the Causal Theory.

2. The Causal Theory as stated by Kripke goes something like this. A speaker, using a name 'NN' on a particular occasion will denote some item x if there is a causal chain of *reference-preserving links* leading back from his use on that occasion ultimately to the item x itself being involved in a name-acquiring transaction such as an explicit dubbing or the more gradual process whereby nicknames stick. I mention the notion of a reference-preserving link to incorporate a condition that Kripke lays down; a speaker S's transmission of a name 'NN' to a speaker S' constitutes a reference-preserving link only if S intends to be using the name with the same denotation as he from whom he in his turn learned the name.

Let us begin by considering the theory in answer to our question about speaker's denotation (i.e., at the level of the individual speaker). In particular, let us consider the thesis that it is *sufficient* for someone to denote x on a particular occasion with the name that this use of the name on that occasion be a causal consequence of his exposure to other speakers using the expression to denote x.

An example which might favourably dispose one towards the theory is this. A group of people are having a conversation in a pub, about a certain Louis of whom S has never heard before. S becomes interested and asks: 'What did Louis do then?' There seems to be no question but that S denotes a particular man and asks about him. Or on some subsequent occasion S may use the name to offer some new thought to one of the participants: 'Louis was quite right to do that'. Again he clearly denotes whoever was the subject of conversation in the pub. This is difficult to reconcile with the Description Theory since the scraps of information which he picked up during the conversation might involve some distortion and fit someone else much better. Of course he has the description 'the man they were talking about' but the theory has no explanation for the impossibility of its being outweighed.

The Causal Theory can secure the right answer in such a case but I think deeper reflection will reveal that it too involves a refusal to recognize the insight about contextual determination I mentioned earlier. For the theory has the following consequence: that at any future time, no matter how remote or forgotten the conversation, no matter how alien the subject matter and confused the speaker, S will denote one particular Frenchman—perhaps Louis XIII—so long as there is a causal connexion between his use at that time and the long distant conversation.

It is important in testing your intuitions against the theory that you imagine the predicate changed—so that he says something like 'Louis was a basketball player' which was not heard in the conversation and which arises as the result of some confusion. This is to prevent the operation of what I call the 'mouthpiece syndrome' by which we attach sense and reference to a man's remarks only because we hear someone else speaking through him; as we might with a messenger, carrying a message about matters of which he was entirely ignorant.

Now there is no knock-down argument to show this consequence unacceptable; with pliant enough intuitions you can swallow anything in philosophy. But notice how little *point* there is in saying that he denotes one French King rather than any other, or any other person named by the name. There is now nothing that the speaker is prepared to say or do which relates him differentially to that one King. This is why it is so outrageous to say that he believes that Louis XIII is a basketball player. The notion of saying has simply been severed from all the connexions that made it of interest. Certainly we did not think we were letting ourselves in for this when we took the point about the conversation in the pub. What has gone wrong? [6]

The Causal Theory again ignores the importance of surrounding context, and regards the capacity to denote something as a magic trick which has somehow been passed on, and once passed on cannot be lost. We should rather say: in virtue of the context in which the man found himself the man's dispositions were bent towards one particular man—Louis XIII—whose states and doings alone he would count as serving to verify remarks made in that context using the name. And of course that context can persist, for the conversation can itself be adverted to subsequently. But it can also disappear so that the speaker is simply not sensitive to the outcome of any investigations regarding the truth of what he is said to have said. And at this point saying becomes detached, and uninteresting.

(It is worth observing how ambivalent Kripke is on the relation between denoting and believing; when the connexion favours him he uses it; we are reminded for example that the ordinary man has a false belief about Gödel and not a true belief about Schmidt. But it is obvious that the results of the 'who are they believing about?' criterion are bound to come dramatically apart from the results of the 'who is the original bearer of the name?' criterion, if for no other reason than that the former must be constructed to give results in cases where there is no name and where the latter cannot apply. When this happens we are sternly reminded that 'X refers' and 'X says' are being used in *technical* senses.[7] But there are limits. One could regard the aim of this paper to restore the connexion which must exist

---

6. Kripke expresses doubts about the sufficiency of the conditions for this sort of reason; see "Naming and Necessity," p. 303.

7. *Ibid.*, p. 348 fn.

between strict truth conditions and the beliefs and interests of the users of the sentences if the technical notion of strict truth conditions is to be of interest to us.)

Reflection upon the conversation in the pub appeared to provide one reason for being favourably disposed towards the Causal Theory. There is another connected reason we ought to examine briefly. It might appear that the Causal Theory provides the basis for a general non-intentional answer to the Problem of Ambiguity. The problem is clear enough: What conditions have to be satisfied for a speaker to have said that p when he utters a sentence which may appropriately be used to say that q and that r and that s in addition? Two obvious alternative answers are

    (a) the extent to which it is reasonable for his audience to conclude that he was saying that p

    (b) his intending to say that p

and neither is without its difficulties. We can therefore imagine someone hoping for a natural extension of the Causal Theory to general terms which would enable him to explain for example how a child who did not have determinative intentions because of the technical nature of the subject matter may still say something determinate using a sentence which is in fact ambiguous.

I touch upon this to ensure that we are keeping the range of relevant considerations to be brought to bear upon the debate as wide as it must be. But I think little general advantage can accrue to the Causal Theory from thus broadening the considerations. The reason is that it simply fails to have the generality of the other two theories; it has no obvious application, for example, to syntactic ambiguity or to ambiguity produced by attempts to refer with non-unique descriptions, or pronouns. It seems inconceivable that the general theory of disambiguation required for such cases would be inadequate to deal with the phenomenon of shared names and would require *ad hoc* supplementation from the Causal Theory.

I want to stress how, precisely because the Causal Theory ignores the way context can be determinative of what gets *said*, it has quite unacceptable consequences. Suppose for example on a T.V. quiz programme I am asked to name a capital city and I say 'Kingston is the capital of Jamaica'; I should want to say that I had said something strictly and literally true even though it turns out that the man from whom I had picked up this scrap of information was actually referring to Kingston-upon-Thames and making a racist observation.

It may begin to appear that what gets said is going to be determined by what name is used, what items bear the name, and general principles of contextual disambiguation. The causal origin of the speaker's familiarity with the name, save in certain specialized 'mouthpiece cases', does not seem to have a critical rôle to play.

This impression may be strengthened by the observation that a causal connexion between my use of the name and use by others (whether or not leading back ultimately to the item itself) is simply not necessary for me to use the name to say something. Amongst the Wagera Indians, for example, 'newly born children receive the names of deceased members of their family according to fixed rules . . . the first born takes on the name of the paternal grandfather, the second that of the father's eldest brother, the third that of the maternal grandfather.' [8] In these and other situations (names for streets in U.S. cities, etc.,) a knowledgeable speaker may excogitate a name and use it to denote some item which bears it without any causal connexion whatever with the use by others of that name.

These points might be conceded by Kripke while maintaining the general position that the denotation of a name in a community is still to be found by tracing a causal chain of reference preserving links back to some item. It is to this theory that I now turn.

3. Suppose a parallel theory were offered to explain the sense of general terms (not just terms for natural kinds). One would reply as follows: 'There aren't two fundamentally different mechanisms involved in a word's having a meaning: one bringing it about that a word acquires a meaning, and the other—a causal mechanism—which operates to ensure that its

---

8. E. Delhaise, "Les Wagera," *Monogr. Ethnogr.*, 1909.

meaning is preserved. The former processes are operative all the time; whatever explains how a word gets its meaning also explains how it preserves it, if preserved it is. Indeed such a theory could not account for the phenomenon of a word's changing its meaning. It is perfectly possible for this to happen without anyone's intending to initiate a new practice with the word; the causal chain would then lead back too far.'

Change of meaning would be decisive against such a theory of the meaning of general terms. Change of denotation is similarly decisive against the Causal Theory of Names. Not only are changes of denotation imaginable, but it appears that they actually occur. We learn from Isaac Taylor's book: *Names and their History*, 1898: "In the case of 'Madagascar' a hearsay report of Malay or Arab sailors misunderstood by Marco Polo . . . has had the effect of transferring a corrupt form of the name of a portion of the African mainland to the great African Island." A simple imaginary case would be this: Two babies are born, and their mothers bestow names upon them. A nurse inadvertently switches them and the error is never discovered. It will henceforth undeniably be the case that the man universally known as 'Jack' is so called because a woman dubbed some other baby with the name.

It is clear that the Causal Theory unamended is not adequate. It looks as though, once again, the intentions of the speakers to use the name to refer to something must be allowed to count in determination of what it denotes.

But it is not enough to say that and leave matters there. We must at least sketch a theory which will enable 'Madagascar' to be the name of the island yet which will not have the consequence that 'Gödel' would become a name of Schmidt in the situation envisaged by Kripke nor 'Goliath' a name of the Philistine killed by David. (Biblical scholars now suggest that David did not kill Goliath, and that the attribution of the slaying to Elhannan the Bethlehemite in 2 Samuel 21 xix is correct. David is thought to have killed a Philistine but not Goliath.[9]) For although this has never been explicitly argued I would agree that

9. Henry Wheeler Robinson, *History of Israel*, rev. ed. (Naperville, Ill.: Allenson, 1964), p. 187.

even if the 'information' connected with the name in possession
of an entire community was merely that 'Goliath was the Philistine David slew' this would still not mean that 'Goliath' referred
in that community to that man, and therefore that the sentence
expressed a truth. And if we simultaneously thought that the
name *would* denote the Philistine slain by Elhannan then both
the necessity and sufficiency of the conditions suggested by the
Description Theory of the denotation of a name are rejected.
This is the case Kripke should have argued but didn't.

4. Before going on to sketch such a theory in the second
part of this paper let me survey the position arrived at and use
it to make a summary statement of the position I wish to adopt.

We can see the undifferentiated Description Theory as the
expression of two thoughts.

(a) the denotation of a name is determined by what speakers
    intend to refer to by using the name.
(b) the object a speaker intends to refer to by his use of a
    name is that which satisfies or fits the majority of descrip-
    tions which make up the cluster of information which the
    speaker has associated with the name.

We have seen great difficulties with (a) when this is interpreted as a thesis at the micro level. But consideration of the
phenomenon of a name's getting a denotation, or changing it,
suggests that there being a community of speakers using the
name with such and such as the intended referent is likely to be
a crucial constituent in these processes. With names as with
other expressions in the language, what they signify depends
upon what we use them to signify; a truth whose recognition is
compatible with denying the collapse of saying into meaning at
the level of the individual speaker.

It is in (b) that the real weakness lies: the bad old Philosophy
of Mind which we momentarily uncovered. Not so much in the
idea that the intended referent is determined in a more or less
complicated way by the associated information, but the specific
form the determination was supposed to take: *fit*. There is
something absurd in supposing that the intended referent of
some perfectly ordinary use of a name by a speaker could be
some item utterly isolated (causally) from the user's community

and culture simply in virtue of the fact that it fits better than
anything else the cluster of descriptions he associates with the
name. I would agree with Kripke in thinking that the absurdity
resides in the absence of any causal relation between the item
concerned and the speaker. But it seems to me that he has
mislocated the causal relation; the important causal relation lies
between that item's states and doings and the speaker's body of
information—not between the item's being dubbed with a
name and the speaker's contemporary use of it.

Philosophers have come increasingly to realize that major
concepts in epistemology and the philosophy of mind have
causality embedded within them. Seeing and knowing are both
good examples.

The absurdity in supposing that the denotation of our contemporary use of the name 'Aristotle' could be some unknown
(n.b.) item whose doings are causally isolated from our body of
information is strictly parallel to the absurdity in supposing
that one might be seeing something one has no causal contact
with solely upon the ground that there is a splendid match between object and visual impression.

There probably is some *degree of fit* requirement in the case
of seeing which means that after some amount of distortion or
fancy we can no longer maintain that the causally operative
item was still being seen. And I think it is likely that there is a
parallel requirement for referring. We learn for example from
E. K. Chambers' *Arthur of Britain* that Arthur had a son Anir
"whom legend has perhaps confused with his burial place". If
Kripke's notion of reference fixing is such that those who said
Anir was a burial place of Arthur might be denoting a person it
seems that it has little to commend it, and is certainly not justified by the criticisms he makes against the Description
Theory. But the existence or nature of this 'degree of fit'
requirement will not be something I shall be concerned with
here.

We must allow then that the denotation of a name in the
community will depend in a complicated way upon what those
who use the term intend to refer to, but we will so understand
'intended referent' that typically a *necessary* (but not sufficient)

condition for x's being the intended referent of S's use of a name is that x should be the source of causal origin of the body of information that S has associated with the name.

II

5. The aim I have set myself, then, is modest; it is not to present a complete theory of the denotation of names. Without presenting a general theory to solve the problem of ambiguity I cannot present a theory of speaker's denotation, although I will make remarks which prejudice that issue. I propose merely to sketch an account of what makes an expression into a name for something that will allow names to change their denotations.

The enterprise is more modest yet for I propose to help myself to an undefined notion of speaker's reference by borrowing from the theory of communication. But a word of explanation.

A speaker may have succeeded in *getting it across* or in *communicating* that p even though he uses a sentence which may not appropriately be used to say that p. Presumably this success consists in his audience's having formed a belief about him. This need not be the belief that the speaker intended to say in the strict sense that p, since the speaker may succeed in getting something across despite using a sentence which he is known to know cannot appropriately be used to say that p. The speaker will have referred to a, in the sense I am helping myself to, only if he has succeeded in getting it across that Fa (for some substitution F). Further stringent conditions are required. Clearly this notion is quite different from the notion of denotation which I have been using, tied as denotation is to saying in the strict sense. One may refer to x by using a description that x does not satisfy; one may not thus denote x.

Now a speaker may know or believe that there is such-and-such an item in the world and intend to refer to it. And this is where the suggestion made earlier must be brought to bear, for *that* item is not (in general) the satisfier of the body of information the possession by the speaker of which makes it true that he knows of the existence of the item; it is rather that item which is causally responsible for the speaker's possession of that body of information, or dominantly responsible if there is more than one. (The point is of course not specific to this intention, or to intention as opposed to other psychological attitudes.) Let us then, very briefly, explore these two ideas: source and dominance.

Usually our knowledge or belief about particular items is derived from information gathering transactions, involving a causal interaction with some item or other, conducted ourselves or is derived, maybe through a long chain, from the transactions of others. Perception of the item is the main but by no means the only way an item can impress itself on us; for example, a man can be the source of things we discover by rifling through his suitcase or by reading his works.

A causal relation is of course not sufficient; but we may borrow from the theory of knowledge and say something like this. X is the source of the belief S expresses by uttering 'Fa' if there was an episode which caused S's belief in which X and S were causally related in a type of situation apt for producing knowledge that something F-s ($\exists x(Fx)$)—a type of situation in which the belief that something F-s would be caused by something's F-ing. That it is a way of producing knowledge does not mean that it cannot go wrong; that is why X, by smoking French cigarettes can be the source of the belief S expresses by 'a smokes Greek cigarettes'.

Of course some of our information about the world is not so based; we may deduce that there is a tallest man in the world and deduce that he is over 6 feet tall. No man is the source of this information; a name introduced in relation to it might function very much as the unamended Description Theory suggested.

Legend and fancy can create new characters, or add bodies of source-less material to other dossiers; restrictions on the causal relation would prevent the inventors of the legends turning out to be the sources of the beliefs their legends gave rise to. Someone other than the ϕ can be the source of the belief S expresses by 'a is the ϕ'; Kripke's Gödel, by claiming the proof, was the source of the belief people manifested by saying 'Gödel proved the incompleteness of Arithmetic', not Schmidt.

Misidentification can bring it about that the item which is the source of the information is different from the item about which the information is believed. I may form the belief about the wife of some colleague that she has nice legs upon the basis of seeing someone else—but the girl I saw is the source.

Consequently a cluster or dossier of information can be dominantly *of* [10] an item though it contains elements whose source is different. And we surely want to allow that persistent misidentification can bring it about that a cluster is dominantly of some item other than that it was dominantly of originally.

Suppose I get to know a man slightly. Suppose then a suitably primed identical twin takes over his position, and I get to know him fairly well, not noticing the switch. Immediately after the switch my dossier will still be dominantly of the original man, and I falsely believe, as I would acknowledge if it was pointed out, that *he* is in the room. Then I would pass through a period in which neither was dominant; I had not misidentified one as the other, an asymmetrical relation, but rather confused them. Finally the twin could take over the dominant position; I would not have false beliefs about who is in the room, but false beliefs about e.g., when I first met the man in the room. These differences seem to reside entirely in the differences in the believer's reactions to the various discoveries, and dominance is meant to capture those differences.

Dominance is not simply a function of *amount* of information (if that is even intelligible). In the case of persons, for example, each man's life presents a skeleton and the dominant source may be the man who contributed to covering most of it rather than the man who contributed most of the covering. Detail in a particular area can be outweighed by spread. Also the believer's reasons for being interested in the item at all will weigh.

Consider another example. If it turns out that an impersonator had taken over Napoleon's rôle from 1814 onwards (post-Elba) the cluster of the typical historian would still be domi-

---

10. The term is D. Kaplan's; see "Quantifying In" in *Words and Objections*, ed. by D. Davidson and J. Hintikka (New York: Humanities Press, 1969). I think there are clear similarities between my notion of a dominant source and notions he is there sketching. However I want nothing to do with vividness. I borrow the term "dossier" from H. P. Grice's paper "Vacuous Names" in the same volume.

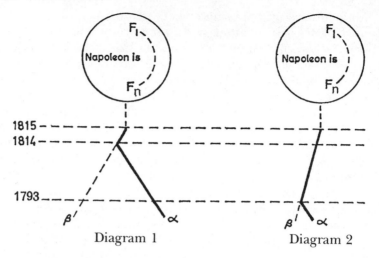

Diagram 1   Diagram 2

nantly of the man responsible for the earlier exploits (α in diagram 1) and we would say that they had false beliefs about who fought at Waterloo. If however the switch had occurred much earlier, it being an unknown Army Officer being impersonated, then their information would be dominantly of the later man (β in diagram 2). They did not have false beliefs about who was the general at Waterloo, but rather false beliefs about that general's early career.

I think we can say that *in general* a speaker intends to refer to the item that is the dominant source of his associated body of information. It is important to see that this will not change from occasion to occasion depending upon subject matter. Some have proposed [11] that if in case 1 the historian says 'Napoleon fought skilfully at Waterloo' it is the impostor β who is the intended referent, while if he had said in the next breath '. . . unlike his performance in the Senate' it would be α. This seems a mistake; not only was what the man said false, what he intended to say was false too, as he would be the first to agree; it wasn't Napoleon who fought skilfully at Waterloo.

With this background then we may offer the following tentative definition:

11. K. S. Donnellan, "Proper Names and Identifying Descriptions" in *Semantics of Natural Language,* p. 371.

'NN' is a name of x if there is a community C

1. in which it is common knowledge that members of C have in their repertoire the procedure of using 'NN' to refer to x (with the intention of referring to x)
2. the success in reference in any particular case being intended to rely on common knowledge between speaker and hearer that 'NN' has been used to refer to x by members of C and not upon common knowledge of the satisfaction by x of some predicate embedded in 'NN' [12]

(In order to keep the definition simple no attempt is made to cover the sense in which an unused institutionally-approved name is a name.)

This distinction (between use-because-(we know)-we-use-it and use upon other bases) is just what is needed to distinguish dead from live metaphors; it seems to me the only basis on which to distinguish the referential functioning of names, which may grammatically be descriptions, from that of descriptions.[13]

The definition does not have the consequence that the description 'the man we call 'NN'' is a name, for *its* success as a referential device does not rely upon common knowledge that *it* is or has been used to refer to x.

Intentions alone don't bring it about that a name gets a denotation; without the intentions being manifest there cannot be the common knowledge required for the practice.

Our conditions are more stringent than Kripke's since for him an expression becomes a name just so long as someone has dubbed something with it and thereby caused it to be in common usage. This seems little short of magical. Suppose one of a group of villagers dubbed a little girl on holiday in the vicinity 'Goldilocks' and the name caught on. However suppose that there were two identical twins the villagers totally fail to distin-

12. For the notion of "common knowledge" see D. K. Lewis, *Convention* (Cambridge: Harvard University Press, 1969), and the slightly different notion in S. Schiffer, *Meaning* (Oxford: Clarendon Press, 1972). For the notion of "a procedure in the repertoire" see H. P. Grice, "Utterer's Meaning, Sentence Meaning, Word Meaning," *Foundations of Language*, 1968. Clearly the whole enterprise owes much to Grice but no commitment is here made to any specific version of the theory of communication.
13. And if Schiffer is right much more as well—see *Meaning*, chap. V.

guish. I should deny that 'Goldilocks' is the name of either— even if by some miracle each villager used the name consistently but in no sense did they fall into two coherent sub-communities. (The name might denote the girl first dubbed if for some peculiar reason the villagers were deferential to the introducer of the name—of this more below.)

Consider the following case. An urn is discovered in the Dead Sea containing documents on which are found fascinating mathematical proofs. Inscribed at the bottom is the name 'Ibn Khan' which is quite naturally taken to be the name of the constructor of the proofs. Consequently it passes into common usage amongst mathematicians concerned with that branch of mathematics. 'Khan conjectured here that . . .' and the like. However suppose the name was the name of the scribe who had transcribed the proofs much later; a small '*id scripsit*' had been obliterated.

Here is a perfect case where there is a coherent community using the name with the mathematician as the intended referent and a consequence of the definition would be that 'Ibn Khan' would be one of his names. Also, 'Malachai' would have been the name of the author of the Biblical work of the same name despite that its use was based upon a misapprehension ('Malachai' means my messenger).[14]

Speakers within such traditions use names under the misapprehension that their use is in conformity with the use of other speakers referring to the relevant item. The names would probably be withdrawn when that misapprehension is revealed, or start a rather different life as "our" names for the items (cf., 'Deutero Isaiah' etc.). One might be impressed by this, and regard it as a reason for denying that those within these traditions spoke the literal truth in using the names. It is very easy to add a codicil to the definition which would have this effect.

Actually it is not a very good reason for denying that speakers within such traditions are speaking the literal truth.[15]

14. See Otto Eissfeldt, *The Old Testament* (New York: Harper and Row, 1965), p. 441.

15. John McDowell has persuaded me of this, as of much else. He detests my conclusions.

But I do not want to insist upon any decision upon this point. This is because one can be concessive and allow the definition to be amended without giving up anything of importance. First: the definition with its codicil will still allow many names to change their denotation. Secondly: it obviously fails to follow from the fact that, in our example, the community of mathematicians were not denoting the mathematician that they were denoting the scribe and were engaged in strictly speaking massive falsehood of him.

Let me elaborate the first of these points.

There is a fairly standard way in which people get their names. If we use a name of a man we expect that it originated in the standard manner and this expectation may condition our use of it. But consider names for people which are obviously nicknames, or names for places or pieces of music. Since there is no standard way in which these names are bestowed subsequent users will not in general use the name under any view as to its origin, and therefore when there is a divergence between the item involved in the name's origin and the speakers' intended referent there will be no *mis*apprehension, no latent motive for withdrawing the name, and thus no bar to the name's acquiring a new denotation even by the amended definition. So long as they have no reason to believe that the name has dragged any information with it, speakers will treat the revelation that the name had once been used to refer to something different with the same sort of indifference as that with which they greet the information that 'meat' once meant groceries in general.

We can easily tell the story in case 2 of our Napoleon diagram so that α was the original bearer of the name 'Napoleon' and it was transferred to the counterfeit because of the similarity of their appearances and therefore without the intention on anyone's part to initiate a new practice. Though this is not such a clear case I should probably say that historians have used the name 'Napoleon' to refer to B. They might perhaps abandon it, but that of course fails to show that they were all along denoting α. Nor does the fact that someone in the know might come along and say 'Napoleon was a fish salesman and was never at

Waterloo' show anything. The relevant question is: 'Does this contradict the assertion that was made when the historians said "Napoleon was at Waterloo"?' To give an affirmative answer to this question requires the prior determination that they have all along been denoting α.

We need one further and major complication. Although standardly we use expressions with the intention of conforming with the general use made of them by the community, sometimes we use them with the *over-riding* intention to conform to the use made of them by some other person or persons. In that case I shall say that we use the expression *deferentially* (with respect to that other person or group of persons). This is true of some general terms too: "viol", "minuet" would be examples.

I should say, for example, that the man in the conversation in the pub used 'Louis' deferentially. This is not just a matter of his ignorance; he could, indeed, have an opinion as to who this Louis is (the man he met earlier perhaps) but still use the expression deferentially. There is an important gap between

intending to refer to the ϕ and believing that $a = $ the ϕ

intending to refer to a

for even when he has an opinion as to whom they are talking about I should say that it was the man they were talking about, and not the man he met earlier, that he intended to refer to.

Archaeologists might find a tomb in the desert and claim falsely that it is the burial place of some little known character in the Bible. They could discover a great deal about the man in the tomb so that he and not the character in the Bible was the dominant source of their information. But, given the nature and point of their enterprise, the archaeologists are using the name deferentially to the authors of the Bible. I should say, then, that they denote that man, and say false things about him. Notice that in such a case there is some point to this characterization.

The case is in fact no different with any situation in which a name is used with the over-riding intention of referring to something satisfying such and such a description. Kripke gives the example of 'Jack the Ripper'. Again, after the arrest of a man a not in fact responsible for the crimes, a can be the dominant source of speakers' information but the intended referent could well be the murderer and not *a*. Again this will be productive of a whole lot of falsehood.

We do not use all names deferentially, least of all deferentially to the person from whom we picked them up. For example the mathematicians did not use the name 'Ibn Khan' with the *over-riding* intention of referring to whoever bore that name or was referred to by some other person or community.

We must thus be careful to distinguish two reasons for something that would count as "withdrawing sentences containing the name"

(a) the item's not bearing the name 'NN' ('Ibn Khan', 'Malachai')

(b) the item's not being NN (the biblical archaeologists).

I shall end with an example that enables me to draw these threads together and summarize where my position differs from the Causal Theory.

A youth *A* leaves a small village in the Scottish highlands to seek his fortune having acquired the nackname 'Turnip' (the reason for choosing a nickname is I hope clear). Fifty or so years later a man *B* comes to the village and lives as a hermit over the hill. The three or four villagers surviving from the time of the youth's departure believe falsely that this is the long departed villager returned. Consequently they use the name 'Turnip' among themselves and it gets into wider circulation among the younger villagers who have no idea how it originated. I am assuming that the older villagers, if the facts were pointed out, would say: 'It isn't Turnip after all' rather than 'It appears after all that Turnip did not come from this village'. In that case I should say that they use the name to refer to *A,* and in fact, denoting him, say false things about him (even by uttering 'Here is Turnip coming to get his coffee again').

But they may die off, leaving a homogeneous community using the name to refer to the man over the hill. I should say the way is clear to its becoming his name. The story is not much affected if the older villagers pass on some information whose source is *A* by saying such things as 'Turnip was quite a one for the girls', for the younger villagers' clusters would still be dominantly of the man over the hill. But it is an important feature of my account that the information that the older villagers gave the younger villagers could be so rich, coherent and important to them that A could be the dominant source of their information, so that they too would acknowledge 'That man over the hill isn't Turnip after all'.

A final possibility would be if they used the name deferentially towards the older villagers, for some reason, with the consequence that no matter who was dominant they denote whoever the elders denote.

6. *Conclusion.* Espousers of both theories could reasonably claim to be vindicated by the position we have arrived at. We have secured for the Description Theorist much that he wanted. We have seen for at least the most fundamental case of the use of names (non-deferentially used names) the idea that their denotation is fixed in a more or less complicated way by the associated bodies of information that one could cull from the users of the name turns out not to be so wide of the mark. But of course that the fix is by causal origin and not by fit crucially affects the impact this idea has upon the statement of the truth conditions of existential or opaque sentences containing names. The theorist can also point to the idea of dominance as securing what he was trying, admittedly crudely, to secure with his talk of the 'majority of' the descriptions, and to the "degree of fit requirement" as blocking consequences he found objectionable.

The Causal Theorist can also look with satisfaction upon the result, incorporating as it does his insight about the importance of causality into a central position. Further, the logical doctrines he was concerned to establish, for example the non-contingency of identity statements made with the use of names, are not controverted. Information is individuated by source; if a is the source of a body of information nothing else could have been. Consequently nothing else could have been *that a*.

The only theorists who gain no comfort are those who, ignoring Kripke's explicit remarks to the contrary,[16] supposed that

16. "Naming and Necessity," p. 302.

the Causal Theory could provide them with a totally *non-intentional* answer to the problem posed by names. But I am not distressed by their distress.

Our ideas also point forwards; for it seems that they, or some close relative, must be used in explaining the functioning of at least some demonstratives. Such an expression as 'That mountaineer' in 'That mountaineer is coming to town tonight' may advert to a body of information presumed in common possession, perhaps through the newspapers, which fixes its denotation. No one can be *that* mountaineer unless he is the source of that information no matter how perfectly he fits it, and of course someone can be that mountaineer and fail to fit quite a bit of it. It is in such generality that defense of our ideas must lie.

But with these hints I must leave the subject.

9 Speaking of Nothing [1]

KEITH S. DONNELLAN

Russell tells us in "On Denoting" to test our logical theories by their "capacity for dealing with puzzles." [2] In this paper I raise the question of how a theory of reference, one of recent origin, might handle one of the major puzzles Russell mentioned. The theory of reference that I have in mind—and one I subscribe to—I will call "the historical explanation theory." (It, or ones similar to it in important respects, has also been called the "causal theory." For various reasons, I prefer a different title.[3])

Among a number of puzzles mentioned by Russell, two stand out as more important than the others. One is the well-known problem of identity statements with which Frege begins his article, "On Sense and Reference," [4] the question of how a statement of the form "*a* is identical to *b*," when true, can differ in "cognitive value" from a corresponding statement of the apparently trivial form, "*a* is identical to *a*," The second puzzle is the topic of this paper. In a large number of situations speakers apparently refer to the nonexistent. The most obvious example

Reprinted from *The Philosophical Review*, LXXXIII (January, 1974), 3–32, by permission of the author and editors.

1. Earlier versions of this paper were read at a number of meetings and colloquia and several important changes have resulted from those discussions. I am particularly grateful for detailed comments by Tyler Burge.

2. Reprinted in *Logic and Knowledge*, ed. by R. C. Marsh (London: George Allen and Unwin, 1956), p. 47.

3. Why I am reluctant to use the word "causal" may become somewhat clearer further on, but the main reason is that I want to avoid a seeming commitment to all the links in the referential chain being causal.

4. *Translations from the Philosophical Writings of Gottlob Frege*, ed. by Peter Geach and Max Black (Oxford: Blackwell, 1960).

of this is, perhaps, the use of singular terms in negative existence statements—for example, "The discoverer of the philosopher's stone does not exist" or "Robin Hood did not exist." The
problem is, of course, well known and ancient in origin: such
statements seem to refer to something only to say about it that
it does not exist. How can one say something about what does
not exist? For a few philosophers, to be sure, these questions
have led to attempts to provide the referent. But in general
such attempts have been met with suspicion. Russell certainly
thought it a merit of his theory of definite descriptions (and his
fully developed views on singular expressions) that such apparent references to the nonexistent were explained without having to entertain the idea of referents of singular terms that are
nonexistent.

Where the singular terms involved are definite descriptions,
"On Denoting" provided a solution to the two puzzles mentioned that was at once a break-through in the treatment of
these expressions and satisfying in the coherent explanation it
gave. Russell's fully developed theory of singular terms, perhaps best represented in "Lectures on Logical Atomism," [5] extends the proposed solution to ordinary proper names, for
these turn out to be concealed definite descriptions. The view
of "On Denoting" now could be made to cover most of the uses
of singular terms in language as we actually speak it and, moreover, seemed to meet the test of solving the various puzzles
about reference. But the fully developed view also introduced a
category of singular expressions that were acknowledged to be
rarely, if ever, found in everyday speech—what Russell called
names in "the strict logical sense" or "genuine" names.

Genuine names and the motivation for giving pride of place
to such exotic singular terms have special interest for the historical explanation theory, because while its treatment of ordinary singular expressions is radically different from Russell's it
has some similarities to his characterization of genuine names.

The question posed, then, is how the historical explanation
theory of reference can handle the puzzle that Russell's view

5. Reprinted in *Logic and Knowledge.*

has no difficulty with, the problem of apparent reference to the nonexistent.

I cannot in this paper plead the full case for the historical explanation theory, though I shall try to give its main features; so it may be best to consider it an exercise in the hypothetical: *if* the theory is correct what follows concerning apparent reference to the nonexistent? [6]

I. Three Kinds of Apparent Reference to the Nonexistent

We need to keep distinct three situations in which apparent reference to the nonexistent occurs. The differences are important in their own right, but I need to call attention to them because one kind of situation will be excluded from consideration in this paper.

I will, in the first place, distinguish what I will call "discourse about fiction" from "discourse about actuality"; and, secondly, within the latter category, the use of "predicative" statements from the use of "existence" statements.[7] What is to be excluded from consideration here is an account of discourse about fiction. (This is not, of course, to say that such an account is not in the end needed.)

Under "discourse about fiction" I mean to include those occasions on which it is a presupposition of the discourse that fictional, mythological, legendary (and so forth) persons, places, or things are under discussion. I believe, for example, that said with the right intention, the following sentences would express

6. If we divide the theory into its negative aspects (see sec. III) and its positive (see sec. IV), what the theory denies and the reasons for doing so have been, perhaps, better delineated in the literature than the content of the positive theory. (This is certainly true of my own contributions.) My papers dealing with various parts of the theory as I see it are: "Reference and Definite Descriptions," *Philosophical Review*, LXXV (1966), 281–304; "Putting Humpty Dumpty Together Again," *Philosophical Review*, LXXVII (1968), 203–215; "Proper Names and Identifying Descriptions," *Synthese* (1970), reprinted in *Semantics of Natural Language*, ed. by D. Davidson and G. Harman (Dordrecht: D. Reidel, 1972). By others, Saul Kripke's paper, "Naming and Necessity," in *Semantics of Natural Language*, is the most important in that it gives not only arguments for the negative aspects of the theory, but also a positive account (that, however, I do not altogether agree with).

7. The terminology, of course, is for convenience and not supposed to reflect a prejudgment that existence cannot be in some sense a genuine predicate.

true propositions: "The Green Hornet's car was called 'Black Beauty,' " "Snow White lived with seven dwarves," and "To reach the underworld, one must first cross the River Styx." (By the "right intention" I mean that the speaker wishes to be taken as talking about fiction, mythology, or legend.) At the same time I also believe it is true that neither the Green Hornet, his car, Snow White, nor the River Styx exists or ever has existed. These two beliefs, however, are entirely consistent. And therein lies the puzzle: how can there be true propositions that apparently involve predicating properties of what does not exist?

Discourse about actuality carries the presupposition that the speaker is talking about people, places, or things that occur in the history of our world. A puzzle arises when the speaker is unfortunate enough to use a singular expression, intending to attribute a property to something, but fails, in his use of that expression, to refer to any thing. This very likely occurred, for example, some years ago following the publication of *The Horn Papers*,[8] that purported to contain the diary of one Jacob Horn and that would, if genuine, have shed light on the colonial history of Washington County, Pennsylvania. Many people believed them to be genuine, but, on the evidence, it seems likely that they are not and that Jacob Horn did not exist. There must have been many believers, however, who made statements using the name "Jacob Horn" with the intention of predicating various properties of a historical figure. For example, someone might well have said, "Jacob Horn wrote about Augusta Town and now we know where it was located." It would have been some sort of inconsistency—exactly what kind is another question—for such a speaker then to affirm the nonexistence of Jacob Horn. This contrasts with discourse about fiction—there one can, for example, consistently deny the existence of Snow White while also stating that she enraptured a prince.[9]

8. See Middleton and Adair, "The Mystery of the Horn Papers," *William and Mary Quarterly*, 3rd series, IV (1947); reprinted in *The Historian as Detective*, ed. by Robin W. Winks (New York: Harper and Row, 1969).

9. The denial of Snow White's existence, it should be noted, is in discourse about actuality, while the statement that she enraptured a prince is in discourse about fiction. (If the question of existence arose in discourse about fiction alone, Snow White existed, whereas Hamlet's father's ghost, again presuming

The puzzle about predicative statements, as I shall call them, in discourse about actuality with a singular expression and no referent is more subtle philosophically than the puzzle about fictional discourse. There is not the same possibility of stating something true. Nor can the speaker with consistency acknowledge the nonexistence of what he speaks about. To see how statements such as those made by believers in the authenticity of *The Horn Papers* can puzzle a philosopher requires the ability to see a difficulty in how one can even speak and be *understood* when using a singular expression with no referent.

The difference between discourse about fiction and discourse about reality, it is important to keep in mind, is a matter of presuppositions about the intent of the speech act. It is not that in the one fictional characters are involved and in the other real people, places, and things. A not too well-informed person might have taken (at least the first part of) the movie *Doctor Strangelove* for a documentary. His statement, "Doctor Strangelove, the top military scientist in the United States, is a psychopath," would then be a bit of discourse about reality, even though Doctor Strangelove is, in fact, fictional. On the other hand, this very same sentence used by someone having seen the whole movie would probably be a comment on the movie, a bit of discourse about fiction.

While I will need often to consider predicative statements about actuality, the problem I want to concentrate on concerns "existence" statements—those that have either the form "*S* does not exist" or the form "*S* exists," where "*S*" is a singular expression. Negative existence statements, unlike predicative statements, are true when there is no referent for the singular expression. If I speak the truth in saying, "Jacob Horn does not exist," I would be apparently referring to what does not exist. But even more paradoxically, the truth of what I say depends directly upon the nonexistence of a referent for "Jacob Horn." Moreover, this is discourse about reality; I do not, clearly, in-

---

we are talking about fiction, probably did not.) This does not disturb the point: no such contrast can be made out for Jacob Horn; if Jacob Horn did not exist there are no true predicative statements to be made about him.

tend to talk about a fictional character. Negative existence statements, of all those mentioned, bring apparent reference to the nonexistent into sharpest focus.

It is of some importance to mention the difference between denying the existence of something altogether and denying its present existence or its existence at some point or during some period in time. To begin with we certainly want to distinguish between

(1) Napoleon no longer exists,

and

(2) Napoleon does not and never did exist.

The first statement is both true and not an apparent reference to the nonexistent in the sense we want. (1) contains a reference to Napoleon in the same way that "Socrates was snub-nosed" contains a reference to Socrates. (1) should, it seems, be put into the class of predicative statements, despite the fact that existence is involved. On the other hand, (2) is a paradigm of the kind of statement that generates the problem of apparent reference to the nonexistent.

What shall we say, however, about a statement such as

(3) Santa Claus does not exist?

Often, I believe, it expresses a statement of the same form as (2), an absolute denial of existence, not confined to any one period in time. But suppose, for example, that someone is unsure whether Jacob Horn ever did exist, but is certain that he does not now exist. He might express this by saying, "Jacob Horn does not exist." So, perhaps, sentences of the surface form of (3) are ambiguous. But what is the other meaning that they might have? The sentence given, in the imagined circumstances, seems to me to be equivalent to

(4) Jacob Horn does not now exist.

This is neither the absolute denial of Jacob Horn's existence nor the predicative assertion that Jacob Horn no longer exists. (4), I believe, amounts to the disjunction of the two: "Either Jacob Horn does not and never did exist or he did exist and does no longer." In which case, the dichotomy illustrated by (1) and (2) is still maintained. In what follows, however, it is the absolute denial of existence that will be of concern and any examples of the form "*N* does not exist" should be construed in that way.

II. A Theory Gone Wrong With Interesting Motives—Russell

Russell's theory of singular terms holds interest for the historical explanation theory, not only because of obvious oppositions on some key issues—several more recent discussions would serve that purpose [10]—but also because certain problems and issues that evidently motivated features of Russell's theory that are nowadays generally ignored or thought obviously wrong are brought to the fore once again by the historical explanation theory. I believe that much of Russell's theory has been accepted by many philosophers with the thought that there was a certain excrescence that could be ignored. Russell's views on ordinary singular terms, definite descriptions, proper names in ordinary language have wide acceptance; his addition of "genuine" names to the ranks has generally been ignored as so much metaphysical meandering. I think there is no doubt that "genuine" names, as Russell characterized them, have no place in a correct theory of reference. But from the first, in "on Denoting," Russell contrasted his account of those singular terms for which his theory provided a way out of puzzles about reference with another kind of singular term, a "genuine" name, for which he seemed to feel there was a theoretical need. But, of course, "genuine" names, if they were to be included in the general theory, could not reintroduce the same puzzles. This, I think, accounts for some of the peculiar properties attributed to "genuine" names: for example, the distinction between "knowledge by acquaintance" and "knowledge by description" that gave the result that we could only genuinely name something we are acquainted with in a very strong sense seems to have been introduced in part to make it impossible to assert negative existence statements using "genuine" names.

The reason this has interest for the historical explanation theory is that Russell's contrast, the radical difference between

10. E.g., J. Searle, "Proper Names," *Mind,* LXVII (1958), and *Speech Acts* (Cambridge: Cambridge University Press, 1968), chap. IV.

most singular terms in ordinary language and "genuine" names, is that the former have descriptive content and the latter do not. Given his view of singular terms with descriptive content, the puzzles about reference yield easily for them. He felt, however, some need to have singular expressions, nonetheless, that do not function in accord with his analysis of definite descriptions and ordinary proper names. The historical explanation theory denies that, for at least many uses of ordinary singular expressions, Russell's view is correct. In particular, it denies that ordinary proper names always have descriptive content. The question is, does this mean that perhaps ordinary singular expressions may fulfill the function that Russell thought only "genuine" names, with all their peculiarities, could? And, if so, how can the historical explanation view deal with the puzzles about reference?

What was the motivation for introducing "genuine" names? Russell often talks in ways that can seem nonsensical—that, for example, when a definite description such as "the author of *Waverly*" is involved, the denotation of the definite description, Scott in this case, is not a "constituent" of the proposition expressed. The implied contrast is that if "Scott" is a genuine name and were there in place of the definite description "the author of *Waverly*" then Scott would be a constituent. But it certainly sounds queer at first glance to find a flesh-and-blood person in a proposition!

Russell's analysis of statements containing definite descriptions and, by extension, ordinary proper names, shows, he believed, that such statements are not really *about,* do not really *mention,* the denotation of the description or the referent of the name. Russell emphasizes this again and again. "Genuine" names, on the other hand, can somehow perform the feat of really mentioning a particular individual. To try to put much weight on such terms as "about" would lead us, I think, into a morass. What it is for a statement to be *about* an individual, if that requires any attempt to define *aboutness,* is a question better avoided if we are ever to get on with the problem. (After all, Russell himself recognized a well-defined relationship that a statement containing a definite description can have to some particular individual—its denotation. It would be a delicate task to show either that in no sense of "about" is such a statement *about* the denotation of the definite description or that there is some clear sense of "about" in which it is not.)

But I believe we can say something useful about the reasons Russell had for talking in this way. On his theory of definite descriptions the singular expression, the definite description, is really a device that introduces quantifiers and converts what might seem at first sight a simple proposition about an individual into a general proposition. "The ϕ is ψ" expresses the same proposition as "There is a ϕ and there is at most one ϕ and all ϕ's are ψ's"; and the latter clearly would express a general proposition about the world. Ordinary proper names, of course, function on his view in the same way, since they are in reality concealed definite descriptions. Now if we contrast these singular expressions with ones, if there are any, that do not introduce quantifiers, that when put as the subject of a simple subject-predicate sentence do not make the sentence express a general proposition, then I think there is a strong temptation to say that only the second kind of singular term can be used to really mention an individual.

Russell clearly believed that there must be the possibility, at least, of singular terms that do not introduce quantifiers; that seems in large part to be his reason for believing in "genuine" names. Whether or not there is some argument that shows the necessity of such singular terms, I believe that prior to theory the natural view is that they occur often in ordinary speech. So if one says, for example, "Socrates is snub-nosed," the natural view seems to me to be that the singular expression "Socrates" is simply a device used by the speaker to pick out what he wants to talk about while the rest of the sentence expresses what property he wishes to attribute to that individual. This can be made somewhat more precise by saying, first, that the natural view is that in using such simple sentences containing singular terms we are not saying something general about the world— that is, not saying something that would be correctly analyzed with the aid of quantifiers; and, second, that in such cases the speaker could, in all probability, have said the same thing, expressed the same proposition, with the aid of other and different singular expressions, so long as they are being used to refer to the same individual. To illustrate the latter point with a different example: if, at the same moment in time, one person were to say, "Smith is happy," a second "You are happy," a third "My son is happy," and a fourth "I am happy," and if in each case the singular expression refers to the same person, then all four have expressed the same proposition, have agreed with each other.

What I see as the natural pre-theoretical view might be captured as a certain way of representing what proposition is expressed. For example, the sentence "Socrates is snub-nosed" might be represented as an ordered pair consisting of Socrates—the actual man, of course, not his name—and the predicate (or property, perhaps), being snub-nosed. (More complicated sentences, involving relations and more than one singular expression of this sort would be represented as ordered triplets, and so forth.) Now if someone were to say to Socrates, "You are snub-nosed," or Socrates were to say about himself, "I am snub-nosed," the proposition expressed would, in each case, be represented by the same ordered pair—propositional identity, given the same predicate, would be a function simply of what individual is referred to.

This way of representing propositions would, I think, meet with at least provisional approval by Russell, but only if it were restricted to those propositions expressed by statements containing "genuine" names. We might even say that the manner of representation gives a respectable sense in which an individual might be a constituent of a proposition. But my examples of statements for which this representation was suggested would, on Russell's view, be incorrect just because they involve singular terms from ordinary language. For Russell, they would be examples of sentences that express complex general propositions and, whatever our view of the nature of propositions, I do not think we would want propositional identity for general propositions to be a function of the individuals that happen to make the propositions true or false.

Russell pays the price, I believe, of giving up the natural view of many uses of ordinary singular terms, a price he is willing to pay—chiefly, perhaps, because he thus can dissolve puzzles about reference. The special properties of "genuine" names, on the other hand, are supposed to rescue them. The "natural" view, on the other hand, seems to generate Russell's budget of puzzles, in particular the one which is the concern of this paper. If I say, "Socrates is snub-nosed," the proposition I express is represented as containing Socrates. If I say, instead, "Jacob Horn does not exist," the "natural" view seems to lead to the unwonted conclusion that even if what I say is true, Jacob Horn, though nonexistent, must have some reality. Else what proposition am I expressing? The "natural" view thus seems to land us with the Meinongian population explosion.

Russell, of course, avoids this problem easily. Since the proper name "Jacob Horn" would, for him, be a concealed definite description, to say "Jacob Horn does not exist" is not to refer to some individual in order to say something about him, but merely to assert that a particular class of things, perhaps the class of writers of diaries about certain events in early Pennsylvania history, is either empty or contains more than one member. (So a singular nonexistence statement of this kind is on all fours with statements such as "There are no flying horses" or "There is more than one living ex-President." It does not mention a particular individual any more than these do.)

The issue has importance for the historical explanation view because it denies that many singular terms in ordinary language, in particular proper names, are concealed descriptions of the sort that Russell had in mind. "Homer," for example, is not a concealed description such as "the author of the Homeric Poems," to use Russell's own example. The question is, does the historical explanation view, if correct, support what I have called the "natural" view? In the next section this question will be considered.

III. The Historical Explanation View: Negative Aspect

I now want to begin to lay out the bare bones of the theory of reference I want to discuss. As I have said, I will not here argue for its correctness nor will I try to fill in all the gaps.

Russell and the majority of philosophers in contemporary times who have discussed (ordinary) proper names have held that by one mechanism or another they are surrogates for descriptions. For Russell, as I have mentioned, they are simply abbreviations for definite descriptions; for others—for example, Searle [11]—they are correlated with a set of descriptions and what one is saying in, say, a simple subject-predicate sentence employing a proper name is that whatever best fits these descriptions has whatever property is designated by the predicate. The descriptions, both on Russell's view and on the looser view of Searle and others, which the proper name masks, are thought of as obtained from the people who use them— roughly speaking, by what they would answer to the question, "To whom (what) are you referring?" This view of ordinary proper names embodies what I have called the "principle of identifying descriptions." [12] The theory of reference I am concerned with holds that the principle of identifying descriptions is false.

What this means, to give an example, is that, supposing you could obtain from me a set of descriptions of who it is that I believe myself to refer to when I say, "Socrates was snub-nosed"—perhaps such things as "the mentor of Plato," "the inventor of the 'Socratic method,' " "the philosopher who drank the hemlock," and so forth—it is theoretically possible that I am referring to something about which no substantial number of these descriptions is true or that although there is something that fits these descriptions to whatever extent is required by the particular variation of the principle, that is not in fact the referent of the name I used.

On this theory, then, ordinary proper names are like Russell's "genuine" names at least in so far as they do not conceal descriptions in the way he thought. This is, I think, a virtue of the theory. As David Kaplan has remarked, there was always something implausible about the idea that a referent of a

11. See references in fn. 10.
12. In "Proper Names and Identifying Descriptions."

proper name is determined by the currently associated descriptions.

IV. The Historical Explanation Theory: Positive Aspect

The first tenet of the theory of reference I have been describing was negative—the view that proper names must have a backing of descriptions that serves to pick out their referents is false. The second tenet is positive, but more tentative. How is the referent of a proper name, then, to be determined? On Russell's view and variants on it, the answer to this question would be simple: the referent is that which fits the associated descriptions best, where "best" may be defined differently by different writers. As I see it, one of the main reasons a backing of descriptions for proper names is so attractive is that it furnishes a simple way of ascertaining what a speaker is saying, and of determining whether what he says is true or false (given that we are dealing only with assertions). We find, so to speak, that thing in the world which uniquely fits the descriptions and then see whether or not it has the properties ascribed to it. If proper names do not have a backing of descriptions, how do we decide whether or not, when someone says, for example, "Russell wrote 'On Denoting,' " he has said something true or false?

Putting existence statements aside, when a speaker says something of the form, "N is ϕ," where "N" is a name and "ϕ" a predicate, we can say that in general the truth conditions will have the following form. What the speaker has said will be true if and only if (a) there is some entity related in the appropriate way to his use of "N" in this sentence—that is, he has referred to some entity, and (b) that entity has the property designated by ϕ. (I say "in general" because there are difficulties for any theory of reference about uses of names for fictional characters, "formal" objects such as numbers, and so forth.) The question is, what is the "appropriate relation" mentioned in condition (a)? How, that is, does an entity have to be related to the speaker's use of the name "N" to be its referent? The principle of identifying descriptions, were it only true, has a simple answer to this: the entity must have (uniquely) the properties or some sufficient number of the properties designated by the "backing of descriptions" for this use of the name "*N*." Roughly speaking, and on the most usual view, it will be the entity that answers to the descriptions the speaker would (ideally) give in answer to the question, "To whom are you referring?"

But even without the arguments that, I believe, show the principle of identifying descriptions not only false, but implausible, putting the matter in this general way is somewhat liberating. It shows that what we need is *some* relation between the speech act involving the name "*N*" and an object in the world— the right one, of course—but the relation supplied by the principle of identifying descriptions is now only a candidate for that office.

But if the principle of identifying descriptions is false, what then is the appropriate relation between an act of using a name and some object such that the name was used to refer to that object? The theory of reference I want to discuss has not as yet, so far as I know, been developed in such a way as to give a completely detailed answer. Yet there are positive things that can be said and enough, I believe, both to contrast it with the principle of identifying descriptions and to give us something like an answer to the original question: how will it handle apparent reference to the nonexistent in such statements as "Santa Claus does not exist"?

The main idea is that when a speaker uses a name intending to refer to an individual and predicate something of it, successful reference will occur when there is an individual that enters into the historically correct explanation of who it is that the speaker intended to predicate something of. That individual will then be the referent and the statement made will be true or false depending upon whether it has the property designated by the predicate. This statement of the positive thesis leaves a lot to be desired in the way of precision, yet with some clarifying remarks I think it has more content than might at first sight be supposed.

Suppose someone says, "Socrates was snub-nosed," and we ask to whom he is referring. The central idea is that this calls for a historical explanation; we search not for an individual

who might best fit the speaker's descriptions of the individual
to whom he takes himself to be referring (though his descriptions are usually important data), but rather for an individual
historically related to his use of the name "Socrates" on this occasion. It might be that an omniscient observer of history
would see an individual related to an author of dialogues, that
one of the central characters of these dialogues was modeled
upon that individual, that these dialogues have been handed
down and that the speaker has read translations of them, that
the speaker's now predicating snub-nosedness of something is
explained by his having read those translations. This is the sort
of account that I have in mind by a "historical explanation."

Several comments are in order here. First, it is not necessary,
of course, that the individual in question be snub-nosed; obviously the speaker may have asserted something false about
the referent of the name "Socrates." Second, if we take the set
of descriptions the speaker could give were we to ask him to
whom he was referring, the historical explanation as seen by
our omniscient observer may pick out an individual as the referent of the name "Socrates" even though that individual is not
correctly described by the speaker's attempt at identification.
For example, the speaker may believe that Socrates—that is,
the person he refers to—was a philosopher who invented the
Socratic method. But it is clearly imaginable that our omniscient observer sees that while the author of the dialogues did
intend one of the characters to be taken as a portrayal of a real
person, he modestly attributed to him a method that was his
own brain child. And, in general, it would be possible to have
the historical connection with no end to mistaken descriptions
in the head of the speaker. The descriptions the speaker gives,
however, may play an important role, though not the one given
to them by the principle of identifying descriptions. The omniscient observer may see, for example, that the reason the
speaker believes himself to be referring to someone who invented a certain philosophical method is that his present use of
the name "Socrates" is connected with his having read certain
translations of these dialogues. Or, to take a slightly different
case, he may see that his descriptions come from a faulty mem-

ory of those dialogues, and so forth. The question for the omniscient observer is "What individual, if any, would the speaker describe in this way even if perhaps mistakenly?"

I have used the notion of an omniscient observer of history and, of course, we ordinary people cannot be expected to know in detail the history behind the uses of names by those with whom we converse. Nor do we often make the sort of historical inquiries which would reveal those details. We often assume, for example, that if another speaker's descriptions of the referent of a name he has used more or less jibe with descriptions we would give of a person, place, or thing that we believe ourselves to know about, then he is referring to that. Also, for example, the context of the use of a name may lead us to assume without question that the speaker refers to someone with whom we are both acquainted. But the historical explanation theory need not deny this or be troubled by it. All it needs to hold is that the *final* test for reference is the kind of historical connection I have described, that the customary assumptions and use of indicators are in the end dependent upon being fairly reliable guides to the existence of such a connection.

What the historical explanation theory must attempt to establish is that when there is an absence of historical connection between an individual and the use of a name by a speaker, then, be the speaker's descriptions ever so correct about a certain individual, that individual is not the referent; and, on the other hand, that a certain historical connection between the use of a name and an individual can make the individual the referent even though the speaker's descriptions would not by themselves single out the individual. This job must be accomplished by building up examples in which these two points are made obvious. We might, for instance, try to show that the historical connection is necessary by constructing a situation in which, for instance, one person begins by assuming that another is referring to a friend of his, perhaps because the descriptions seem accurate, the context is appropriate, and so forth, and who then discovers that it is practically impossible for the speaker to have been acquainted with or otherwise related to his friend. In such an event, surely confidence that the speaker was referring to the friend would be shaken despite the apparent accuracy of description or appropriateness of context. But, as I have said, I cannot here undertake the full defense of the historical explanation theory.

There are, however, two further points of clarification that ought to be mentioned here. It should be obvious that I have only provided an example of what counts as a historical explanation rather than a formula for obtaining the referent of a particular use of a name. Even in the illustration several individuals entered into the account, only one of which was the referent. Of the individuals who are in some way or other part of the historical explanation of a use of a name, which is the referent? What kind of theory is this if it does not give us the means to make this determination?

In defense against this charge that the theory is excessively vague, it is helpful, I think, to compare it with another philosophical theory about a quite different problem. The causal theory of perception can be taken as holding that an observer, O, perceives an object, M, only if M causes O to have sense impressions. The theory seems to me to have content and to be important, whether or not it is correct. For one thing, if true it means that certain other theories are mistaken. But the theory as stated does not, obviously, allow us to say which among the various causal factors involved in an observer having sense impressions is the thing he perceives; nor does it tell us which ways of causing sense impressions are relevant. Possibly no philosophical analysis can determine this, although in any particular case we may be able to say that this is or is not the right sort of causal connection. Analogously, the historical explanation theory lacks this sort of specificity. But for all that, if it is true, certain other theories, in particular the identifying descriptions theory, will be wrong and the theory does tell us something of importance.

Because there have sometimes been misunderstandings about this, I think I should point out that the history to which the historical explanation theory alludes is not the history of the use of a name. It is not the history of the use of, say, the name "Socrates" that is important. Socrates may not have been, as far as theory goes, called "Socrates"; corruption of names is just as possible as corruption of information. (The history of such a corruption, however, *might* enter into the historical explanation.) Nor, I think, should the theory be construed as holding that the historical connections end with some original "dubbing" of the referent. It may be that people, places, and things usually receive names by some such ceremony and that we generally use names (or corruptions of them) as a result of such a ceremony, but it is not a theoretical necessity that names enter our linguistic transactions in this way.[13]

What the historical explanation does, then, is to provide the relationship between the use of a referring expression and the referent which the principle of identifying descriptions presupposes could be provided only by some measure of correct descriptions of the referent known to the speaker. I think there are counterexamples to the principle of identifying descriptions [14] and, of course, if there *are* that defeats it straight off. Still a plausible, if not clearly correct, alternative theory in this case also acts as an objection. For one of the principle reasons that many philosophers have for adopting the principle of identifying descriptions is that they cannot see how there *could* be an appropriate relation otherwise that would pick out the referent of (as the main example) a proper name.

I have, in describing this theory of reference, talked about a "historical explanation." I hope it is obvious that "historical" is being used in the broadest sense possible; that all of what I have said could just as well be applied to cases in which one refers, by use of a name, say, to someone still extant, to someone who has just gone out of the room, or to someone pres-

13. That is to say, the first use of a name to refer to some particular individual might be in an assertion about him, rather than any ceremony of giving the individual that name. (In fact, my own name is an example: I discovered that colleagues were pronouncing my last name differently than my parents do—so, orally, they referred to me by a different name—and I let it stand. But I was never dubbed by that new name. I am sure that the first use of it was either an assertion, question, or whatever about me and not a kind of baptism. And I think it is probable that whatever audience there was knew to whom the speaker referred.)

14. See my "Proper Names and Identifying Descriptions."

ently in one's company. The "historical explanation," in other words, can involve as brief an interval of time as one pleases.

V. A Solution to the Puzzle Rejected

My problem, then, is to show how such a theory of reference can deal with simple existence statements expressed by the use of a proper name, the difficulty being that on this theory, proper names do not have a backing of descriptions and, in general, they function to refer via what I have called a historical connection with some individual. But a true negative existence statement expressed by using a name involves a name with no referent and the corresponding positive existence statement, if false, will also. But in other contexts, when a name is used and there is a failure of reference, then no proposition has been expressed—certainly no true proposition. If a child says, "Santa Claus will come tonight," he cannot have spoken the truth, although, for various reasons, I think it better to say that he has not even expressed a proposition.[15]

One apparently possible solution to the problem must be rejected. Russell and others, as we have seen, thought of (ordinary) proper names as concealed definite descriptions; he held a version, that is, of the principle of identifying descriptions. Existential statements involving ordinary proper names were therefore no problem for him—they were really existential statements involving definite descriptions and could be analyzed in accordance with his theory of definite descriptions. The suggestion I want to look at is that while our theory tells us that names in predicative statements do not obey the principle of identifying descriptions and are not concealed definite descriptions, existential statements may represent a special case. Thus, so this suggestion would run, "Santa Claus" in "Santa Claus will come tonight" is not a concealed definite description, but *is* one in the special context of "Santa Claus does not exist" and "Santa Claus exists." This would, of course, immediately solve our problem, but unfortunately it is not a solution that

15. Given that this is a statement about reality and that proper names have no descriptive content, then how are we to represent the proposition expressed?

our theory can accept. The difficulty is not that names would be treated as functioning differently in different contexts; in fact, as will become evident, my own view is that they do behave differently in existence statements. Rather, the trouble is that any theory that rejects the principle of identifying descriptions for predicative statements must also reject it for existence statements.

To simplify matters, let us restrict ourselves to Russell's version of the principle of identifying descriptions in which a name simply stands in place of some definite description. If we adopt the principle for existence statements involving names, this will come to saying that, for example, "Socrates did not exist" means the same thing as (expresses the same proposition as) some other sentence formed from this by replacing "Socrates" by a definite description—perhaps, say, the sentence, "The Greek philosopher who was convicted of corrupting the youth and drank hemlock did not exist." But, now, on any view we must, I think, accept the following:

(*E*) That Socrates did not exist entails that it is not true that Socrates was snub-nosed.

Our theory tells us that the second occurrence of "Socrates" in (*E*) is not a concealed definite description. But then neither can the first occurrence be one. For if we take some definite description such as the one suggested as what the first occurrence of "Socrates" stands for, rejection of the principle of identifying descriptions for the second occurrence means that it *could* be true that Socrates was snub-nosed even though no unique individual existed who satisfied that description. That is to say, if "Socrates" in "Socrates did not exist" is a concealed definite description, but is not in "Socrates was snub-nosed," then the antecedent of (*E*) could be true while the consequent is false. Since we want to accept the entailment expressed by (*E*) our theory cannot treat "Socrates" as a concealed description in existential statements.

This solution not being open to us, we cannot on the other hand go to the opposite extreme and handle existential statements involving ordinary proper names in the way Russell did for what he called names "in the strict logical sense." There simply are no meaningful existential statements involving these "genuine" names and so the problem does not arise about how to deal with them. But, of course, we cannot countenance this about ordinary proper names, for it does make sense to say, "Homer existed" or "Santa Claus does not exist."

VI. Truth Conditions and "Blocks"

What we need to do first is see what, on our theory of reference, the truth conditions are going to look like for existence statements involving names. In predicative statements, such as "Homer was a great poet," if everything goes well, there will be some individual related to this use of "Homer" "historically," as I have put it, and the statement will be true if that individual had the property expressed by the predicate and false otherwise. This, of course, cannot be so for a negative existence statement such as "Homer did not exist." This statement would be true, in fact, just in case there is a failure of reference, not in the statement itself, but in other possible or actual predicative statements involving the name. That is, if there is no individual related historically in the right way to the use of "Homer" in, say, the statement "Homer was a great poet," no individual whose possession or nonpossession of poetic genius makes this true or false, then we can truly state that Homer did not exist.

Initially then the question comes to this: "What, on our theory, constitutes a failure of reference in a predicative statement involving a proper name?" (As we shall see there is more to the matter than just this.) Since the positive part of our theory, the part that attempts to say what successful reference to an individual consists in, has been, perhaps because of the nature of things, left more suggestive than in a rigorously formulated state, it cannot be hoped that we shall do much better with failure of reference. But we can say some things of a nontrivial nature.

Suppose a child who believed in Santa Claus now learns the truth, the truth which he expresses by saying, "Santa Claus does not exist." He comes to learn this, as usual, from cynical older children; what has he learned? Our account is that he has learned that when in the past he believed something, for example, which he would have expressed by saying, "Santa Claus comes tonight," and would have thought himself in saying this to be referring to someone, the historical explanation of this belief does not involve any individual who could count as the referent of "Santa Claus"; rather it ends in a story given to him by his parents, a story told to him as factual. I do not mean, of course, that the child would or could express the knowledge he has in his new state of disillusionment in this fashion—that would require him to know the correct account of reference. But if *we* are approaching the correct theory, then this is how we can state what he has discovered.

When the historical explanation of the use of a name (with the intention to refer) ends in this way with events that preclude any referent being identified, I will call it a "block" in the history. In this example, the block is the introduction of the name into the child's speech via a fiction told to him as reality by his parents. Blocks occur in other ways. For example, children often invent imaginary companions whom they themselves come to speak of as actual. The block in such a case would occur at the point at which a name for the unreal companion gets introduced by the child himself via his mistaken belief that there is a companion to name. A somewhat different example would be this: suppose the Homeric poems were not written by one person, but were a patchwork of the writings of many people, combined, perhaps, with fragments from an oral tradition. Suppose, further, that at some point in time an ancient scholar for whatever reasons—he might have seen a name attached to some written version of the poems and supposed it to be the name of the author—attributed the poems to a single person he called "Homer." If this were the historical explanation of our saying, for example, "Homer wrote the *Iliad*," then the block occurs at the point at which this scholar enters the picture.

On theories that subscribe to the principle of identifying descriptions, examples of failure of reference such as occur in this last example would be treated as a failure to satisfy a uniqueness condition. The reason that Homer would not have existed given these circumstances is that no single individual satisfies the descriptions we associate with Homer (or satisfies a "sufficient" number, according to certain views). But according to our theory this is not the reason for failure of reference; it is rather that the history of our use of the name, a history with which we may not be familiar, does not end in the right way. One way to see that the opposing account, though plausible, is wrong is to think of the possibility of someone existing who *does* satisfy the descriptions we might supply of the referent of a name we use, but who has no historical connection with us whatsoever. Suppose, for example, that contrary to what we adults believe we know, there is, in fact, a man with a long white beard and a belly like a bowl full of jelly who comes down chimneys on Christmas night to leave gifts (the ones whose labels are missing about which parents worry because they don't know to what aunt the child should write a thank-you note). We must, of course, imagine that it is absolutely fortuitous that our descriptions of Santa Claus happen to fit so accurately this jolly creature. In that case I do not think that he *is* Santa Claus. The fact that the story of Santa Claus, told to children as fact, is historically an invention constitutes a block even if the story happens to contain only descriptions that accurately fit some person.

VII. A Rule for Negative Existence Statements

Using the technical, but admittedly not well-defined, notion of a "block," we can now sketch the way the historical explanation theory may treat negative existence statements involving names. A similar treatment could then be given for positive existence statements.

I will suggest a rule, using the notion of a block, that purports to give the truth conditions for negative existence statements containing a name. This rule, however, does not provide an *analysis* of such statements; it does not tell us what such statements mean or what proposition they express. This means that in this case we are divorcing the truth conditions from meaning.

With the deletion of some qualifications that would be

needed to make it strictly correct, the rule can be expressed as follows:

(R) If N is a proper name that has been used in predicative statements with the intention to refer to some individual, then ⌜N does not exist⌝ is true if and only if the history of those uses ends in a block.

The rule as stated obviously requires some modifications. For one thing we would need some way of distinguishing, for example, the denial of the existence of Aristotle the philosopher, from Aristotle the ship magnate. To accomplish this we must do two things: first, find a means of collecting together the uses of "Aristotle" in predicative statements that were, so to speak, attempts to refer to the philosopher, separating them from a similar collection of uses of the name that were attempts to refer to the ship magnate, and do this without, of course, assuming that any of these uses succeeds in referring. Second, we must be able to relate a particular negative existence statement using the name "Aristotle" to one such collection rather than any other.

The way of amending Rule (R) that seems to me in keeping with the historical explanation theory and to accomplish these tasks is this. Certain uses of the name "Aristotle" in predicative statements will have similar histories, histories that will distinguish them from other uses of the name. Each use of the name will, of course, have its own historical explanation, but these may, at a certain point, join up. So, in tracing back several uses of the name "Aristotle" by me and several uses by you, we may find a common root in certain ancient writings and documents, while other uses of the name by me or by you may have nothing in common with the history of the first set of uses. It is possible that the histories may join at what I have called a block. Another possibility, however, is that although different uses of the name end in different blocks, these blocks are themselves historically connected. This might occur, for example, for the use by different children of the name "Santa Claus." I have suggested that the block in this example occurs where the parents tell the children a fiction as if it were fact. The block, however, would be a different one for each child. Still the blocks themselves are historically related in an obvious way since the parents' deception is rooted in a common tradition.

Still another possible source of difficulty with Rule (R) as stated is that it makes use of prior instances of the name in predicative statements. Is it possible meaningfully to assert "*N* does not exist" when *N* has never been used in predicative statements (about actuality)? If it is, then Rule (R) would have to be amended in some way, perhaps by talking of potential or possible uses. But at the moment I am not sure how this would go and I will not attempt it.

Even without worrying about the vagueness of the idea of a "block," Rule (R) may look unexciting, but its consequences are interesting. In the first place its form is completely antithetical to the principle of identifying descriptions, for it has nothing to do with whether an individual of a certain description existed or not. Second, it does not involve our theory of reference in any difficulties: there is the connection with the notion of historical explanation and so it ties in neatly with the positive aspects of the view, but it has no Meinongian implications, no overpopulation with entities whose existence is being denied. This result is bought, to be sure, at the price of making a name function differently in existence statements as opposed to predicative statements. But, as I have said, I think that this is not an unintuitive result.

While the above are important consequences of (R), what interests me about (R) is that it gives the truth conditions for statements that assert that some *individual* does not exist in terms of a linguistic failure—the failure of a name to refer on account of a "block." And it should occur to one that there may be something wrong with this. How, it might be asked, can Homer's existence or nonexistence be a matter of a fact about language, a fact about the name "Homer"? One is reminded, at this point, of a similar problem connected with the other puzzle about reference mentioned at the beginning of this paper. In "On Sense and Reference," immediately after propounding the puzzle about identity statements, Frege mentions a solution that he had formerly thought correct, but which he now repu-

diates just because it seems to involve turning identity statements, which apparently express facts about the world, into
statements about a particular language.

Rule (R), in so far as it is supposed to express truth conditions for negative existence statements of a certain kind, seems
objectionable for the same reasons. The crux of the problem in
both cases seems to be this. We are inclined to say that the
propositions expressed by us as "The Evening Star is identical
with the Morning Star" and "Homer did not exist" can be the
very same propositions that someone else may express using
entirely different names. Therefore, how can we give a rule,
such as (R), which makes the truth conditions of what we say
depend upon facts about particular names?

The child who has become disillusioned expresses his new-
found knowledge by saying "Santa Claus doesn't exist." A
French-speaking child, with a similar history of being deceived
by adults, might express his discovery by saying, *"Père Noël n'existe pas."* Although the names are different, I believe we should
want to say that the two children have learned the same fact
and, on that account, that they have expressed the same proposition. Yet if we apply Rule (R) to each case it seems that the
truth conditions must be different; they involve a block in the
history of the use of the name "Santa Claus" for the English-
speaking child and a block for the French-speaking child in the
history of the use of the different name, "Père Noël."

Perhaps we can see the problem more clearly by looking for
a moment at predicative statements. If we consider a simple
(grammatically) subject-predicate statement, such as "Socrates
is bald," and think of this as divided into its referring element,
"Socrates," and its predicative element, "is bald," then if a certain change in the predicative element—for example, from "is
bald" to "is short"—results in a change in the truth conditions
for the statement, we want to say that the result expresses a different proposition. In general only interchange of synonymous
predicates will maintain the same truth conditions and the
same proposition. *If* referring expressions such as "Socrates"
were concealed descriptions—that is, introduced predicate elements into a statement—then the same could be said about

them: substituting a different referring expression, unless it happened to conceal the same or synonymous descriptions as the one it is substituted for, would shift both the truth conditions and the proposition expressed (and, in fact, this is the heart of Frege's way of avoiding his puzzle about identity statements).

But our theory of reference denies that referring expressions such as "Socrates" conceal descriptions or introduce predicate elements. If we keep the predicative element the same and substitute a different referring expression—say, "Plato" for "Socrates"—then whether or not we have the same proposition expressed depends solely upon whether or not the same thing is referred to. And this in turn depends upon whether the historical explanation of the use of these two expressions traces back to the same individual. If you say "Henry is bald" and I say "George is bald" we express the same proposition if the person you referred to by using the name "Henry" and I by using the name "George" are the same person. But what you say is true if and only if the person you referred to—that is, the person historically connected—when you used the name "Henry" has the property of being bald; whereas what I say is true if and only if what I referred to by using the name "George" has the property of being bald. The truth conditions are different because they must be stated in terms of what is referred to by different expressions, in the one case my use of the name "George" and in the other your use of the name "Henry." Yet we may express the same proposition.

So with predicative statements involving proper names, given the same predicate, sameness or difference of propositions comes down to sameness or difference of the referent of the names. It seems that if we try to state the truth conditions for a particular use of such a statement, we are not going to arrive at what we should like to call the proposition expressed. But although we thus are separating truth conditions from propositions expressed, the latter notion is still a fairly clear concept. It seems, however, that we cannot in the same way preserve a clear notion of what proposition is expressed for existence statements involving proper names.

Our problem arose because we wanted on the one hand to make it possible that one child saying "Santa Claus does not exist" may express the same proposition as another who says *"Père Noël n'existe pas."* But, on the other hand, our explanation of the truth conditions for such statements in Rule (*R*) made them different for the two cases. We have seen, however, that if the historical explanation theory is correct, a difference in truth conditions without a shift in proposition expressed can occur in any case with predicative statements. This can occur when there is a difference in names used without a change in referent. So this seems to be a general feature of the theory's treatment of names. When we turn to negative existence statements and Rule (*R*), however, we cannot give as a criterion for propositional identity sameness of referent. For, of course, if true, the name in such a statement has no referent.

What we would like, still continuing with the example, is a reason for saying that both children express the same proposition that is at once in line with our theory and intuitively satisfying. I want to suggest that we may find such a reason once more by using the idea of a historical connection, that, in our example, it is the blocks in the historical explanation of the use respectively of the names "Santa Claus" and "Père Noël" that are themselves historically connected. Once again, I do not have the resources to spell out a general principle for what this historical connection must be, any more than I did with the notion of a block itself. Yet in the example before us, and others one can think of, our inclination to say that people using different names express the same negative existence proposition seems to be a matter of historical connection between the blocks involved. In our example, it seems to me that the reason we think both children express the same proposition is that the story of Santa Claus and the story of Père Noël, the stories passed on to the two children as if they were factual, have a common root. And if there were not this common history, I think we should rather hold that the two children believed similar, perhaps, but not identical falsehoods, for example, when the one attributed gifts to Santa Claus and the other to Père Noël and that they expressed different truths when one said

"Santa Claus does not exist" and the other said *"Père Noël n'existe pas."*

VIII. Concluding Remarks

If this discussion has been on the right track, then at least the outline of a solution to some problems concerning nonexistence statements is available to the historical explanation theory. One point emerged in the course of the last sections. We can perhaps point to criteria for saying when two existence statements involving names express the same proposition, but these criteria take a different form from those for predicative statements involving names. In particular, it cannot be a matter of sameness of referent. For predicative statements we were able to suggest a way of representing propositions, as ordered n-tuplets, but no obvious way of representing propositions expressed by existence statements suggests itself. This does not seem to me to count against the theory, since the notion of a proposition is not, I think, a clear one that has established use outside of a theory. The fact that the representation suggested for predicative statements involving proper names has no counterpart for existence statements, however, may account in part for the fact that Russell took the alternatives for proper names to be either a Meinongian view or a concealed descriptions view. For the representation of propositions suggested is, I think, essentially Russellian and either of these views of ordinary proper names would allow him to apply it to existence statements.

10 Transworld Identity or Worldbound Individuals?

ALVIN PLANTINGA

Calvin College

I

The idea of *possible worlds* has seemed to promise under-standing and insight into several venerable problems of modal-ity—those of essence and accident, for example, necessary and contingent truth, modality *de dicto* and *de re*, and the nature of subjunctive conditionals. But just what is a possible world? Sup-pose we take it that a possible world is a *state of affairs* of some kind—one which either obtains, is real, is actual, or else *could have* obtained. But then how shall we understand "could have" here? Obviously no *definition* will be of much use: Here we must give examples, lay out the connections between the concept in question and other concepts, reply to objections, and hope for the best. Although I cannot do this in detail here,[1] I do wish to point out that the sense of possibility in question is wider than that of *causal* or *natural* possibility—so that *Agnew's swimming the Atlantic Ocean,* while it is perhaps causally or naturally impos-sible, is not impossible in the sense under discussion. On the other hand, this sense is narrower than that captured in first-order logic, so that many states of affairs are necessary, in the sense in question, although their corresponding propositions are not provable in first-order logic. Examples of such states of affairs would include those corresponding to truths of arithme-

Reprinted by permission of New York University Press, from *Logic and Ontology,* edited by Milton K. Munitz, © 1973 by New York University, pp. 193–212.
    1. See my *"De Re et De Dicto", Nous,* III (September, 1969) and "World and Essence," *Philosophical Review,* LXXIX (October, 1970).

tic and mathematics generally, as well as many more homely items such as *Nobody's being taller than himself, red's being a color,* (as well as *a thing's being colored if red*), *Agnew's not being a composite number,* and the like. Other and less homely candidates include *every person's being conscious at some time or other, every human person's having a body at some time during his career,* and *the existence of a being than which it's not possible that there be a greater.*

In the sense of necessity and possibility in question, furthermore, a pair of states of affairs S and S' may be so related that it is not possible that both obtain, in which case S *precludes* S'; and if it is impossible that S obtain and S' *not* obtain, then S *includes* S'. So, for example, *Agnew's having swum the Atlantic* includes *Agnew's having swum something or other* and precludes *Agnew's not being able to swim.* Still further, a state of affairs S may be such that for any state of affairs S', S either includes or precludes S', in which case S is *maximal.* Now we may say that a possible world is just a maximal possible state of affairs. Corresponding to each possible world W, furthermore, there is a unique class of propositions, C, of which a proposition P is a member just in case it is impossible that W be actual and P be false. Call this class *the book on W.* Like possible worlds, books too have a maximality property: each book contains, for any proposition P, either P or the negation of P. And the book on the actual world, obviously, is the set of true propositions.

Now it is plausible and natural to suppose that the same individual exists in various different states of affairs. There is, for example, the state of affairs consisting in *Paul R. Zwier's being a good tennis player;* this state of affairs is possible but does not in fact obtain. It is natural to suppose, however, that if it *had* obtained, Zwier would have existed and would have been a good tennis player. That is, it is natural to suppose that Zwier *exists in* this state of affairs. But, of course, if he exists in this state of affairs, then he exists in every possible world including it; that is, every possible world including *Zwier's being a good tennis player* is such that, had it been actual, Zwier would have existed. So Zwier exists in many possible worlds. I say it is natural to make this supposition; but many philosophers otherwise kindly disposed toward possible worlds are inclined toward its denial.

Among them, there is, for example, Leibniz, whose credentials on this subject are certainly impeccable; Leibniz apparently held that each object exists in just one world.[2] The idealists, furthermore, in arguing for their doctrine of internal relations, were arguing in essence that an object exists in exactly one possible world—indeed, some of them may have thought that there is only one such world. More recently, the view that individuals are thus confined to one world—let's call it The Theory of Worldbound Individuals—has been at least entertained with considerable hospitality by David Kaplan.[3] Roderick Chisholm, furthermore, finds difficulty and perplexity in the claim that the same object exists in more than one possible world.[4] Still further, The Theory of Worldbound Individuals is an explicit postulate of David Lewis' Counterpart Theory.[5] In what follows I shall explore this issue. Now perhaps the most important and widely heralded argument for the Theory of Worldbound Individuals (hereafter 'TWI') is the celebrated *Problem of Transworld Identification*, said to arise on the supposition that the same object exists in more than one world. Accordingly I will concentrate on these two topics: TWI and the problem of Transworld Identity.

Why, then, should we suppose that an individual is confined to just one world—that you and I, for example, exist in this world and this world only? According to G. E. Moore, the idealists, in arguing for their view that all relations are internal, were really arguing that all relational properties are essential to the things that have them. The argument they gave, however, if it is sound, establishes that *all* properties—not just relational properties—are thus essential to their owners. If this is correct, however, then for no object x is there a possible state of affairs in which x lacks a property that in fact it has; so x exists only in the actual world, the world that does in fact obtain.

2. As has been argued by Benson Mates, "Leibniz on Possible Worlds," *Logic, Methodology, and Philosophy of Science*, 3rd ed. (Amsterdam: Van Rootsclaar and Staal, 1968).
3. "Transworld Identification," read at an APA Symposium, Chicago, 1967.
4. "Identity through Possible Worlds: Some Questions," *Nous*, I (1967), 1.
5. "Counterpart Theory and Quantified Modal Logic," *Journal of Philosophy*, LXV (March, 1968), 113.

Now an argument for a conclusion as sweeping as this must pack quite a punch. What did the idealists come up with? A confusion, says Moore. What the idealists asserted is

    (1) If P be a relational property and A a term to which it does in fact belong, then, no matter what P and A may be, it may always be truly asserted of them, that any term which had *not* possessed P would necessarily have been other than numerically different from A. . . .[6]

Perhaps we may put this more perspicuously as

    (1′) If x has P, then for any object y, if there is a world in which y lacks P, then y is distinct from x

which clearly entails the desired conclusion. What they suggested as a reason for accepting (1), however is

    (2) If A has P and x does not, it *does* follow that x is other than A.[7]

If we restate (2) as the claim that

    (2′) For any object x and y, if x has P and y does not, then x is distinct from y

holds in every world, we see that (2) is just the thesis that the Indiscernibility of Identicals is necessarily true. This thesis seems accurate enough, but no reason at all for (1) or (1′). As Moore, says, (1) and (2) are easily conflated, particularly when they are put in the idealists' typically opaque and turgid prose; and the idealists seized the opportunity to conflate them.

Initially, then, this argument is unpromising. It has a near relative, however, that we may conceivably find in Leibniz and that often surfaces in contemporary discussion. Leibniz writes Arnauld as follows:

Besides, if, in the life of any person and even in the whole universe anything went differently from what it has, nothing could prevent us from saying that it was another person or another possible universe which God had chosen. It would then be indeed another individual.[8]

---

6. "External and Internal Relations," *Philosophical Studies* (London: Routledge and Kegan Paul, 1922), p. 287.

7. *Ibid.*, p. 289.

8. Letter from Leibniz to Arnauld, July 14, 1686. Leibniz makes very nearly the same statement in a letter to Count von Hessen-Rheinfels, May 1686 (p. 111), *Discourse on Metaphysics* (LaSalle, Ill.: Open Court, 1962), pp. 127–128. Published in the *Discourse* as well.

This is on its face a dark saying. What Leibniz says here and elsewhere, however, may suggest the following. Suppose Socrates exists in some world W distinct from the actual world (which for purposes of easy reference I shall name "Charley"). Taking the term 'property' in a broad sense, we shall be obliged to concede that there must be some property that Socrates has in Charley but lacks in W. (At the very least, if we let 'π' name the book on Charley, then one property Socrates has in Charley but lacks in W is that of being such that every member of π is true.) So let us suppose that there is some property—snubnosedness, let us say—that Socrates has in Charley but lacks in W. That is, the Socrates of Charley, Socrates-in-Charley, has snubnosedness, while the Socrates of W does not. But surely this is inconsistent with the Indiscernibility of Identicals, a principle than which none sounder can be conceived. For according to this principle, if Socrates-in-Charley has snubnosedness but Socrates-in-W does not, then Socrates-in-Charley is distinct from Socrates-in-W. We must conclude, therefore, that Socrates does not exist both in Charley and in W. There may be some person in W that much resembles our Socrates, Socrates-in-Charley; that person is nonetheless distinct from him. And of course this argument can be generalized to show that nothing exists in more than one world.

Such an argument, however, is less than impeccable. We are asked to infer

(3) Socrates-in-Charley is snubnosed and Socrates-in-W is not

from

(4) Socrates is snubnosed in Charley but not in W

We need not quarrel with this request; but the Indiscernibility of Identicals in no way licenses the inference that Socrates-in-Charley and Socrates-in-W are distinct. For, contrary, perhaps, to appearances, there is no property that (3) predicates of Socrates-in-Charley and withholds from Socrates-in-W. According to (3) [so taken that it follows from (4)], Socrates-in-Charley (that is, Socrates) has the property of being snubnosed, all right, but *in Charley*. Socrates-in-W, however, lacks that property *in W*. But this latter, of course, means only that Socrates-in-*W* has the property of being such that, if *W* had obtained, he would not have been snubnosed. And, of course, this property—the property an object *x* has iff *x* would not have been snubnosed, had *W* obtained—is not the complement of snubnosedness. Indeed, this property is not even incompatible with snubnosedness; Socrates himself is snubnosed, but would not have been had *W* been actual. So the Indiscernibility of Identicals does not apply here; there is no property *P* which (3) asserts that Socrates-in-Charley has but Socrates-in-*W* lacks. To suppose that Socrates has *P* in the actual world but lacks it in *W* is to suppose only that Socrates does in fact have *P* but would not have had it, had *W* been actual. The Indiscernibility of Identicals casts not even a hint of suspicion upon this supposition. This objection, therefore, is a snare and a delusion.

A more popular and more promising argument for TWI is the dreaded *Problem of Transworld Identity* said to confront anyone who rashly supposes the same object to exist in more than one world. Here the claim is that there are deep conceptual difficulties in *identifying* the same object from world to world—difficulties that threaten the very idea of Transworld Identity with incoherence. These difficulties, furthermore, presumbaly do not arise on TWI.[9]

But what, exactly, *is* the problem of Transworld Identity? What difficulties does it present for the notion that the same object exists in various possible worlds? Just how does this problem go? Although published statements of it are scarce,[10] the problem may perhaps be put as follows. Let us suppose again that Socrates exists in some world *W* distinct from this one—a world in which let us say, he did not fight in the battle of Marathon. In *W,* of course, he may also lack other properties he has in this world—perhaps in *W* he eschewed philosophy, corrupted no youth, and thus escaped the wrath of the Athenians. Perhaps in *W* he lived in Corinth, was six feet tall, and remained a bachelor all his life. But then we must ask our-

9. So David Lewis: "P_2 [the postulate according to which nothing exists in more than one world] serves only to rule out avoidable problems of individuation" ("Counterpart Theory").

10. But see Chisholm, "Identity through Possible Worlds," pp. 1–8.

selves how we could possibly *identify* Socrates in that world. How could we *pick him out*? How could we *locate* him there? How could we possibly tell which of the many things contained in W is *Socrates*? If we try to employ the properties we use to identify him in *this* world, our efforts may well end in dismal failure—perhaps in that world it is Xenophon or maybe even Thrasymachus that is Plato's mentor and exhibits the splendidly single-minded passion for truth and justice that characterizes Socrates in this. But if we cannot identify him in W, so the argument continues, then we really do not understand the assertion that he exists there. If we cannot even identify him, we would not know whom we were talking about, in saying that Socrates exists in that world or has this or that property therein. In order to make sense of such talk, we must have a *criterion* or *principle* that enables us to identify Socrates from world to world. This criterion must include some property that Socrates has in each world in which he exists—and if it is sufficient to enable us to *pick him out* in a given world, distinguish him from other things, it must be a property he alone has in these worlds. Further, if the property (or properties) in question is to enable us to pick him out, it must in some broad sense be "empirically manifest"—it must resemble such properties as having such-and-such a name, address, Social Security number, height, weight, and general appearance in that we can tell by broadly empirical means whether a given object has or lacks it. How, otherwise, could we use it to *pick out* or *identify* him? So, if it is intelligible to suppose that Socrates exists in more than one world, there must be some empirically manifest property that he and hc alone has in each of the worlds in which he exists. Now obviously we do not know of any such property, or even that there is such a property. Indeed, it is hard to see how there *could* be such a property. But then the very idea of Transworld Identity is not really intelligible—in which case we must suppose that no object exists in more than one world.

The first thing to note about the objection outlined above is that it seems to arise out of a certain *picture* or *image*. We imagine ourselves somehow peering into another world; we ask ourselves whether Socrates exists in it. We observe the behavior and characteristics of its denizens and then wonder about which of these, if any, is Socrates. Of course, we realize that he might look quite different in *W,* if he exists there at all. He might also live at a different place, have different friends and different fingerprints, if, indeed, he has fingers. But how then can we tell which one he *is?* And does it so much as make sense to say that he exists in that world, if there is no way in principle of identifying him, of telling which thing there *is* Socrates?

Now perhaps this picture is useful in certain respects; in the present context, however, it breeds nothing but confusion. For it is this picture that slyly insinuates that the proposition *Socrates exists in other possible worlds* is intelligible to us only if we know of some empirically manifest property that he and he alone has in each world in which he exists. But suppose we consider an analogous temporal situation. In Herbert Spiegelberg's book *The Phenomenological Movement* there are pictures of Franz Brentano at ages 20 and 70 respectively. The youthful Brentano looks much like Apollo; the elderly Brentano resembles nothing so much as Jerome Hines in his portrayal of the dying Czar in Boris Godounov. Most of us will concede that the same object exists at several different times; but do we know of some empirically manifest property *P* such that a thing is Brentano at a given time *t* if and only if it has *P?* Surely not; and this casts no shadow whatever on the intelligibility of the claim that Brentano existed at many different times.

Still, isn't the argument made above available here? No doubt there was a time, some fifty years ago, when Spiro Agnew was a precocious baby. But if I understand that assertion, must I not be able to *pick him out, locate* him, at that time? If I cannot identify him, if I cannot tell which of the things that existed at that time was Agnew, then (so goes the argument) I cannot make sense of the claim that he existed at that time. And I could identify him, at *t,* only if I know of some empirically manifest property that he and he alone has at *t.*

But here the argument is manifestly confused. To suppose that Agnew was a precocious baby at *t* it is not necessary that I be able to pick his picture out of a gallery of babies at *t.* Of course I must know *who he is* to understand this assertion; and perhaps to know that I must know of some property that he and he alone has. Indeed, we might go so far as to concede that this property must be 'empirically manifest' in some sense. But surely it is asking too much to require that I know of such a property that he and he only has *at every time at which he exists.* Of course I must be able to answer the question "Which of the things existing at *t* is Agnew?" But the answer is trivial; it's that man sitting right over there—the Vice President of the United States.

If this is correct, however, why suppose otherwise in the Transworld case? I understand the proposition that there is a possible world in which Socrates did not teach Plato. Now let *W* be any such world. Why suppose that a condition of my understanding this is my knowing something about what he would have looked like or where he would have lived, had *W* been actual? To understand this proposition I must know who Socrates is. Perhaps this involves my knowing of some property that is empirically manifest (whatever exactly that comes to) and unique to Socrates. But what earthly (or otherwise) reason is there for supposing that I must know of some empirically manifest property he has *in that world W?* The picture suggests that I must be able to look into *W* and sift through its inhabitants until I run across one I recognize as Socrates—otherwise I cannot identify him, and hence I do not know whom I am talking about. But here the picture is not doing right by us. For, taken literally, of course, this notion makes no sense. All I know about this world *W* is that Socrates would not have taught Plato had *W* obtained. I do not know anything about which other persons would have existed, or—except for his essential properties—which other properties Socrates has in that world. How could I know more, since all I have been told about *W* is that it is one of the many worlds in which Socrates exists but does not teach Plato?

Accordingly, the claim that I must be able somehow to identify Socrates in *W*—pick him out—is either trivial or based on a confusion. Of course, I must know which of the persons existing in *W*—the persons who would have existed, had *W* been actual—I am talking about. But the answer, obviously, and trivially, is Socrates. To be able thus to answer, however, I need know nothing further about what Socrates would have been like had W been actual.

But let us imagine the objector regrouping. "If Socrates exists in several worlds," he says, "then even if there need be no *empirically manifest* property he and he alone has in each of them, there must at any rate be some property or other that he and only he has in each world in which he exists. Let us say that such a property is an essence of Socrates. Such an essence meets two conditions: (1) Socrates has it in every world he graces, and (2) nothing distinct from him has it in any world. (By contrast, a property need meet only the first condition to be *essential* to Socrates.) Now a property P entails a property Q if there is no world in which there exists an object that has P but lacks Q. So any essence of Socrates entails each of his essential properties—each property that Socrates has in every world in which he exists. Furthermore, if E is an essence of Socrates, then the class C of his essential properties—the properties he has in each world in which he exists—will obviously entail E in the sense that there is no world in which something exemplifies all of these properties but does not exemplify E. (What makes this particularly obvious is that any essence of Socrates is essential to him and hence is a member of C.) An essence of Socrates, therefore, is, in this sense, equivalent to the class of his essential properties; and Socrates exists in more than one possible world only if he has at least one essence in the explained sense. But at best it is far from clear which (if any) of Socrates' properties are essential to him and even less clear that he has an essence. Nor does there seem to be any way of determining whether he has such a property or, if he does, which properties are entailed by it. So is not the suggestion that he has an essence both gratuitous and problematic? We can and should avoid this whole problem by accepting TWI." Thus far the objector.

What can be said by way of reply? First, that if we follow this counsel, we gain all the advantages of theft over honest toil, as Russell says in another connection. The question is whether Socrates has an essence and whether objects do or do not exist in more than one world—not whether we would be saved some work or perplexity if we said they did not. But more fundamentally, TWI does not avoid the question which of Socrates' properties are essential to him. Obviously it gives an answer to that question, and an unsatisfactory one at that; for it says that *all* of his properties are essential to him and that any property he alone has—that of being married to Xantippe, for example—is one of his essences.

These caveats entered, however (and I shall return below to the second), let us consider the objector's main complaint. Is it really so difficult, on The Theory of Transworld Identity, to determine whether Socrates has an essence? In fact, in the actual world, Socrates has the property of being snubnosed. But now consider a world W in which he is not snubnosed. Had W obtained, Socrates would not have been snubnosed; we may say, therefore, that Socrates is non-snubnosed-in-W. In general, where P is a property and W a world, to say that x has P-in-W is simply to say that x would have had P if W had been actual. So Socrates has the property of *being-non-snubnosed-in-W;* that is, he has this property in Charley, the actual world. In W, on the other hand, Socrates has the property of *being-snubnosed-in-Charley.* Indeed, in *any* world in which Socrates exists, he has the property of being snubnosed-in-Charley.[11] This property, therefore, is essential to him. And of course we can generalize the claim: Where P is any property Socrates has, the property of having-P-in-Charley is essential to him. But now consider some property P that Socrates has in fact and that he alone has—*being married to Xantippe,* perhaps, or *being born at such and such a place and time,* or *being A. E. Taylor's favorite philosopher.* The property *having-P-in-Charley* will, of course, be essential to Socrates. Furthermore, each thing distinct from Socrates has its complement essentially, for everything distinct from Socrates has the complement $\bar{P}$ of P; hence each such thing has $\bar{P}$-in-Charley, and has it essentially, that is, in every world in which it exists. But then everything distinct from Socrates has the com-

---

11. If, as I do, we make the S_2-like opposition that if a given state of affairs (or proposition) S is possible, then S is possible in every world. See "World and Essence," p. 475.

plement of *having-P-in-Charley* and has that property essentially. So there is no possible world in which some object distinct from Socrates has the property of having *P*-in-Charley. Not only, then, is this property essential to him; it is also one of his essences. And obviously we can find as many essences of Socrates as you like. Take any property *P* and world *W* such that Socrates alone has *P* in *W*; the property of having *P* in *W* is an essence of Socrates.[12]

Now you may think the very idea of a property like *being-snubnosed-in-Charley* is muddled, perverse, ungainly, or in some other way deserving of abuse and contempt. But where, exactly (or even approximately), is the muddle? We must not let this terminology mislead us into thinking that if there is such a property, then Charley must be a geographical unit or place—like Wyoming, for example—so that this property would be like *being mugged in New Jersey*. Socrates elected to remain in Athens and drink the hemlock, instead of fleeing to Thebes. He had the opportunity to take the latter course, however, and it was certainly possible that he do so. So there are possible worlds in which Socrates flees to Thebes and does not drink the hemlock. Now let *W* be any such world. Certainly it is true of Socrates that if *W* had been actual, he would have fled to Thebes; but that is all that is meant by saying that Socrates had the property of fleeing-to-Thebes-in-*W*. It is certainly not easy to see that this property is mysterious, underhanded, inelegant, or that it merits much by way of scorn and obloquy.

The objector, therefore, is right in claiming that if Socrates exists in several worlds, he must have an essence. His objection to the latter idea, however, is not impressive. Is there really something problematic or untoward in the idea of Transworld Identity? Is there really a problem of Transworld Identification? If there is, I am at a loss to see what it might be.

Of course there are legitimate problems in the neighborhood—problems that often are exposed when the subject ostensibly under discussion is Transworld Identity. For we

12. For more discussion of his essences (and for discussion of more of his essences) see "World and Essence," pp. 487ff.

might ask such questions as these: Is there a world W and an object x existing in W such that x is identical with Socrates, and x, let us say, was born in 1500 B.C. or was an eighteenth-century Irish washerwoman? These questions advertise themselves as questions about Transworld Identity; in fact they are questions concerning which of Socrates' properties are essential to him. Could he have had the property of being disembodied-at-some-time-or-other? Or the property of having-an-alligator-body-at-some-time-or-other? These are legitimate questions to which there are no easy answers. (Socrates himself suggests that everyone actually has the former property, while some of his more snappish acquaintances may have the latter.) These are real questions; but they need not shake our confidence that some of Socrates' properties are ones he could have lacked, so that Charley is not the only possible world in which he exists. The fact that we are not confident about their answers means only that Socrates has *some* properties such that we cannot easily tell whether or not they are essential to him; it does not so much as suggest that *all* his properties are thus inscrutable. And further, of course, the Theory of Worldbound Individuals, as so far explained, does not avoid these questions; it simply answers them by fiat in insisting that each of Socrates' properties is essential to him.

II

The arguments for the Theory of Worldbound Individuals, then, are based upon error and confusion. But are there positive reasons for rejecting it? I think there are. The basic thrust of the theory is the contention that no object exists in more than one possible world; this implies the outrageous view that—taking property in the broadest possible sense—no object could have lacked any property that in fact it has. Had the world been different in even the tiniest, most Socrates-irrelevant fashion, Socrates would not have existed. Suppose God created n electrons. The theory in question entails the absolute impossibility of His having created both Socrates and $n + 1$ electrons. It thereby fails to distinguish the relation in which he stands to inconsistent attributes—being both married and unmarried, for example—from his relation to such attributes as *fleeing to Thebes*. It is as impossible, according to this theory, that Socrates should have had the latter as the former. Consider furthermore, a proposition like

(5) Socrates is foolish

a proposition which predicates of Socrates some property he lacks. Now presumably (5) is true, in a given possible world, only if Socrates exists in that world and has the property of being foolish therein. But on TWI, there is no such world, and (5) accordingly, is necessarily false, as will be any proposition predicating of Socrates a property he does not in fact have. In the same vein, consider any proposition *P* that is false but contingent. Since *Socrates exists* is true only in Charley, where *P* is false, there is no world in which *P* and *Socrates exists* are both true. The latter, therefore, entails the denial of the former. Accordingly, *Socrates exists* entails every true proposition. And all of this is entirely too extravagant to be believed. If we know anything at all about modality, we know that some of Socrates' properties are accidental, that *Socrates is foolish* is not necessarily false, and that *Socrates exists* does not entail every true proposition.

But here we must consider an exciting new wrinkle to this old theory. Embracing the Theory of Worldbound Individuals, David Lewis adds to it the suggestion that a worldbound individual typically has *counterparts* in other possible worlds:

The counterpart relation is our substitute for identity between things in different worlds. Where some would say that you are in several worlds, in which you have somewhat different properties and somewhat different things happen to you, I prefer to say that you are in the actual world and no other, but you have counterparts in several other worlds. Your counterparts resemble you closely in content and context in important respects. They resemble you more closely than do the other things in their worlds. But they are not really you. For each of them is in his own world, and only you are here in the actual world. Indeed we might say, speaking casually, that your counterparts are you in other worlds, that they and you are the same; but this sameness is no more a literal identity than the sameness between you today and you tomorrow. It would be better to say that your counterparts are men you *would have been,* had the world been otherwise.[13]

Fortified with Counterpart Theory, TWI is no longer obliged to hold that each of Socrates' properties is essential to him; instead, a property is essential to him if and only if each of his counterparts (among whom is Socrates himself) has it. Accordingly, while indeed there is no world in which Socrates, *our* Socrates—the object that in our world is Socrates—lacks the property of being snubnosed, there are no doubt worlds containing *counterparts* of Socrates—counterparts which are not snubnosed. So the property of being snubnosed is not essential to him.

And let us now return to

(5) Socrates is foolish,

TWI seems to imply, paradoxically enough, that this statement is necessarily false. Can Counterpart Theory be of help here? Indeed it can, for, no doubt, Socrates has foolish counterparts in other worlds; and this is sufficient, according to TWI fortified with Counterpart Theory, for the contingency of (5). This proposition is contingently false if there is another world in which it is true; but its truth in a given world does not require the existence, in that world, of what is denoted by 'Socrates' in this. Like 'the first man to climb Mt. Rainier', 'Socrates', according to the present view, denotes different persons in different worlds. Or, as we may also put it, in different worlds different things have the property of being Socrates— just as, in different worlds, different things have the property of being the first man to climb Rainier.

Socrateity, then, or the property of being Socrates, is not the property of being identical with the person who in Charley, the

13. "Counterpart Theory," pp. 114–115. I said David Lewis embraces TWI; but this is not entirely accurate. Speaking of the Counterpart Relation, he says, "Yet with this substitute in use, it would not matter if some things *were* identical with some of their counterparts after all! P_2 [the postulate according to which objects are worldbound] serves only to rule out avoidable problems of individuation." One may offer and study means of formalizing modal discourse for a variety of reasons, and TWI is not really essential to Lewis' program. What I shall be quarrelling with in ensuing pages is not that program, but the view which takes TWI as the sober, metaphysical truth of the matter.

actual world, is Socrates; it is not the property of being that person. It is, instead, a property that could have been had by someone else; roughly, it is the property that is unique to Socrates and his counterparts. You may think it difficult to see just what property that is; and indeed that *is* difficult. In the present context, however, what is important to see is that Socrateity is had by different objects in different worlds. Indeed, on Counterpart Theory an object may have more then one property in a given world; so no doubt there are worlds in which several distinct things exemplify Socrateity. And the point is that (5) is true, in a world *W,* just in case *W* contains an object that is both Socratic and foolish—that is, just in case Socrates has a foolish counterpart and Socrateity a foolish instance in *W.* So what (5) says is or is equivalent to

(6) Something exemplifies both Socrateity and foolishness.

And, of course, this proposition will be true in some but not all worlds.

But what about

(7) Socrates exists?

If nothing exists in more than one world, then presumably Socrates does not, in which case on TWI, (fortified with Counterpart Theory though it be), (7) still seems to be true in just one world and still seems paradoxically to entail every true proposition. But here perhaps appearances are deceiving. Counterpart Theory affords the means of denying that (7) is true in only one world. For this proposition, we may say, is true in any world where Socrateity has an instance; since there are many such, there are many worlds in which it is true; hence there are many worlds in which both (7) and some false propositions are true. So the former does not entail every true proposition. But if (7) is true in many worlds, how does the central claim of TWI—that nothing exists in more than one—fit in? If Socrates, along with everything else, exists in only one world, that is, if

(8) Socrates exists in more than one world

is false, how can (7) be true in more than one world?

But perhaps the partisan of TWI can go so far as to deny that his theory commits him to the falsity of (8). Perhaps he can construe it as the entirely accurate claim that *Socrates exists* is true in more than one world. But how, then, does (8) comport with the central claim of TWI? According to the latter, nothing has the property of existing in more than one world. How, then, can TWI sensibly hold that (8) is true? As follows, perhaps. Suppose the predicate "exists in more than one world" expresses a property that, according to TWI, no object has. Then (8), if true, must not, of course, be seen as predicating that property of Socrates—if it did, it would be false. Perhaps it *looks* as if it predicates that property of Socrates; in fact, however, it does not. What it does instead is to predicate *truth in more than one world* of *Socrates exists.* There is an instructive parallel between (8) so construed and

(9) The number of planets is possibly greater than nine.

Read *de dicto*, (9) quite properly predicates possibility of

(10) The number of planets is greater than nine.

It is plausible to add, furthermore, that the words "is possibly greater than nine" express a property—the property a thing has just in case it is possibly greater than nine. Every number greater than nine enjoys this property; that is to say, each number greater than nine is *possibly* greater than nine. The number of planets, however, being nine, does not have the property in question. (9), therefore, can be read as a true *de dicto* assertion; but, thus read, it does not predicate of the object named by "the number of planets" the property expressed by "is possibly greater than seven."

Similarly, then, for (8); the words "exists in more than one world" express a property that (if TWI is true) nothing has; the proposition in question, however, does not predicate that property of anything and hence need not (at any rate on that account) be false. Furthermore the argument from

(11) Nothing exists in more than one world

to the falsehood of (8) is to be rejected. We may compare this argument with another:

(12) Every number greater than seven is necessarily greater than seven.

(13) The number of planets is greater than seven.

Hence

(14) The number of planets is necessarily greater than seven.

If we construe (14) as the *de dicto* claim that

(15) The number of planets is greater than seven

is necessarily true, then it obviously fails to follow from (12) and (13). (12) says that every number meeting a certain condition has a certain property—that of being necessarily greater than seven. According to (13), the number of planets meets that condition. (14), however, is not the consequent *de re* assertion that the number of planets has that property; it is instead the false (and inconsequent) *de dicto* assertion that (15) is necessarily true. But now the same can be said for (8). This is not the *de re* assertion that some specific object has the property that (11) says nothing has. *That* assertion, indeed, is precluded by (11) and thus is false on TWI. Instead, we must look upon (8) as the *de dicto* allegation that *Socrates exists* is true in more than one world—an allegation quite consistent with (11). What we have here, then, as in the inference of (14) from (12) and (13), is another *de re–de dicto* ambiguity.

So the partisan of TWI need not hold that Socrates has all his properties essentially, or that *Socrates exists* entails every true proposition. Indeed, he can go so far as to join the upholder of Transworld Identity in affirming the truth of sentence (8). You may think this course on his part less ingenuous than ingenious; and so, perhaps it is. Indeed, as we shall see, a certain disingenuousness is perhaps a salient feature of TWI. But so far the addition of Counterpart Theory seems to provide TWI with a solution for difficulties it could not otherwise cope with.

Despite its fortification with Counterpart Theory, however, the Theory of Worldbound Individuals is open to a pair of decisive objections. Perhaps we can approach the first of these as follows. Consider the following eccentric proposition:

(16) Everyone is at least as tall as he is.

It is plausible to consider that this proposition predicates a certain property of each person—a property that is universally shared. It predicates of Lew Alcindor, for example, the property of being at least as tall as he himself is, a property that in no way distinguishes him from anyone else. But the proposition also predicates of each person a property he need not share with others. For what it also says of Lew Alcindor is that he has the property of being at least as tall as Lew Alcindor—a property he shares with nearly no one. The same things hold for

(17) Everything is identical with itself.

This proposition predicates of each object the property of being self-identical—a property it shares with everything else. But it also says of any given object x that it has the property of being identical with x—a property unique to x. Socrates, for example, has the property of being essentially identical with Socrates, as well as that of being essentially self-identical. It is natural to say that these two properties *coincide* on Socrates in the sense that it is impossible that he have one but not the other.

But in TWI (henceforth understood to include Counterpart Theory) these two properties come apart. For while Socrates, of course, has no counterparts that lack self-identity, he does have counterparts that lack identity-with-Socrates. He alone of all of his counterparts, in fact, has the property of being identical with Socrates—the property, that is, of being identical with the object that in fact instantiates Socrateity. It is true, no doubt, that each of Socrates' counterparts has Socrateity, so that a counterpart (Socrates$_w$, say) of Socrates in a world W has the property of being identical with the thing that *in W* is Socrates or has Socrateity. But, of course, Socrates$_w$ is *distinct from* Socrates—the person who *in fact* is Socrates. Accordingly, some of Socrates' counterparts have the property of being distinct from Socrates. This means that (according to Counterpart Theory) the two properties predicated of Socrates by (17) do not coincide on Socrates. Indeed he has the property of being essentially self-identical, but he does not have the property of being essentially identical with Socrates. And this is the first of the two objections I promised. According to Counterpart Theory, the property of being identical with myself, unlike the property of self-identity, is not essential to me. Hence I could have been someone else. And this, I take it, is genuinely paradoxical. I could have been different in many ways, no doubt; but it makes no sense to suppose that I could have been someone else—someone, who, had he existed, would have been distinct from me. And yet Counterpart Theory, thus explained, implies not merely that I *could* have been distinct from myself, but that I *would* have been distinct from myself had things gone differently in even the most miniscule detail.

We can approach the same matter a bit differently. According to Counterpart Theory,

(18) I could have been taller than I am

is no doubt true. For what (18) requires is that there be a world in which I have a counterpart whose height exceeds the height I actually enjoy. But then similarly

(19) I could have been a different person from the one I am

will be true just in case there is a world in which I have a counterpart who is a different person from the one I actually am. And of course the Counterpart Theorist will hold that I do have such counterparts; so he must hold that (19) is true. Indeed, he must put up with something even worse; Counterpart Theory implies, not merely that I *could* have been a different person from the one I am, but that I *would* have been a different person, had things gone differently in even the most miniscule detail. More exactly, what Counterpart Theory implies is the truth of

(20) If *S*, then either I would not have existed or I would have been a different person from the one I am

where '*S*' is replaced by any false sentence. For such an instance of (20) will be true if every world in which *S* holds is one in which I lack a counterpart or have one that is a different person from the one I am. And, of course, if *S* is false, then every world in which it holds *is* one in which I either lack a counterpart or have one who is a different person from the one I am. If a leaf deep in the mountain fastness of the North Cascades had fallen in October 31, 1876, the day before it actually fell, then (according to Counterpart Theory) I should have been either nonexistent or else a different person from the one I am. And surely this is false.

According to TWI-Counterpart Theory, therefore, I have self-identity essentially but identity with myself accidentally. Although I could not have had self-diversity, I could have been diverse from myself, I could have been someone else. But there is a related and perhaps more important objection. The characteristic feature of TWI is that each of us (and everything else) would not so much as have existed had things been different in even the most insignificant fashion. This is itself not at all easy to believe. Asked to think of possible but non-actual states of affairs, we come up with such items as *Paul's being a good tennis player;* we suppose that there is a possible state of affairs such that, had it obtained, Paul himself—the very person we know and love so well—would have existed and had some property that, lamentably enough, he lacks. Perhaps this point becomes even more poignant if we take it personally. According to TWI, I would not have existed had things been in even the slightest way different. Had I had an extra cornflake for breakfast, I should not now exist. A narrow escape if there ever was one! The very idea fills one with existential Angst; the merest misstep has dramatic consequences indeed.

But of course the Angst is misplaced. For, according to TWI, there is no world in which I have that extra cornflake; it is not logically or metaphysically possible that I should have done so. And this holds whether or not TWI is fortified with Counterpart Theory; the latter's promise to relieve the former of this embarrassing consequence is not fulfilled. I am now confronted with what seems to me to be a choice; I can load my pipe with Dunhill's Standard Mixture or with Balkan Sobranie, both being available and congenial. I believe that it is possible for me to do either of these things and that which I do is up to me. According to TWI, however, one of these events will take place and the other has not so much as a ghost of a chance. For one of these takes place in the actual world and the other occurs in no possible world whatever. If I shall, in fact, smoke Sobranie, then smoking Dunhill is as far out of the question as smoking the number 7. No doubt the partisan of TWI will protest that it is possible for me to take an action A if there is a world in which I have a counterpart who takes that action. But is not this just to redefine, change, the meaning of the locution 'it is possible for me'? Of what relevance to my being able to take an action A is the fact, if it is a fact, that there is a possible state of affairs such that, had it obtained, someone very like but distinct from me would have taken A? Surely this gives me no reason at all for supposing it possible that *I* take this action. Of course we can give a new sense to the terms involved; but to do so is just to change the subject.

The difficulty with TWI in its original Leibnizian forms, I said, was that it implied that each object has each of its properties essentially; and the original attractiveness of Counterpart Theory was its promise to overcome that difficulty. This promise, I think, is illusory. Of course we can define the locution 'has *P* essentially' in the way suggested by Counterpart Theory; and then we will be in verbal agreement with the truth that objects have some of their properties accidentally. But the agreement, I suggest, is *only* verbal. For according to TWI, if in fact I have a property *P,* then there is no possible world in which I lack it. It is not possible that I should have lacked it. Of course there may be a state of affairs *S* such that had it obtained, there would have existed someone similar to me that would have lacked *P;* but how is this even relevant to the question where *I* could have lacked *P*—whether it is possible that *I* should not have had *P*? This seems no more to the point than the possibility that there be someone with my *name* who lacks *P*. And hence I do not think Counterpart Theory succeeds in overcoming the main objection to TWI; that difficulty remains.

By way of summary and conclusion, then: our initial insight into these matters is that objects have only some of their properties essentially; and an object *x* has a property *P* contingently only if there is a possible state of affairs *S* such that *x* would not have had *P* had *S* obtained. This joint affirmation obviously implies that the same object exists in more than one possible world—an idea that some find difficult or incoherent. The objections to this idea, however, do not withstand careful scrutiny. To reject it, furthermore, is to hold that an object exists in exactly one possible world, and this alternative entails—with or without the fortification of Counterpart Theory—that each object has each of its properties essentially.

Bibliography

Abbreviations

A	*Analysis*
AJP	*Australasian Journal of Philosophy*
APQ	*American Philosophical Quarterly*
CJP	*Canadian Journal of Philosophy*
JP	*Journal of Philosophy*
M	*Mind*
N	*Nous*
P	*Philosophy*
PR	*Philosophical Review*
PS	*Philosophical Studies*
S	*Synthese*

Ackerman, Diana. "Propositional Attitudes and the Causal Theory of Names." Unpublished paper, Brown University, Providence, Rhode Island.

Altham, J. E. J. "The Causal Theory of Names: Part II." *Aristotelian Society Supplementary Volume*, 1973, 209–225.

Barker, John A. "Pragmatics and Definite Descriptions." *Tulane Studies in Philosophy*, XXI (1972), 63–84.

Bell, J. M. "Opacity and Identity." *A*, 31 (October, 1970), 19–24.

Benfield, David and Edward Erwin. "Identity, Schmidentity—It's not all the Same." *PS*, (February, 1975), 145–148.

Blumenfeld, Jean Beer. "Kripke's Refutation of Materialism." *AJP*, 53 (August, 1975), 151–156.

Boer, Steven E. "Reference and Identifying Descriptions." *PR*, LXXXI (April, 1972), 208–228.

——. "The 'Sense' of Proper Names: A Demurrer." *AJP*, 52 (December, 1974), 232–239.

Boer, Steven E. and William G. Lycan. "Knowing Who." *PS*, 28 (November, 1975), 299–344.

Brody, Baruch A. "Why Settle for Anything Less than Good Old-

Fashioned Aristotelian Essentialism." *N*, VII (November, 1973), 351–365.

Camp, Joseph L., Jr. "Plantinga on De Dicto and De Re." *N*, V (May, 1971), 215–225.

——. "Defining Art." *British Journal of Aesthetics,* 15 (Summer, 1975), 191–206.

Carney, J. D. "Kripke and Materialism." *PS,* 27 (April, 1975), 279–282.

Carney, J. D., and Philip Von Bretzel. "Modern Materialism and Essentialism." *AJP,* 51 (May, 1973), 78–81.

Carter, W. R. "On A Priori Contingent Truths." *A,* 36 (January, 1976), 105–106.

Chandler, Hugh S. "Rigid Designation." *JP,* LXXII (July 17, 1975), 363–368.

Chastain, Charles. "Reference and Context," in *Language, Mind, and Knowledge,* edited by Keith Gunderson. Minneapolis: University of Minnesota Press, 1975.

Corrado, Michael. "Proper Names and Necessary Properties." *PS,* 24 (March, 1973), 112–116.

De Sousa, R. B. "Kripke on Naming and Necessity." *CJP,* III (March, 1974), 447–464.

Devitt, Michael. "Singular Terms." *JP,* LXXI (April 18, 1974), 183–204.

Donnellan, Keith S. "Necessity and Criteria." *JP,* LIX (October 25, 1962), 647–658.

——. "Proper Names and Identifying Descriptions." *S,* 21 (October, 1970), 335–358.

——. "Putting Humpty Dumpty Together Again." *PR,* LXXVII (April, 1968), 203–215.

——. "Substances and Individuals" (abstract). *JP,* LXX (November 8, 1973), 711–712.

Dummett, Michael. "Note on an Attempted Refutation of Frege." Appendix to Chapter 5 of *Frege: Philosophy of Language.* New York: Harper and Row, 1973.

——. " 'Postscript.' " *S,* 27 (1974), 523–534.

Durrant, Michael. "Essence and Accident." *M,* LXXXIV (October, 1975), 595–600.

Enc, Berent. "Necessary Properties and Linnaean Essentialism." *CJP,* V (September, 1975), 83–102.

Fales, Evan. "Definite Descriptions as Designators." *M,* LXXXV (April, 1976), 225–238.

Feldman, Fred. "Kripke on the Identity Theory." *JP*, LXXI (October, 1974), 665–676.

——. "Kripke's Argument Against Materialism." *PS*, 24 (November, 1973), 416–419.

Fine, Arthur. "How to Compare Theories: Reference and Change." *N*, IX (March, 1975), 17–30.

Fisk, Milton. "Are There Necessary Connections in Nature?" *Philosophy of Science*, 37 (September, 1970), 385–404.

Freed, Bruce. "Saying of and Saying That." *JP*, LXVII (November 19, 1970), 969–978.

Geach, P. T. "The Perils of Pauline." *Review of Metaphysics*, XXIII (December, 1969), 287–300.

Gibbard, Allan. "Contingent Identity." *Journal of Philosophical Logic*, 4 (May, 1975), 187–222.

Grandy, Richard. "Reference, Meaning, and Belief." *JP*, LXX, (August 16, 1973), 439–452.

Hacking, Ian. "All Kinds of Possibility." *PR*, LXXXIV (July, 1975), 321–338.

Hintikka, J. "The Semantics of Modal Notions and the Indeterminacy of Ontology." *S*, 21 (October, 1970), 408–424.

Hollinger, Robert. "Natural Kinds, Resemblances, and Conceptual Change." *Personalist*, LV (Autumn, 1974), 323–333.

Kahan, Howard. "Thomason on Natural Kinds." *N*, III (November, 1969), 409–412.

Kaplan, David. "Quantifying In." *S*, 19 (December, 1968), 178–214.

Katz, Jerrold. "Logic and Language: An Examination of Recent Criticisms of Intentionalism," in *Language, Mind, and Knowledge*, edited by Keith Gunderson. Minneapolis: University of Minnesota Press, 1975.

Korner, Stephan. "Individuals in Possible Worlds," in *Logic and Ontology*, edited by M. K. Munitz. New York: New York University Press, 1973.

Kripke, Saul. "Naming and Necessity," in *Semantics of Natural Language*, edited by Donald Davidson and Gilbert Harman. Dordrecht: D. Reidel, 1972.

Levin, Michael E. "Kripke's Argument against the Identity Thesis." *JP*, LXXII (March 27, 1975), 149–167.

Locke, Don. "The Necessity of Analytic Truths." *P*, XLIV (January, 1969), 12–32.

Lycan, William G. "Kripke and the Materialists." *JP*, LXII (October 24, 1974), 677–689.

———. "Mental States and Putnam's Functionalist Hypothesis." *AJP*, 52 (May, 1974), 48–62.

MacKay, Alfred F. "Mr. Donnellan and Humpty Dumpty on Referring." *PR*, LXXVII (April, 1968), 197–202.

Mackie, J. L. *"De* What *Re* is *De Re* Modality?" *JP*, LXXI (September 19, 1974), 551–560.

———. "Locke's Anticipation of Kripke." *A*, 34 (June, 1974), 177–180.

Margolis, Joseph. "On Names: Sense and Reference." *APQ*, 5 (July, 1968), 206–211.

Matson, Wallace I. "How Things Are What They Are." *Monist*, 56 (April, 1972), 234–239.

McGinn, Colin. "A Note on the Essence of Natural Kinds." *A*, 35 (June, 1975), 177–183.

———. "On the Necessity of Origins." *JP*, LXXIII (March 11, 1976), 127–134.

McKinsey, Michael. "Searle on Proper Names." *PR*, LXXX (April, 1971), 220–229.

Morrison, Paul G. "Reply to Putnam's 'Is Semantics Possible?' " in *Language, Belief, and Metaphysics*, edited by Howard E. Kiefer and Milton K. Munitz. Albany: State University of New York Press, 1970.

Oliver, W. Donald. "Essence, Accident, and Substance." *JP*, LI (November 11, 1954), 719–730.

Peacocke, Christopher. "Proper Names, Reference, and Rigid Designation," in *Meaning, Reference, and Necessity*, edited by Simon Blackburn. Cambridge: Cambridge University Press, 1975.

Plantinga, Alvin. *"De Re et De Dicto."* *N*, III (September, 1969), 235–258.

———. *God, Freedom, and Evil.* New York: Harper and Row, 1974.

———. *The Nature of Necessity.* London: Oxford University Press, 1974.

———. "What George Could Not Have Been." *N*. V (May, 1971), 227–232.

———. "World and Essence." *PR*, LXXIX (October, 1970), 461–492.

Putnam, Hilary. "The Analytic and the Synthetic," in *Minnesota Studies in the Philosophy of Science*, Vol. III, edited by H. Feigl and G. Maxwell. Minneapolis: University of Minnesota Press, 1966.

———. "Comment on Wilfrid Sellars." *S*, 27 (1974), 447–454.

———. "Dreaming and 'Depth Grammar';" in *Analytical Philosophy*, edited by R. J. Butler. Oxford: Blackwell, 1962.

———. "Explanation and Reference," in *Conceptual Change*, edited by Glenn Pearce and Patrick Maynard. Dordrecht: D. Reidel, 1973.

———. "It Ain't Necessarily So." *JP*, LIX (October 25, 1962), 658–671.

——. "The Meaning of 'Meaning'," in *Language, Mind, and Knowledge,* edited by Keith Gunderson. Minneapolis: University of Minnesota Press, 1975.

——. "On Properties," in *Essays in Honor of Carl Hempel,* edited by Nicholas Rescher et al. Dordrecht: D. Reidel, 1969.

——. "Psychological Concepts, Explication, and Ordinary Language." *JP,* LIV (February 14, 1957), 94–100.

——. "Psychological Predicates," in *Art, Mind, and Religion,* edited by W. H. Capitan and D. D. Merrill. Pittsburgh: University of Pittsburgh Press, 1965.

Ravnkilde, Jens. "How to Get Rid of Essentialism." *Danish Yearbook of Philosophy,* 12 (1975), 7–64.

Squadrito, Kathy. "Locke, Quine, and Natural Kinds." *The Modern Schoolman,* XLIX (January, 1972), 135–143.

Stalnaker, Robert C. "Possible Worlds." *N,* X (March, 1976), 65–75.

——. "Pragmatics." *S,* 22 (December, 1970), 272–289.

Stalnaker, Robert C., and Richmond H. Thomason. "Modality and Reference," *N,* II (November, 1968), 359–372.

Swinburne, R. G. "Analyticity, Necessity, and Apriority." *M,* LXXXIV (April, 1975), 225–243.

Teller, Paul. "Essential Properties: Some Problems and Conjectures." *JP,* LXXII (May 8, 1975), 233–248.

Thomason, Richmond H. "Modal Logic and Metaphysics," in *The Logical Way of Doing Things,* edited by Karel Lambert. New Haven: Yale University Press, 1969.

——. "Species, Determinates, and Natural Kinds." *N,* III (February, 1969), 95–102.

Tichy, Pavel. "Plantinga on Essence: A Few Questions." *PR,* LXXXI (January, 1972), 82–93.

Titiev, Robert J. "Kripke, Rigid Designators, and Cartesian Dualism." *PS,* 26 (December, 1974), 357–376.

Troyer, John. "Locke on the Names of Substances." *The Locke Newsletter,* 6 (Summer, 1975), 27–39.

Vendler, Zeno. "On the Possibility of Possible Worlds." *CJP,* V (September, 1975), 57–72.

Vision, Gerald. "Essentialism and the Senses of Proper Names." *APQ,* 17 (October, 1970), 321–330.

Wiggins, David. "Essentialism, Continuity, and Identity." *S,* 23 (1974), 321–359.

Wilder, Hugh T. "Quine on Natural Kinds." *AJP,* 50 (December, 1972), 263–270.

Yoshida, R. M. "De Sousa on Kripke and Theoretical Identities." *CJP*, V (September, 1975), 137–141.

Zemach, Eddy M. "Putnam's Theory on the Reference of Substance Terms." *JP*, LXXIII (March 11, 1976), 116–126.

Index

Library of Congress Cataloging in Publication Data
(For library cataloging purposes only)

Main entry under title:
Naming, necessity, and natural kinds.

Bibliography: p.
Includes index.
1. Semantics (Philosophy)—Addresses, essays, lectures. 2. Reference (Philosophy)—Addresses, essays, lectures. 3. Description (Philosophy)—Addresses, essays, lectures. 4. Necessity (Philosophy)—Addresses, essays, lectures. 5. Names—Addresses, essays, lectures. I. Schwartz, Stephen P. 1938–
B840.N34   121   76-28021
ISBN 0-8014-1049-5
ISBN 0-8014-9861-9 pbk.